Growing Up S

HQ 27 .S723 1996

Starks, Kay Johnston.
                gift
Growing up sexual

HarperCollinsCollegePublishers

Acquisitions Editor: Chris Jennison
Project Coordination and Text Design: York Production Services
Manufacturing Manager: Hilda Koparanian
Electronic Page Makeup: York Production Services
Printer and Binder: R. R. Donnelley & Sons Co.
Cover Printer: Color Imetry Corp.

Growing Up Sexual, Second Edition

Copyright © 1996 by HarperCollins College Publishers

HarperCollins ® and ® are registered trademarks of HarperCollins Publishers Inc.

All rights reserved. Printed in the United States of America. No part of this book may be reproduced in any manner whatsoever without written permission, except in the case of brief quotations embodied in critical articles and reviews. For information address HarperCollins College Publishers, 10 East 53rd Street, New York, NY 10022. *For information about any HarperCollins title, product, or resource, please visit our World Wide Web site at* **http://www.harpercollins.com/college**.

Library of Congress Cataloging-in-Publication Data

Starks, Kay Johnston.
   Growing up sexual / Kay Johnston Starks, Eleanor S. Morrison. — 2nd ed.
    p. cm.
   Rev. ed of: Growing up sexual / Eleanor S. Morrison. c1980.
   Includes bibliographical references and index.
   ISBN 0-673-99417-1
   1. Youth—United States—Sexual behavior. 2. Youth—United States—Attitudes. 3. Sex customs—United States. 4. Sexual ethics—United States. I. Growing up sexual. II. Title.
HQ27.S74 1996
306.7'0835—dc20   95-49011
                                                                   CIP

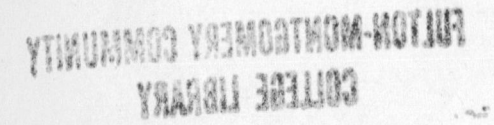

95 96 97 98   9 8 7 6 5 4 3 2 1

Contents

Preface v
Introduction: To Teachers and Students vii

Chapter 1
Variations in Family Style and Patterns — 1

Chapter 2
Discovering My Own Body: Masturbation — 16

Chapter 3
Childhood Sexual Experience — 28

Chapter 4
Sex Roles and Expectations — 42

Chapter 5
Sex Education, Formal and Informal — 59

Chapter 6
Variations in Sexual Orientation — 90

Chapter 7
Adolescence: Emerging Sexuality — 106

Chapter 8
Intimacy: Sexual and Emotional   *130*

Chapter 9
Self-Image and Sexuality   *154*

Chapter 10
STDs, Pregnancy, and Prevention   *168*

Chapter 11
Abuse: Painful and Confusing Experiences with Sexuality   *182*

Chapter 12
Sexuality and Personal Values: Drifting, Rebelling, Acquiescing, or Deciding   *213*

Chapter 13
Prices of Silence: Some Concluding Remarks   *239*

References 253
Index 260

Preface

Growing Up Sexual offers a unique view of human sexual development. This book is based on anonymous autobiographical papers written by students in human sexuality courses at Michigan State University and Central Michigan University. As the authors (faculty for the courses) read these personal documents term after term, they were made aware of the common experiences that are involved in psychosexual development.

The organization of the book traces these common experiences. The book begins with chapters describing childhood experiences: family approaches to sexuality, masturbation, juvenile sexual play, learning about being a boy or a girl, and sex education (or lack of it). Apparent in these chapters is a common burden of ignorance, misinformation, and guilt *and* participation and pleasure in activities perceived by young people as condemned by their elders.

Chapters on adolescent sexuality deal with the physical and emotional changes that accompany puberty and first sexual experiences. Sexual orientation, sex roles, self-image, decisions (or lack of them) about sexual activity and contraception, and abuse are among the experiences explored. Throughout, the authors allow their students' own words to express their pain and pleasure in sexuality and their yearning for knowledge and understanding.

A primary purpose of this book is to reduce the sense of isolation and uniqueness young adults often feel about their sexual growing up and current experience. The chapters may help students increase their self-knowledge, and their appreciation both for the diversity and commonality in growing up experiences.

The material is intended to stimulate reflection and discussion. Each chapter closes with questions directed toward the individual reader as a stimulus to self-examination through journal-writing or note-keeping. There are also questions designed for group discussion of the materials.

This edition of the book includes anecdotal materials included in the earlier edition (from the mid-1970s) as well as materials from graduate and undergraduate students in the late 1980s and early 1990s. As the authors indicate in their Introduction, there is a surprising continuity in the themes and experiences revealed in recent papers with those from 20 years earlier.

Growing Up Sexual is appropriate as a supplementary text for courses on human sexuality and/or developmental psychology offered in departments of psychology, sociology, family studies, women's studies, health education, and home economics, and also as a supplementary text for graduate level courses for mental health professionals. The chapters are sequenced developmentally, but each chapter stands alone and can be used independently to supplement topics as appropriate in courses designed differently.

Introduction: To Teachers and Students

BACKGROUND

The idea for this book originally grew out of a human sexuality course at Michigan State University, where we served as faculty and teaching assistants. This second edition is supplemented by experience in a similar course at Central Michigan University, taught by one of the authors.

A personal autobiographical paper submitted anonymously was one of the requirements of the courses. The assignment was as follows:

> "Who I Am Sexually"—a paper about yourself as a sexual being. The paper will not be graded, since it is both impossible and inappropriate for one person to evaluate another person's sexual reflections. However, failure to turn in the paper will affect your grade in the course. Put your birth date on the paper, but do not put your name; instead, put it on another sheet, which you will separate from the paper as you turn it in. This process will assure anonymity to the student and provide a method for the instructor to record the fact that the paper was received.
>
> This is a paper for you—an occasion for you to look at yourself from a sexual standpoint. It is intended as a personal learning exercise—therefore, be as personal as you wish.
>
> Do some disciplined reflection about your sexual development, your family background, your personal sexual values, and any other things that seem pertinent. You may want to include (but need not) such matters as early memories relating to sexuality; early feelings about your gender and your body; feelings, past and present, about sex; things that delight and disturb you about yourself and your sexuality; things that disturb you about societal sexual norms; helpful and not-so-helpful experiences in your sexual development; strong convictions you have in any area about sexuality; ambivalences, doubts, confusion you have about sexual matters; anything else pertinent, unique, and useful to you.

Each term, a new group of students wrote papers, and each term, the staff members reading the papers were moved by the pathos, humor, confusion, delights, agony, isolation, ignorance, guilt, and embarrassment continually appearing. The papers were human documents reflecting diverse attitudes, values, and experiences about sexuality. They mirrored the almost universal lack of coherent and accurate information received during the years of growing up.

The assignment was intended purely as a personal focusing and learning activity for the student. The idea for using these papers in a book occurred a year and a half after the last group of papers included in the first edition had been written.

Because the papers were anonymous and ungraded, there was no way for the faculty to control what material was included or left out in any given paper. The rough guidelines quoted above were often, but not always followed. Out of this relatively unstructured writing, a rather remarkable convergence of experience and themes emerged. This led us to conclude that these papers might be somewhat representative of the developmental experiences of other Americans. The categories we have used for chapter headings reflect areas recurrently cited in the papers. Three areas have appeared in the papers from more recent courses: sexual abuse, violence, and the experience of growing up with an awareness of being gay or lesbian. With the increase in public awareness of childhood sexual abuse, and the increase in public awareness of the gay and lesbian communities' existence, students in recent years have apparently felt safer to include these experiences in their papers.

Very frequently, students wrote about having received fragments of information from home, church, school, or peers, but those segments were seldom consistently integrated with personal and interpersonal experiences of genital exploration, discovery, and exploitation. The consistent separation of experience and information very frequently led to the following:

- Self doubt: "Am I normal?"
- Guilt: "If my church or parents feel so negative about what I'm doing, then I must be a bad person."
- Isolation: "I mustn't let anyone know what terrible thoughts, fantasies, and experiences I am having".... "I am the only one doing this."
- Ambivalence: "How could anything that is so pleasurable be such a sin?"
- Indecision: "I am probably foolish not to be using contraception, but if I do, then I am *planning* to be sexually active!"

The students also said that there was seldom a continuing opportunity to get any kind of "reality check" on these doubts and fears. Nor was there a chance to safely express real concerns, ignorance, and/or fears. Even at best, parents frequently seemed eager to terminate any question-and-answer period or any talk that dealt explicitly with sexual matters. Religious teachings often only served to make sexual activities seem wrong. Peers often shared misinformation, contributing to confusion and mistakes. So, the process of growing up sexually was often lonely, chaotic, and confusing.

As these patterns continued to appear term after term, we decided that these personal experiences and statements might serve two significant purposes:

1. To provide a kaleidoscope of what it was like to grow up as a sexual being in mid- to late-twentieth-century America.
2. To provide a much-needed "reality check" for those now growing up, and for the adults (parents, teachers, clergy, medical personnel, counselors, and others) who are concerned about helping young people come to maturity with more information, more interpersonal skills, and more clearness about their own self-chosen sexual values.

Now, almost 20 years later, it is disconcerting to find a repetition of the same themes and experiences in the current student generation. Students in both graduate and undergraduate level courses at Central Michigan University, responding to the same assignment of writing an anonymous "Who I Am Sexually?" paper identify the same (mostly negative) experiences.

As we come to the second edition, we have included many of the excerpts from the earlier edition, and have added new ones from more recent papers. We have been unable to find many discernible differences except, as indicated above, there have been recent papers reporting sexual abuse, sexual violence, and the experience of coming to affirm oneself as lesbian or gay.

A WORD ABOUT PROCEDURE

As we began in 1978 to consider publishing these materials, our first problem concerned the right to use the very personal stories in the papers. We had been elaborately careful in the courses to protect students' anonymity. However, a birth date had been asked for, as a means for the students' retrieving their own paper in order to write a second paper at the end of the term, turning both back to the instructors.

We sent letters to 580 Michigan State University students who had been enrolled in the course during the nine terms for which we had papers (papers had been returned to students during eight other terms). In the letter, we indicated that we were considering writing a book for young people, their parents, and other adults concerned with healthy sexual development. We asked that they return a reply card without signing it, giving us their birth date and the term in which they took the course. By furnishing this information, they would be giving us permission to use excerpts from their papers. We stated that identifiable names, places, and other data would be changed. We received affirmative responses from 228 students who had taken the course between the winter term of 1972 and the spring term of 1975. Their birth dates ranged from 1930 to 1956, with the majority born between 1950 and 1954.

Students enrolled in the courses at Central Michigan University in the years 1989 through 1994 were informed by the faculty at the end of the term about the planned revision of this book. At that time, they were invited to hand in their paper with a note giving permission for its inclusion, if they so chose. Sixty-seven students, out of a total of 172, gave their permission.

We want the reader to be strongly aware that we do not consider this material in any sense to be research findings that are statistically representative of the general population. The material is drawn from a relatively small sample of persons, all of whom were enrolled in one of two midwestern state universities. A large majority of students selected human sexuality as an elective course. About 35 (at Central Michigan University) were fulfilling a requirement in their program, and all were responding to a faculty assignment in writing the papers. Although there was diversity in age, ethnic and racial background, and residence (rural or urban), the majority of students were from Michigan.

PURPOSE

We offer these anecdotal, personal materials in the hope that they may trigger some heightened consciousness or remembrance of the reader's own growing up, and that such a process may be useful to readers in reflecting on their own sexuality and its meaning.

A second hope is that these documents of human journeys to adult sexuality may be illuminating to parents, teachers, and counselors. Possibly, these materials may evoke a sensitivity to what may be going on in the lives of young people with whom the reader lives or has a relationship, or for whom she or he has professional responsibility.

Our hope is also that it might impact action on a variety of levels: personal, community, institutional, legislative, judicial. Such action is urgently needed in mobilizing community support for comprehensive educational programs, for comprehensive health and counseling services for children and young people, for resources for parent education and peer education projects. Hopefully, through such concerned and concerted efforts, subsequent generations may find more wholeness and fulfillment in sexual development, and less anxiety and confusion in the search for the nature and meaning of human sexuality.

SOME COMMENTS

Working together has been exhilarating and exhausting. Making decisions, choosing excerpts to be used, and maintaining a unity of focus and direction would probably have been simpler if one person were doing these tasks. We feel the manuscript is richer for having multiple authors. We want to acknowledge the colleagueship of Don Crawford, Nina Ronzio, and Cynda Hyndman in working on the first edition.

We would like to express appreciation to the students who wrote the introspective papers for their willingness to allow them to be published.

Eleanor S. Morrison was the originator of the sexuality course at Michigan State University; Kay Johnston Starks was the faculty person for the course at Central Michigan University.

Kay Johnston Starks and Eleanor S. Morrison

Chapter 1

Variations in Family Style and Patterns

INTRODUCTION

Family attitudes and practices directly affect an individual's sexuality from birth throughout life. Gender roles are at least initially defined by family expectations (Beal, 1994). "Much initial sexual learning takes place in the home.... Who do you show your body to? Under what conditions may you be naked—see other people naked? May you go into the bathroom when somebody else is there? May you take a bath with other people? May you freely touch your own body or other people's bodies? May other people touch you? Who may you kiss? Who may kiss you? . . . People who have sex are going to have to touch people, be undressed with someone else, and have someone else undressed with them. The kind of training they have had about touching and nudity becomes part of the repertoire they bring to sexually oriented situations" (Gagnon and Greenblatt, 1978, pp. 53–55). Parents demonstrate by their behavior with each other and with their children how to talk about sex, how to express caring, and how to behave in intimate relationships. Children draw conclusions from this experience with their parents. The conclusions they draw, according to Gagnon and Simon (1973), are often based on unclear and incomplete parental messages—messages often not clarified as the child grows up because of the reluctance parents feel about discussing sexuality with their children. Many of the students supported Gagnon's premise when they indicated that they felt their current attitudes, positive and negative, about sexual matters were directly related to their childhood experiences of their parents' attitudes. In this chapter we intend to explore attitudes that apparently grew out of family interaction.

One of the basic areas identified by many students as having had impact on their feelings about themselves, about the other gender, and about sexuality in general, had to do with the kind of direct or indirect communication about sexuality that they experienced in their homes.

FEMALE

My parents' views about sex are pretty old-fashioned. My father never discussed sex with me. My mother is a little embarrassed and amazed when I bring up the subject. Having an older brother has helped; he has helped me know something about male bodies and has given me some clues about male feelings about sex. None of my siblings, male or female, and I ever really talked about sex directly. I guess my parents' quietness on sex matters has affected the whole family.

FEMALE

My home life was not conducive to being open about sex. My mother has a way of talking circles around me—imposing her attitudes even if she thinks she's not. Since I could never explain to her how I felt about nonsexual matters, I knew sexual matters would be hopeless too. And my father was impossible to talk to—he never talked to us kids about anything. He doesn't know how. I think he's scared of us or something. My image of a father for the longest time was someone who earned money for the family. The thought of a father playing with his kids or taking them places was inconceivable to me.

FEMALE

I consider it my good fortune that I never thought sexuality was dirty or horrible like so many people do. I never learned to be ashamed of my body. My parents didn't overtly teach me this. Their behavior did. I was never punished for exploring my own body or for being curious and finding out what other bodies were like. Our family just didn't make a big deal out of sex. A lot of my girlfriends hated having periods, but I enjoyed it. I was prepared for what it would be like and was eager to begin developing into a woman. It made me feel very female and I enjoyed that feeling. At the time I first started, I can also remember feeling sort of awed that I could reproduce. I feel lucky to have grown up with the idea that sexuality is a normal thing, but just as you must learn to control the time and place you urinate, the same holds true for sex, which meant it's better to wait until you're married.

FEMALE

My mother is a fanatic about cleanliness and so when I started my period I thought Mother would be furious that I'd soiled my underwear, so I used to put them into the top of the piano. I'd still rather throw away underwear that is soiled from my period than have to wash it.

Students observed and learned from the way their parents expressed or did not express affection and caring to each other.

FEMALE

Mom and Dad are neat; they still act like lovers. Mom will see Dad coming up the walk from work and she'll say, "Ooh, I love that man!" with a loving smile. And Dad will sneak up in back of her and give her a kiss on the neck (on the side where it tickles) or a pinch on the rear—they enjoy each other.

One of the family practices that varies from family to family has to do with the amount of nudity in the home—nudity on the part of both parents and children. Considerable diversity in this regard was reported in the student papers.

FEMALE

Since there was no male around when I was growing up, another shocking experience was the realization that males had pubic hair. When I felt a boy's penis for the first time I was really shocked and afraid to look at male genitals.

FEMALE

My father was never nude—that I remember—and once when I was nine years old, I was lying on the bottom bunk and he climbed to the top bunk, in a night shirt. I saw these big genitals hanging down and had a negative reaction to the color, texture, shape, roughness, and size. I never had had anything else to compare it to except my brother's little teeny weenie penis which was white and smooth.

FEMALE

I never saw my father any way but completely dressed, so for many years I would grab any book to find out about male anatomy.

FEMALE

My parents were open about their bodies and proud of them. This led our family to be the same way—we were not immodest but we were not unnaturally modest. I recall one time in high school when a friend stayed all night. My brother heard us talking in the morning and came to the bedroom door in just his underwear to see who was there (he was 20 at the time). My friend was terribly embarrassed. I hadn't even noticed until she mentioned it to me. When I came to Michigan State, I recall girls in the dorm who made a point to close the blinds whenever they changed their clothes and who would die if a guy saw them in their pajamas, even a long flannel nightgown (which has got to be the most unrevealing thing you could wear). I figured that most people had seen a female body by that time, so why worry? My body isn't, after all, the fantastic type of body that one runs for binoculars to see.

MALE

My dad and I took showers together. I was curious about his genitalia and asked him questions about it—like how come his had hair on it and mine didn't. He reassured me that I would someday have hair on mine too and said that the time would be when I was older. For the time being this satisfied my curiosity. Other early sexual discoveries came to me when my mother bathed me and my sister, who is nineteen months older, together. Of course I noticed that her body and my body were different.

As children grew older many families permitted less nudity and cross-gender bathing than when the children were very young.

FEMALE

When my brothers, sisters, and I were small, we were allowed to roam around the house nude, occasionally taking baths with Mommy and Daddy. But clothing became very essential as we grew older.

MALE

My earliest reflections regarding my sexuality take me back to my early childhood when I was bathed with my sister. I noticed the differences between my sister and myself, but gave very little thought to them. When we were slightly older my mother began to bathe us in our undershorts and I didn't know why. When the age came that we were bathed separately, I simply assumed that there had been something wrong with the dual bathing and my mother had corrected the error. As I grew older, I began to feel my mother should no longer see me in the raw. I don't know what brought about the change, but somehow it had become embarrassing.

One of the older graduate students with children of her own reported that the developing sense of modesty and demand for privacy came more from her children as they reached a certain age than from her own convictions or practices.

FEMALE

As my four children approached puberty, they each in turn developed a sense of modesty: bedroom doors were closed, the bathroom was used by only one person at a time, and they no longer casually walked from bedroom to bathroom nude. Cross-gender nudity in our family was no longer appropriate. As each child gradually became comfortable in their new adult bodies their extreme modesty decreased, but the new awareness of their sexuality (I think) prevented a return to the total uninhibited nudity of childhood.

This new modesty collided with the lack of privacy in public exercise and swimming facilities.

MALE

I remember trauma and confusion after my first visit to the "Y" with my dad. No one was wearing a swimming suit and it seemed odd to me; after all, even though I had never been told that the human body was anything to be ashamed of, it had been made clear to me that one did not exhibit oneself—at the "Y" nobody seemed to care.

MALE

I remember a junior high locker room lecture about how the time in life had come that we would not be able to be quite so particular about getting dressed or undressed in front of others. Mindsets don't change so easily!

FEMALE

I know that it was not until I went to college that I stopped trying to hide my body in situations like a locker room. Coming from 12 years of parochial schooling, it took me a while to realize that there were better attitudes to take toward my body than being ashamed of it.

Parents often do not talk about themselves as sexual beings and assume that their children don't and won't know about their sexual relationships. Occasionally children inadvertently witness parental sexual activity and reported reactions were varied.

ANGER

MALE

It so happened my bedroom was beside my parents'. On many occasions I awoke to the raised voice of my mother, protesting about something. It seemed as though my father was hurting her in some way, and she wanted him to stop. I would lie awake hearing this for up to an hour, getting madder and more upset every minute. I would get so mad at my father. I promised myself I would never hurt a woman. I couldn't understand how he could be such a heartless bastard and hurt my mother. Although I never really knew or understood what was going on, these episodes made me absolutely livid.

CONFUSION

MALE

Ignorant of the taboos associated with walking into my parents' bedroom unannounced, I encountered sexual activity for the first time. My father and my Aunt Ruth were standing facing each other and he was feeling her breasts. It seemed strange to see my father with someone other than my mother. I had never seen a breast before but I remember what hers looked like—young, firm, pointed, and sensuous. I was not noticed so I left, sensing that I shouldn't be there.

AROUSAL

MALE

From my parents I got the idea that sex was okay only if the two people were married, and even then it was something private and secret. Sometimes I would come into my parents' bedroom after they had had intercourse the night before. I would know this because my mother's pants would be on the floor next to the bed and she would be wearing an open pajama top without her bra on. I could sometimes see her breasts and I knew that she was naked under the cover.

SKEPTICISM

FEMALE

I also recall mistakenly surprising my parents (and myself) by entering their room while they were engaged in intercourse. They later assured me they had been "Indian wrestling," and I rather skeptically accepted the explanation, having had no visualization of intercourse, or Indian wrestling, for that matter. I suppose that I had thought intercourse to be a rather quiet, inactive, immobile activity like most other adult activities. (Incidentally, my husband and I recently used the same cop-out with our small son upon being discovered in the act.)

ANYTHING GOES

FEMALE

Growing up on the farm showed me what sex was. I guess that I always knew that my parents had sex in the bedroom. This was normal and of course I knew firsthand what sex was. There were no surprises in their relationship sexually.

I was very upset when my dad moved downstairs before they got the divorce. I couldn't understand how they could separate with us kids at home. I knew they were fighting but. . . .

I remember one time I came home from school early one day and caught my dad in bed with his girlfriend. I was so embarrassed because I had brought a friend with me. My dad did not get mad at me; he only tapped me on the arm and said "darn you" and smiled because I had caught him.

I remember that one time he told me that one-half of the world was made to have sex with the other half. That was a very dangerous thing to tell a 12-year-old.

I soon started dating and of course I wanted to make sure that I got my half, which was easy most of the time. Boys and girls will be boys and girls. I was not told anything about any birth control. I sure was lucky I guess. I never did get into trouble anyway.

"Research, based on approximately 650 college student questionnaires, suggests that it is quite difficult for youth to think of their parents as sexual beings" (Pocs and Godow, 1977, p. 33). According to Calderone and Johnson (1989, p. 129), "most children don't particularly want to think about the lives of their own parents in sexual terms; most adolescents find it really hard to believe that their parents, much less their grandparents, actually have intercourse for enjoyment. In fact, quite a few children have the idea that their parents, if they have had three children, for example, have had intercourse only three times."

FEMALE

My mother was morally conservative and Dad always referred to her as Victorian. I could not picture Mom and Dad making love. I knew they had to and that they did, but really facing it was hard. I guess I felt intercourse was a bad or dirty thing. Only bad kids did it. And there was always the thing about respect. Mom used to give me the line—"A boy won't respect you if you let him touch you."

MALE

It kind of strikes me as odd to think of how easy it has been to be open about sex in my family. I can remember when my brother and I were the only ones left at home. We asked Mom, at the dinner table, to rate Dad as a lover. She said PDG (pretty darn good). Dad has always had a pat on the fanny and a kiss for Mom and has always told her he loves her. I was bumming around this summer after I got out of the service. One of the times I was home I was talking with Mom in their bedroom when I saw a book by David Reuben. It automatically switched my train of thought, and I asked if she and Dad still have sex. She said yes and I asked her how often. She kind of laughed and said, "Well, that depends on your father, but generally once or twice a week." We got talking and I found out that Mom almost always has an orgasm with Dad. Finding these things out was truly amazing for me. When I was in high school I'd believed that Mom and Dad had stopped having sex long ago. I was also under the impression that Mom didn't enjoy sex because it was only a rare woman who could ever have an orgasm and I was willing to bet she didn't. I was amazed that I had asked these questions and that she had answered.

FEMALE

Mom and Dad have made sex a natural (not hidden or "dirty") part of life for me (as well as for my brothers and sisters, I'm sure), though I'm not sure they fostered it intentionally. How many kids' parents have fantastic water fights in the bathroom, chasing each other into the bedroom (nude), laughing like little kids? How many girls have their Mom turn with sparkling eyes to say, "Someday I'll have to tell you about the time you were conceived (reflectively)—umm! That sure was a beautiful field up on Granddad's farm...." Whenever Mom would start to say something like that I'd always say, "Oh, Mother!" and laugh. I still feel kind of funny when she tells me anything about her and Dad—partly because I feel as if I'm intruding and partly because it's hard to imagine my mother and my father having intercourse, and playing and loving the same as anybody else. I supposed it's always hard for a child to imagine parents making love, even when, like mine, they kiss and hug in front of the child.

One of the adult students in the class wrote of her concern about attitudes toward the sexuality of older adults.

FEMALE

Is it possible to continue a satisfactory sex life until death? I have read articles recently concerning the sexual needs of the elderly—articles recommending that the privacy needed for sex be made available in nursing and old people's homes. Somehow the idea repulsed me, even though I know my feeling is ridiculous. Here again, I think I am influenced by my mother. A year ago when she was in a depressed state, she confided in me that my father had tried to have intercourse with her—"And at age eighty, isn't that terrible? That was over for us long ago!" But did it need to be over? That act might have given him the comfort and security he needed in his last days (he died in March), and I have a great sense of sadness when I think of the loneliness and isolation both of them must have felt many times in their later years, which might have been avoided if our culture had encouraged in my mother an acceptance of this very basic means of communication.

Students gave examples of the impact the experiences had on their ability to develop productive male-female relationships.

FEMALE

Lacking a father, I was unaware of how two people react to each other in a husband-wife situation and I still at times wonder about this; to what extent do or should husbands and wives show affection toward one another when in the presence of their children?

MALE

One thing that my father believed in, although never directly stated, was that sexual contact and flirtation with other women in the presence of my mother was acceptable. In his eyes mother held a second-class rating. I often resented him for the hurt he caused her, and I often resented her for her lack of spine in not confronting the situation with more strength. Because I disapproved, I am now particularly uncomfortable at finding myself acting out my father's attitude unconsciously.

Behaviors and attitudes modeled by parents are often unconsciously learned so well by the children that they replicate them automatically as adults. Frank Pittman (1993, pp. 116, 120) speaks of his own experience:

> Dad came back after the war was over, but I never quite found a use for him, and he didn't seem to find a use for me. I needed something from him that I wasn't getting. I didn't know how to ask for it, and he didn't know how to give it to me. I kept trying to get him to tell me the secrets of being a man, and he kept avoiding talking to me . . . What I did not realize until I became a father myself was that there was very little to talk about . . . Boys just learn to be men by being with their fathers, experiencing the world and living life. But if they haven't had that experience, they may never feel comfortable with an awareness of what it means to be a man, what they are supposed to do with their masculinity, and how they can become fathers themselves.

FEMALE

My parents were divorced a couple years ago. All I can remember about their relationship is that I never saw them act very lovingly toward each other. For a long time, perhaps from the time I was old enough to think about it, they were at odds with each other. I remember waking in the middle of the night to the sound of them arguing downstairs; I would listen at the top of the stairs, cry a little, and then go back to bed. I remember small things: my parents sleeping in twin beds, but pushed together and made up separately. This bothered me for quite a while, for I heard that other married couples slept in one double bed. Then I learned that Dad snored and Mom couldn't sleep if someone was moving around and wiggling the bed. There was a time when my parents were going to a marriage counselor—my mother bought sheets to fit over both beds, but that didn't last very long. Anyway, what this says to me is that I don't have a very good example to learn from. On top of that, there has been a divorce on my mom's side of the family for three generations now, and the next suspect is me. Therefore, I am a bit worried, not overly, but I really want to be sure my marriage lasts when I do get married.

Parents too often act on their own assumptions about their adolescents' sexual behavior, instead of helping them think through their choices.

FEMALE

My mother was none too facilitative to my sexual development. Throughout my adolescent years, I can recall many instances of my mother giving me a powerful double message—"Be popular at any cost but don't do anything that has sexual implications." My mother approved of my going steady (she thought it was a cool thing to be doing), and encouraged my boyfriend and me to spend considerable amounts of time together. However, once she came back early (quite unexpectedly!) from an evening out on the town and found my boyfriend unbuttoning my blouse and feeling my breasts. He was immediately ordered to leave and we were forbidden to see each other for several months. The only discussion that ensued was one which centered around "that" activity not being appropriate for a thirteen-year-old girl. No further explanation from Mom.

FEMALE

My mom used to tell Paul (my boyfriend) and me that if after a date we wanted to go parking, she'd much rather have us come home and go downstairs. She never bothered us; it's a great feeling to know that your parents trust you. They always trusted me when Paul and I were together. Their trust was a little naive. When I told my mom what we were doing, she wasn't thrilled but she didn't condemn me either.

Some women recalled very specific warnings, with little or no explanation given them about proper and improper sexual behavior. Many of them were told to maintain their virginity until marriage; they were not to indulge in petting, partic-

ularly heavy petting, "because of what it would lead to." No men in our sample reported similar parental injunctions.

FEMALE

My mom and her friends were discussing the girls in the church who "had" to get married. Then as I walked in the room the phrase came out, "Instead of a wedding at the Clark house, a funeral would be appropriate, and I'd wear black." My mom agreed and said to me, "Remember this conversation, it may come in handy one day or night," and smiled. Well, I never did forget it. This is just one example of how I'm sure I am deeply affected by my family and the beliefs that influenced my sexuality.

FEMALE

My mother hammered into my head that there were some things nice girls don't do, and having premarital sex was the main taboo. Heavy petting was unthinkable because it could lead to bad things and a good girl would not be good anymore. Sex after marriage was the only way and a girl must not ruin herself for her husband. A man was to marry a pure woman and the only pure woman was a virgin. My mother would give me lots of static if a boy called me too often, if I stayed out late, or hung around with the wrong crowd. My mother continually pointed out indecent actions on the part of young girls that were not considered ladylike. "A woman must constantly be on guard so as not to ruin her reputation. She can degrade and lower herself if she does not act like a woman at all times. Nothing in this world is worse than a cheap and common woman." All during my teen years I was constantly being hounded by my mother to remain a good girl.

FEMALE

A majority of the time my parents have helped me make the right decision. They have given me some very strict values to follow, from which I have strayed on occasion, but never without guilt. Of course, I'd just suffer through this guilty feeling, rationalize why I did it, and then turn around and do it again. For instance, in high school I'd have girls over for slumber parties. We'd sneak out late at night and meet guys. I never really wanted to hurt my parents or have them lose faith in me, so naturally, sneaking out made me feel bad. But I figured if I never got caught they would never know. As if sneaking out wasn't nerve wracking enough, I'd always run into a guy who had a thousand hands. My parents thought it a mortal sin to lie next to a guy or to let him touch you, but I thought it was romance. I always felt if my parents ever found out that Bob or Tom touched me a lot they would half kill me.

FEMALE

My parents raised me with strict rules for my behavior. They feel any sex before marriage is wrong and that men only respect a pure virgin as their wife. Religion reinforced this attitude. My girlfriends at school differed. Some thought it was nasty, others teased you for being a chicken. Needless to say, I felt confused and very ashamed of my sexual feelings. When questioned, my parents reacted with strict rules and lectures. I was expected to accept those rules and abide by them. "A man respects a woman who will wait until her wedding night" was the answer to why you must be a virgin.

FEMALE

Ever since I can remember, my mother has told me that most men are out after one thing and one thing alone—sex. I am constantly told to be sure I don't tease men and that if I lose my virginity no man will ever want to marry me. Logically, I know this is garbage yet when I date men, this idea that sex is first and foremost in a man's mind scares me away from a deep relationship. This has had a great deal to do with the rift between my current boyfriend and me. I keep thinking that if I give in then he'll just up and leave.

Some students discovered that although their parents communicated strong disapproval of premarital sex, they had been involved in such a relationship.

FEMALE

Once when I was sixteen, I had to find my birth certificate so that I could get a driver's license. While searching through our family's strongbox, I accidentally came upon my parents' marriage certificate and was extremely shocked to discover that they had been married only five months before my birth. My parents' having to get married was beyond my coping ability. I was stunned. I experienced shock, disbelief, denial and finally hurt. I felt they had betrayed all of the moral values that they had tried to instill in me. Eventually Dad asked me to come into his room to discuss "something." Carefully and with love, he explained about the relationship he and Mother had before their marriage—a relationship between two young adults who loved one another.

FEMALE

I was brought up to believe that premarital sex is not good. The longer I dated John, the more my mother reminded me of this. One day I found out why she was so concerned about this. She told me that she and my father "had" to get married. She was crying at the time. It was like she was confessing to a murder or something. It made me feel like crying to see her feeling so guilty about something so natural and beautiful. Maybe she thought I'd lose respect for her. I don't know. I tried to comfort her as best I could. I think this brought us closer than ever.

MALE

My great-grandmother was a full-blooded American Indian who gave birth to a boy fathered by an Englishman who settled in the area. They never married officially, but she was his common law wife. My grandmother was a tough old Christian woman who chewed tobacco and believed in righteousness, and if her "chillers" didn't mind her she switched 'em good. Grandpa Jerry, her husband, worked himself to death in the coal mines, so Grandma had to raise her kids alone. My parents had their first child while Mom was 15. A year later they decided to get married which was no big deal in their community. We all moved to Michigan when I was two. Imagine, six kids, two adults and all they owned, stuffed into an old beat-up Chevy, headed north to begin a new life in a totally foreign country.

Another student struggled with the contradiction between what her mother said and did.

FEMALE

My mother admonished me against sexual activity of any variety besides kissing, especially emphasizing "You should be a virgin when you marry." Yet as she spoke these words, she was often having her boyfriends spend the night with her. That entire scene embarrassed me. I didn't know how to react when I would wake up and find my mom's bedroom door locked. I was mortified at the thought that my friends might find out. Basically, I was pretty confused about the "proper" value of sexual activity. I finally decided that it must be okay to be physical with men and I have a history of being very receptive (though not aggressive) to sexual advances made by men.

Our students say that what they were taught as children had a great impact on how they feel about sexual issues as adults.

MALE

I am just now beginning to reevaluate my traditional upbringing. The key question is, how much of it can I peel off before I bleed? Although I rationally disagree with much of what I was taught as a child, I wonder to what extent it will continue to direct my actions.

After reading about or observing new models of how to express caring, some students want to institute changes in their families.

FEMALE

I could sense a certain closeness in my boyfriend's family. He always kissed his mother and sister good-bye and told them, "I love you." I thought—"Wouldn't it be nice if my family were this close?" I started thinking what I could do about it and decided to try a few things. Well, I kissed my mother good-bye and talked more about marriage, love, and children. She responded very well. I still can sense a little shyness when I talk about children, but it has helped open up our emotions toward each other.

FEMALE

I guess if there is one feeling I have about sex and sexuality it is that we can be honest and open with Mitchell (our son) about all his concerns and interests. We have tried to treat sex as a normal, healthy activity—not something bad. We don't hide our bodies from him and indeed, at three and one-half he knows more about the male and female bodies than I did at 23! He sees us both dressing; takes showers with both of us. When he was learning body parts he asked, "What's this?" "Your penis," I said. "Penis?" (in a nervous voice). "Sure, like arm or leg—it's part of your body." After that it was penis, just like arm or leg—nothing bad or nasty—just a sexual fact. I hope we can continue to be as open and honest and that he'll feel free to come to us with questions and concerns.

SUGGESTED ISSUES FOR PERSONAL REFLECTION, GROUP DISCUSSION AND INTERACTION, PERSONAL JOURNAL

In your family of origin—

1. What were the accepted behaviors in your family regarding modesty and nudity? Did they change as you grew older? From what to what?

2. How was affection demonstrated (physically, verbally, etc.)—or was it? That is, by whom and to whom? Parents to each other? Parent to child? Child to parent? Sibling to sibling?
3. What attitudes were expressed toward your developing sexual maturity during adolescence?
4. What messages did you get about special boyfriends or girlfriends, dating, and/or going steady?
5. What generalizations would you make about the impact of your family on your current sexual beliefs and practices?
6. What differences existed in the messages given to males and females in the same family? Do you think these have changed over the past two to three generations?

Chapter 2

Discovering My Own Body: Masturbation

INTRODUCTION

*H*istorically, there have been several viewpoints about the practice of masturbation. Some have been condemnatory: Some people have viewed it as harmful to health, leading to a variety of physical and mental difficulties; others, because of religious teaching, view masturbation as sinful because it is for pleasure, not for reproduction. Others recognize masturbation as a common practice, but would prefer not to encourage or condone it.

Current research supports a more positive viewpoint toward masturbation. A fact unknown to many people is that human beings have the physiological capability for sexual arousal and orgasm at birth. One of the first behaviors observable in the delivery room is erection by male babies and lubrication by females. As infants develop, they begin to explore their world, including their own bodies, and they soon find their genitals. In our society, this discovery gives many parents an unexpected problem, and their immediate reaction is sometimes punitive and condemnatory (McDougall, 1986).

In recent research, (Atwood and Gagnon, 1987; Hunt, 1974) data indicate both sexes are beginning to masturbate at earlier ages than revealed in the Kinsey research of the 1940s and 1950s. In Hunt's sample, 63 percent of the males masturbated by age 13, whereas only 45 percent of all males had masturbated by age 13 in the Kinsey sample. Of the females in Hunt's sample, 33 percent had masturbated by age 13, whereas only 15 percent of the females in the Kinsey sample had masturbated to orgasm by the time they were 13 (Kinsey, 1953). On the average, females begin masturbating a good deal later than males, often not until the dating or early marital years. However, although people begin masturbating at earlier ages, it does not mean that they do so without struggle or inner conflict (Crooks and Baur, 1993).

Masturbation is one of several ways people have for finding out about their own bodies and discovering sensual pleasure. It is a common, rather than an unusual practice and was a subject which appeared frequently in the papers used in this book. People reported varying ages at which they discovered they could experience sensual pleasure by touching their genitals. The meanings they attached to masturbation varied widely from the simple "good feelings" of childhood experience to intentional sexual expressions as adults. "Bad feelings" of guilt, worry, fear, and shame often accompanied sensual pleasure.

As with other sexual topics, many students revealed they had never talked about masturbation with anyone. They kept intense physical and emotional feelings to themselves.

FEMALE

I've never been able (wanted?) to talk openly with anyone about masturbation.

MALE

The only thing that really bugs me about sex is the topic of masturbation. Am I the only one? Do other people do it as often as I?

MALE

I was an avid masturbator from about age ten on. Climax back then was unreal. The intense feelings kept building until I could no longer bear to manipulate my penis. All the while I was masturbating I was sure that no one else did, and I never told anyone.

FEMALE

I feel my past experiences are "normal" and that I should not feel peculiar or overly sexual because I masturbated as a child.

Research reveals that for women, masturbation usually offers the most specific and quickest means for reaching orgasm (Kinsey, 1953). Masters and Johnson (1966) report that orgasms from masturbation are more intense physiologically, although not necessarily as emotionally satisfying as those resulting from intercourse. Some students corroborated these findings.

FEMALE

It wasn't until I was sexually stimulated by my boyfriend in my senior year of high school that I realized I had been having orgasms since I was five. Sometimes I think that having stimulated myself for so long it was hard at first to get used to my boyfriend doing it, and the results were not satisfying for a long time. It has also taken me a long time (and I'm still working on it) to realize that masturbation is normal, and that girls do it as well as boys. For a long time I thought I must be a very sexually oriented being.

Many of the early childhood memories had to do with accidentally discovering pleasurable sensations during play, sensations which were not "sexual" in an adult sense.

FEMALE

The first sexual feeling I ever remember having is when I was about four years old and I remember a certain feeling from sliding down the clothesline pole.

MALE

I noticed that my penis became hard when I touched it. In first grade I would sit in the reading circle with a book on my lap, aware that it was covering my penis. I always had a difficult time hiding my "hard on." If I got called on to read, the whole thing became very apparent.

For children, "good feelings" may be the only meaning of masturbation. However, negative adult reactions about touching one's genitals create a sense of guilt or embarrassment. One persistent theme in these excerpts is that children often continue to masturbate despite conflicting messages from parents, siblings, or peers. Children discover that the threatened physical consequences simply do not occur. The private activity continues with an overlay of worry, guilt, and anxiety. Such feelings of guilt instilled at early ages persist at least until contradicted by a person's own experience and learning.

FEMALE

I began to masturbate when I was three years old. My parents, who both disapproved of my behavior (mainly because it embarrassed them), tried long and hard to discourage me. They told me it wasn't nice for a young lady to have her hands between her legs. However, even with this negative attitude, I remember always having masturbated except for a period between the ages of 11 and 13 when for some unknown reason I stopped.

MALE

Looking back, the most interesting comment my parents made, and the one that sticks in my mind the most, had to do with masturbation. Though neither my father nor mother condemned masturbation, they did say something to the effect that it was an unhealthy practice, and that I shouldn't continue. That one comment stayed with me and promoted feelings of guilt until I was old enough to realize for myself that what I did was in fact not unhealthy.

FEMALE

When I was five I remember my mother discovering that I masturbated with a rag doll I slept with. She was upset, but she didn't make a big deal about it. She just told me in a matter-of-fact way, "Do you know what you're doing is called masturbating?" That didn't make much sense to me, except I got the impression she didn't want me to do it. One night she discovered me again and made me sleep on the floor. When she took my rag doll I bunched up the sheets. I can remember getting a very pleasurable sensation that tired me out and helped me go to sleep.

FEMALE

I remember that I used to like to masturbate when I was a little girl. At the time I had no idea that's what I was doing—only knew that what I was doing felt good. I used to rub my pelvis against the arms of the living room chairs. My mother would come along and spank me for doing that, but I don't think she ever explained why or said anything about what I was doing. She just scolded and spanked me, and I knew I was bad because I liked to do it and she didn't want me to. I started sneaking around, trying to do it when she wasn't watching.

MALE

My first recognizable interest in sex that I recall is of stimulating myself probably around the age of three or four. One day Pa or Ma or someone (I really don't remember who it was) walked in and simply said not to do that. I sort of wondered why, but didn't ask. I'm glad I didn't, considering some of the ridiculous stories I might have been told.

These "ridiculous stories" were especially prevalent in the males' accounts. Parents were sometimes named as the source of inaccurate information, but for others the rumors simply existed.

MALE

A parent, I can't remember which one, observed me with an erection while I was getting dressed. He or she mentioned I shouldn't play with my penis because that would make it grow over to the neighbor's house.

MALE

When I was about ten, stories about masturbation got me worried. A friend and I went to a friend's older brother whom we respected and asked, "Is it really bad?" His reply stuck in my mind for years. "Well, it's like a bottle of olives—every time you take one out, there is one less in there." We were very worried because we thought we'd run out before we got to girls.

MALE

Good boys slept with their hands above the covers. Hands below the covers were a personal offense to God, and violation of this taboo resulted in dire and disfiguring penalties. At about age ten I started masturbating anyway. It felt good! I reasoned that if doing it would make the back of my head cave in, I would chance it until the back of my head started to soften, at which time I would quit—cold turkey.

MALE

I heard that if I masturbated, my hand would fall off, my nose would grow long, and I'd probably get warts and pimples. But I did it anyway and nothing happened.

MALE

By seventh grade I could hardly wait for my pubic hair to grow because my brothers told me that when it did I could start to masturbate.

Even when parents reassure a child that masturbation is not harmful, they often do not give enough information so that the child really understands.

MALE

My parents told me there was nothing wrong with "playing with yourself," but I still felt funny doing it. I often wondered if I did it too much, or worried that I would get caught.

Many children learn from peers or siblings about masturbation. Some discover it on their own.

FEMALE

I used to play with a girl, Julie, about three years older than I—when I was in second grade and she was in fourth grade. She once told me of a neat thing to do to make you feel really good. She explained to me how to wrap my legs around the poles of our swing set and squeeze. I used to love doing this and remember reaching states of euphoria, and losing consciousness of present reality. I remember hoping no one would see me because they would think I was crazy. I suppose I has having orgasms because I'd tense my leg muscles and the genital area. Then there would be a release of tension. Not until years later, late high school, when I reflected back, did I realize that I was masturbating.

FEMALE

When I was seven years old, one of my friends introduced me to an activity that felt good, but which I at first felt apprehensive about—masturbation. I have consistently masturbated since then without guilt feelings.

MALE

There weren't too many kids my age in the neighborhood, so I usually wound up playing with older kids. We had built a tree house, and one day when I was up there, one of them told me how to masturbate. I was too young to have any semen, but it still felt good.

FEMALE

My morals always held me back from anything but kissing, except when I was alone. That's when I started exploring my genitals with my hands. I had had biology, so I knew what each part was, especially the clitoris. By gently rubbing it I found that I could reach orgasm and I loved it. And so I was masturbating, and I still do.

MALE

I accidentally discovered that I could get gratification from pressure on my pubic area at a very young age. I was doing this without knowing what I was doing or why it was that way. Let it be known that this was quite awhile ago, before I could get erect.

Some students reported masturbatory arousal was aided by books, pictures, and other activities.

FEMALE

I discovered that reading some of the explicit scenes in some of my father's books gave me a pleasant tingling feeling in my lower abdomen. I didn't know what caused it, but I knew I enjoyed the feeling. When reading no longer sufficed to give it to me, I searched a little farther and found that by pressing my legs together in a certain way or by rubbing gently while reading, I could achieve this feeling. I soon found that I didn't even need to read in order to fantasize in my mind. Of course, visual aids helped so if one was available, I would base my fantasy on that.

MALE

In eighth grade I remember getting erections when I would stare at girls' bodies. I kept *Playboy* magazines that I would fish out of our Boy Scout paper drives. I remember wishing I could someday release the desire I developed after looking at the pictures. In the tenth grade I figured out how to masturbate, and boy did I use it with the pictures. Once I masturbated six times in one afternoon.

FEMALE

I learned to masturbate with a stream of water from a bathtub spout. It seems though that I was a slow learner because I didn't pick up this skill until I was about 14 years old. Although I was taught nothing about this practice directly either from my parents or from books, I did feel that it was somehow harmful, and did experience guilt feelings over it.

Some people reported never discovering or engaging in masturbation.

FEMALE

Masturbation is a word and topic I never heard of until I heard about it in a play. It really repelled me; I never had the urge to masturbate. For some reason, I can accept the fact that men do it much easier than that women do. I know I could never get excited enough by self-stimulation. It seems really unnatural to me.

FEMALE

I have never consciously masturbated; I've never had the desire. I've known what the word meant and implied for years, at least since I was a freshman in high school. But I can honestly say that I was never interested enough to try it.

FEMALE

I must have never thought to inspect myself until I knew there was something down there. I've learned that masturbation is a common thing, but I can honestly say that I never remember doing it. I inspected myself around the age of ten to see my extra hole which I hadn't known

I had, but found nothing pleasurable about touching it, so the thought of masturbating never occurred to me.

It is not surprising that this individual found nothing pleasurable about touching herself if she confined her exploration to her vagina. Instead of direct stimulation to the clitoris where the high concentration of nerve endings make it too sensitive for much direct touch, women most often stimulate the clitoris by stroking the shaft. A more common way is by manipulation of the entire vulva which stimulates the clitoris but in a less direct but more pleasurable manner (Kelly, 1988).

FEMALE

I did my first masturbating during a period when I began to wake up sexually. I didn't really feel guilty—I'd done enough reading to know that a person shouldn't—yet I don't think my family ever knew. I don't think I ever made it a frequent habit, and I haven't done it at all for about a year. I just don't enjoy it very much and I don't think I will ever resume the practice unless I have no other way to be satisfied.

Strong feelings often accompany the act of masturbation when it is first experienced as an adolescent or adult.

MALE

I learned about masturbation, put my guilt aside, and decided to try it. I went down to the basement bathroom. My heart started to pound till it wanted to burst through my chest. I still had some doubts about what I was going to do. Maybe, I thought, it was mortal sin. But I went ahead anyway. I was so nervous; my penis vacillated between being turgid and flaccid. My heart kept beating madly. I finally had an ejaculation. It was not much of an ejaculation because I was so nervous; I was only semi-hard. But it felt good. After a few times I lost my nervousness about masturbating. It became a completely enjoyable, everyday experience.

FEMALE

After hearing about it, I immediately tried masturbation, and I'll be damned, it worked!! For a year or so I had guilt feelings and said many times, "This is the last time," but it never was. After I realized I was not going to stop masturbating I thought the whole situation out. What is wrong with it? It doesn't hurt anyone, not even myself. Orgasm is very natural, not to mention enjoyable. Since then masturbation comes and goes (no pun intended). For a while it is rather intense, once or twice a day. Then it slacks off to once every one to two weeks. I think masturbation has been nothing but an asset.

Sometimes students associated frequent masturbation with emotional difficulties they had experienced. According to Patrick Carnes (1991), children living in a supportive family may find frequent masturbation comforting during times of emotional stress. A less healthy situation develops for children living in families which fail to provide warmth and acceptance, and they may begin to turn to things like food, sex, and whatever it takes to ease the pain.

FEMALE

I recall a period of occasional, even frequent, preteen bedtime masturbation. It seems to have been tied up to loneliness: babysitting for my younger brother on a Saturday night and being in bed and aware of the empty house—empty of the adults.

MALE

I only started masturbating when I moved and my insecurity and self-doubts were at their height. At this time my feelings about masturbation were provincial in that I believed I would have a weak mind and be sterile. This of course compounded my problems, and about this time acne made its first appearance. My brothers were also very badly affected. I really felt down. My major form of recreation was masturbation and also fantasizing about other things. I was a complete introvert.

MALE

I developed a pattern of masturbation at a very young age. I developed the urge to masturbate frequently. At first this was just a free-floating desire to masturbate; however, as I've gotten older this has become clearly a sexual desire. The older I get, the more inferior I feel in that I can't satisfy this drive in any other way than through masturbation. I still masturbate pretty much daily and can't seem to stop, except for the short times when I've had some kind of relationship with a woman.

For others it is a substitute for sexual activity with a partner.

FEMALE

We broke up in October of our freshman year at college and for quite a while I just dated casually. I enjoyed just dating around because I didn't want to get into anything serious for quite a while. It was somewhere in this period that I began to masturbate once in a while. I felt really guilty about this at first, but then after reading that it was normal, and that a lot of people do it, I didn't worry about it. There would be periods of months when I would not think of it, and periods when I would do it often.

FEMALE

Masturbation allows me to have sexual feelings and orgasms when I want or feel the need of it myself. It is an honest personal recognition of my feelings. I could not have or would not want to have a sexual relationship with someone merely for the sake of sex—I want it to be out of love and feeling. So, masturbation involves only me. It allows me to have sexual feelings but still only have sex with another person I care about and feel close to.

Some women experienced masturbation as a positive learning experience, including reducing inhibitions and discovering bodily sensations. These may be helpful in achieving full sexual functioning with a partner (Kaplan, 1987).

FEMALE

I've masturbated since I was sixteen or so and it has been enjoyable to explore my own body—testing my feelings, reactions, and what I like and dislike.

FEMALE

Masturbation has helped me tune into my own body functions and feelings. It has helped me become aware of my sex organs. Also, masturbation has left me feeling not at all ashamed of my sex organs and their functions. In general I think masturbation has helped me achieve a very healthy, open attitude about sex.

FEMALE

The first time that I ever masturbated was during sexual foreplay with my husband. I felt so dirty after that I didn't want him to touch me for weeks. The one thing that I am feeling the best about is that this fall I finally successfully masturbated and felt good about it. It left me with feelings that were just the opposite of how I'd felt in previous experiences. I feel more in control of myself now and more sure of exactly what it is that sexually satisfies me. I've only done it once, but I'm sure if I desire it I can do it again and again and have none of the old bad feelings.

FEMALE

I can remember the first time I masturbated. I was in my early thirties, and had recently learned that it was something women could do. It felt powerful, but afterwards I just lay there waiting to feel really guilty. I never did, and eventually relaxed and enjoyed it!

FEMALE

I started masturbating about two and one-half years ago at the point of desperation. I didn't think I was capable of coming at all, but found out I was. It was a great feeling. I have found that masturbating has helped me in having sex with a guy. I know now exactly where I get excitement and stimulation and can guide my partner.

>As can be seen from these anecdotal materials, masturbation serves a number of purposes. It is useful for children in learning about the pleasurable capabilities of their own bodies (Crooks and Baur, 1993). Research has also disclosed that self-pleasuring can become a legitimate substitute for undesired sexual intimacy, can avoid transmissions of STDs, and "provides a healthy, appropriate way to relieve sexual tension (especially for adults when there is no partner available and for persons of all ages choosing abstinence)" (Leight, 1988, p. 48). Researchers working with sexual dysfunction have found that masturbation is useful as a way to discover what is pleasurable in order to relay this information to a partner for a more mutually satisfying experience. Males can learn how to delay ejaculation (Kaplan, 1987) so they may satisfy their partner, and women who are not orgasmic can learn through masturbation their own sexual response.
>
>A 1970 publication from the Sex Information and Education Council of the United States (SIECUS) had the following wisdom for parental response to masturbation. It is as applicable today as when it was originally published:

>>As a general rule, parents and adults concerned with youth are best advised to disregard evidence of private masturbation in juveniles; not to look for it nor try to prevent it directly, or even indirectly by attempting to divert the youngster's attention to other activities. As with other bodily functions, however, young children can be helped to become aware of the distinction that every individual must learn to make between what is acceptable as public and as private behavior, without implying that the private behavior must be in any way inferior or bad. In adulthood as well as in childhood, masturbation by individuals in private is coming more and more to be regarded as an acceptable means of releasing sexual tension. (SIECUS, 1970)

SUGGESTED ISSUES FOR PERSONAL REFLECTION, GROUP DISCUSSION AND INTERACTION, PERSONAL JOURNAL

1. What memories, if any, do you have of masturbation as a child or adolescent?
    a. What feelings did you have about such activity?
    b. How did you learn about masturbation?
    c. What messages, if any, did you receive about this activity?
2. Indicate on the continuum where you would place each of the following by writing the letter above the appropriate number.

1	2	3	4	5
Highly unacceptable				Highly acceptable

    a. Masturbation for yourself
    b. Masturbation for your preschool child
    c. Masturbation for your school-age child
    d. Masturbation for your teenage children
    e. Masturbation for your partner
    f. Masturbation for your parents
    g. Masturbation for times when you have no partner

Think about what the different placements mean to you.

3. Do you think masturbation should be explained to a child?
    a. If so, how would you do it?
    b. If not, why not?
4. Do you think everyone should masturbate? Why or why not?

Chapter 3
Childhood Sexual Experience

There are few human activities about which there is greater curiosity, greater social concern, and less knowledge than child sexuality. (Wolman and Money, 1980, p. 30)

INTRODUCTION

Children, by the age of two or three, begin to investigate differences between their bodies and those of other children. They usually start by looking at, and sometimes touching, each others' genitals. As they get older (four or five years), this exploration is often done in the context of "playing doctor" or "playing house." According to figures in the Kinsey research (1948, 1953), 45 percent of females and 57 percent of males reported having had experiences of play that could be viewed as sexual in nature. More recently, a survey was done, asking parents of six- and seven-year-olds about their observations of their children's sex play. The results indicated that 76 percent of the girls and 83 percent of the boys had participated in some sex play with friends or siblings (Crooks and Baur, 1993).

These higher figures seem more accurate, based on the university student papers in our classes. Experiences of genital and bodily experimentation, with a wide range of accompanying feelings, appeared so frequently in the papers that one might hypothesize an almost universal occurrence. Many students indicated, however, that they had forgotten such incidents until they began to probe consciously for early memories about sexuality. Such "forgetting" is often a response to strong negative parental reactions. One woman wrote in her paper at the end of the term:

FEMALE

I feel better now about some of my childhood "sexual experiences"—to know that other people had similar experiences and that it's all very normal and natural. A girlfriend and I used to explore each other's bodies when we were small. I "forgot" these experiences for a time because I thought it was wrong and I was embarrassed.

Sexual activity between children has raised controversy among sex educators, researchers and the population in general with regard to the distinction between sex play and exploitation. We propose a working definition of exploitation: Sex play becomes exploitation when there is a significant difference in age, knowledge, or experience. Such difference usually results in the noninitiator experiencing being coerced or manipulated by a more powerful child.

FEMALE

When I was in the first grade, two boys (also in first grade) grabbed me and pulled down their pants and mine and lay on top of me. I was very ashamed of this and never told anyone until recently.

The rest of the childhood activities described in the student writing in this chapter are in the category of sex play or exploration rather than exploitation. The latter will be documented in Chapter 11.

FEMALE

Mike Compton was my very best friend. My boyfriend—as serious a boyfriend as any first grader would dream of. In fact, he was the first person I ever kissed. We planned it all out. He lived on the edge of a field with some woods. That warm summer day we set out for the woods, hand in hand, looking for that perfect place to experience our first kiss. We finally decided on a clearing where the sun shone through the trees in the woods. We turned toward one another holding one another's sweaty hands and I said, "On the lips, but just a short one—not a mushy one like on TV." And with that, we kissed. That wasn't so bad now was it? It wasn't bad at all, but we never did it again. I suppose one kiss is enough among best friends.

> *While toddlers are being toilet trained, they naturally become more aware of their genitals. They notice very quickly that boys and girls are different, and they often like to undress and show each other their bodies, to watch each other go to the toilet and to play together in the bath. Penises, being more conspicuous than girls' genitals, are particularly fascinating. Boys often like to look at or touch each others' penises, and girls may be intrigued by them too. At this stage the interest shown in other children's bodies is mostly due to simple curiosity reinforced by a fascination with toilet functions, and this exploratory play is usually full of laughter. (Lansdown and Walker, 1991, p. 239)*

Many of the early experiences had to do with looking. For most, this was a primary way of checking out whether their own bodies looked like other people's, both same and other gender (Katchadourian, 1989). Much of this play can be misinterpreted by adults who have different perceptions.

FEMALE

I remember a time when a girlfriend and I had gone to the circus and had seen some clowns pull their pants down. We thought this was the funniest thing ever, so we thought we would try it. We went into the backyard and both pulled our pants down. Well, my mother found out what we had done, and she told us we shouldn't do that any more. I remember what a good time we were having "playing circus," and I just couldn't understand why it was "bad."

FEMALE

Once my younger sister and I were over at a girlfriend's house playing in her bedroom. For some reason she pulled her pants down and exposed her rear to us. We were amazed to see she had an extra opening down there we didn't know about. My sister reciprocated by pulling her pants down so we could see if she had the same extra opening. We were amazed at our discovery, our mother not having mentioned to us that we had one.

FEMALE

My first real encounter with sexuality was in the first grade. Bathrooms were very crowded and the girls envied the boys who were done so fast. So, instead of wasting precious break time waiting in line, we decided to try standing like they did. Several girls entered the bathroom together for the experiment. Suddenly we realized the boys were peeping in, so going to the bathroom became a gathering of giggling, screaming, amused girls. I'm not sure we really knew what all that was about, but I remember the sexual tension in the air: a mixture of excitement, pleasure and fear.

FEMALE

When I was four, I remember being behind my house with a neighbor boy who undressed. He was wearing long johns (which I'd never seen) and there were blue veins in his penis. My mother caught us. I don't remember what she said to me but it implied that I was doing something wrong. I remember feeling ashamed.

MALE

I can remember the comparative anatomy studies held in the garage with a female playmate. We were both about four. It was interesting even though it was mostly "looky" and little "touchy." We were never caught at that pastime.

MALE

I remember taking the little girl from down the street into the closet to play doctor. We pulled down our pants, and sort of stood there and looked at each other. Finally, we said, "Humpf!" and went back outside to ride our tricycles.

Touching one another's bodies was also reported in the early years.

FEMALE

I'll never forget my first sexual experience when I was a child. I was four at the time and playing with my cousin. He asked if I would pull down my pants so he could see my "personal spot." He agreed to do the same so I could see his "personal spot." We were amazed at what we saw, and even dared to touch each other. We were just a couple of young, curious children wanting to know what the opposite sex was like. Neither of us told our parents of the experience for fear of being punished.

FEMALE

When Johnny and I were six, he told me about his "little trick." I knew I wanted to see it, so he took off his underwear. Then he asked me to take mine off so he could see what I had. I was a little hesitant for a minute then I said yes. After I removed my shorts and my panties we stared at each other for a while.

Johnny then touched me "there" and asked me to touch him. As we did this I had an incredible feeling and Johnny's penis got bigger and stood up. We stopped what we were doing and started laughing because his penis looked so funny. We quickly got our clothes back on when we heard his brother coming down the stairs. But he didn't suspect anything, and we kept our secret. I remember thinking how good it felt and that we had just discovered something totally new.

Playing doctor seemed an almost universal vehicle for sex play.

MALE

Nancy was a willing playmate and we spent many hours together examining each other's bodies as doctor and nurse. We even once figured out a pact that we would continue these examinations and watch each other develop. This was before we had started school.

FEMALE

At the age of five, a couple of neighbor boys undressed me in a tent in their backyard. I got caught—came home with my blouse outside the straps of my jumper instead of inside. It's amazing the details I can still recall from so many years ago! Until the age of about seven I played doctor with a couple of girlfriends occasionally. I remember enjoying being examined and touched.

FEMALE

The first thing I can remember is playing that game of doctor (we called it "checking") with my little brother, one year younger than I. "Let's go play doctor" ... furtive glances (Mom's not around) and up we'd go to a bedroom. It was basically mutual masturbation, accompanied by guilt ("Can God see us?" ... "Is Mom coming?"), and a kind of fascination with the other person's genitals. I can't remember any real sexual feelings accompanying any "check" (no tingles or excitement). I do remember when I got older (fourth grade) being scared that I would get pregnant. At that time, we attempted intercourse, and were so scared we barely touched.

Children sharing sleeping space are provided opportunities for mutual exploration.

FEMALE

In kindergarten my girlfriend and I always took naps together and underneath the blankets we would explore our own bodies and each others'. In second and third grades, I slept over at the neighbor boy's house, and we would often look at each other, and occasionally touch each other.

FEMALE

A significant thing happened when I was five. My female cousin, age seven, and I began to play "doctor." However, my cousin knew how to do direct clitoral stimulation and taught me how to do it. So, whenever there was a chance to sleep over at her house we could hardly wait to go to bed! We only played our "game" in bed, in the dark, under the covers. This probably went on for about four months and then stopped. I was glad because I was starting to feel guilty about it.

MALE

The seven kids in our family all shared the same large bedroom. A couple of times, I would be put in with my sister to sleep. During the nights, we would explore each other in our sleep [sic] but never talk about it.

As children grew older, the sex play was sometimes more imitative of adult activities.

FEMALE

During the summer between third and fourth grade I became involved in sex play with boys. I was nine then. My friend, Donna, a year older was already growing breasts, was a pretty wild and worldly kid and I was fascinated with her. She was the first to teach me about masturbation. She had learned to stimulate herself by rubbing against the edge of a door. Interestingly, she called it peter-tickle. I wonder why it had a male connotation. Led by Donna, we got together with my brother and the boy next door who was my age. I can see us vividly: walking down the railroad tracks smoking Marvel cigarettes we'd all chipped in to buy (22 or 23 cents) and talking about fucking. We felt so grown up. When we got out in the country we went into the woods and undressed. Richard would lie on top of me and we'd pretend to have intercourse. I remember his limp penis feeling cool against my thigh. My brother and Donna did the same. I wasn't very impressed with the sex play with Richard. He seemed to be real passive about it all; I don't think he ever did anything but just lie there. I think I was disappointed, because after masturbation, this was a real let-down. I guess the novelty wore off. We stopped experimenting and Donna and I drifted apart.

Some children engaged in activities that went on over time, sometimes involving pretend games.

FEMALE

My friend Sharon and I were inseparable playmates. She moved in across the street during kindergarten, and if she wasn't at my house, I was at hers. Endless hours of playing dolls eventually led to playing doctor with our dolls. We used to have elaborate setups of calling, making appointments, and performing "procedures." With the most serious faces we would confer and solemnly nod that yes, this one too needed a "body wash." "Body wash" consisted of putting tubes at the doll's genital area. Placing the tubes gave me all kinds of tingly excitement. Eventually, we ourselves became the patients needing a "body wash." I don't remember ever taking off our clothes, but do remember the bodily pleasure, excitement and anticipation of placing some old rubber tubing next to the genital area, even through layers of underpants and jeans. I also remember we never played this game at my house—always at hers. She had a younger brother; we never allowed him to join us—likewise, my older brother never joined us.

FEMALE

I was aware of the physical differences between boys and girls at an early age. Most of my young playmates were older than I, and taught me all about the "pussy." It was just a matter of rubbing your body against his. Of course we never removed any clothes. No one ever explained that to us, so we just rubbed away, clothes and all. Many times guys were not available to do the "pussy," but girls worked just as well.

FEMALE

Thankfully, I also had many "normal" experiences with nieces, cousins, and neighborhood friends as a young child. We engaged in the usual sex-play activities, such as playing "house" and "doctor," having "beauty pageants" at slumber parties—where the less you wore, the more likely you were to "win." I had a couple different boyfriends between the ages of seven and twelve. We did fun, everyday things like riding bikes, playing ball, walking and talking through the woods, berry-picking, and just playing in general. Sometimes, when we were sure no one else was around, especially our friends, we'd hold hands or put our arms around each other—a couple times we even kissed—quick, shy little pecks, but thrilling to us. I treasure these memories—they were all too few to suit me. I've drawn on them many times—I believe they've often kept me from believing that I really was "bad" or "tainted." I know now, of course, that I did nothing wrong except trust people I should have been able to trust. But without the good memories, I may never have believed this.

Childhood sex play provided the opportunity for learning the pleasurable possibilities of one's own body.

FEMALE

One of my delights was playing married and playing doctor. Playing house and married was done with my cousin, Tom. Playing doctor was done with him and his two sisters who were older than we were. When we were seven or eight they already had breasts, and that was one of the nicest parts about playing doctor—to touch their breasts and look at them—they were so soft and round. These exploratory activities went on for several years without discovery. In fact, whenever my cousins and I would visit my grandmother, Tom and I were always put into the same bed to sleep—a deep feather bed. It was fun to have the feather tick cover us up on all sides as we touched and explored each other's bodies. Our parents and grandparents were apparently unaware of what was going on. In puberty I was quite inhibited and inactive, and it wasn't until late adolescence, as I began to date, that I remembered with gratitude those early experiences of genital arousal.

REACTIONS OF SIGNIFICANT ADULTS

Parents, teachers, and other adults associated with children often feel alarmed when they discover a child exploring his or her genitals or engaged in mutual exploration with a playmate. They feel shock and concern about children's behavior which they interpret as sexual. It awakens fears that the child may be either sexually precocious or perverted.

A frequent response of parents is to attribute adult meanings to childhood experimentation (McKinney, 1989). They may even mistakenly predict future behavior and functionality based on such childhood activity. In order to discourage the behavior, parents may fairly frequently make a moral interpretation: "dirty," "bad," "good boys and girls don't . . . . " In the face of such strong reactions, the child often learns to mask his or her curiosity and satisfy it clandestinely with peers.

In this area of life where the child may get the strongest and most powerfully negative (and confusing) reactions from adults, there is little opportunity for a reality check on misinformation, impressions, and fantasy. Progressive relearning and reinterpretation of adult messages, a characteristic and natural part of learning in other areas of life, is often unavailable, thus leaving the pleasure of the activity tinged with feelings of guilt and shame.

FEMALE

By playing doctor and nurse, I found out the major difference between a boy and a girl. It was an educational experience, but it was awful because my mother caught us behind the garage. She spanked me and forbade the boy to come into our yard again. I think it was the hardest spanking I ever received. I can remember my mother saying, "You ought to be ashamed" and at that time I was. But now I think, "Should I have been ashamed? . . . For what?"

FEMALE

Another memory I have of sex play was when my female cousin and I progressively took off our clothes and showed off in front of my brother and male cousin. We were in about third or fourth grade at the time.

Each time we would take off a piece of our clothing, we would model in front of the bedroom doorway so our brothers could see us, and they would cheer us on. This was a fun game until my father caught us. I don't remember feeling guilty about what I had done, but I was scared because I knew I would be disciplined. However, I don't remember for sure how I was disciplined or whether I was disciplined at all.

FEMALE

My first sexual experience involved a neighbor boy and me. We were playing doctor down in the basement and my mother caught us. She sent him home and me to my room. For a long time I thought sex was bad. I was afraid of it, and also afraid of asking my mother questions about sex.

MALE

I had a very close friend, a boy, who lived a couple of houses away from me, and we used to do everything together. One day we started to show our penises to each other. We hid in a closet, and all of a sudden my mother burst in. She sent my friend home; I suspect she called his mom to tell her what had happened. She didn't really yell at me or hit me but I remember feeling very bad, very guilty. It's funny how I haven't thought of that in years.

> *How parents respond to sex play in children begins to set the stage for later sex-related values. If a parent constantly punishes a child's attempts at genital exploration or sex play, the child may rapidly learn that her or his sex organs and exploratory behaviors are bad. At times the reactions of anxious adults can transform an innocent, natural phase of sexual exploration into a traumatic event with lasting negative consequences for the child. Children often begin to see their sexuality in very clearly defined terms, resulting from parental attitudes toward anything sexual. If parents accept sexual exploration as a natural, positive part of growing up and help children to understand what will be socially acceptable in later life, they may contribute enormously to a healthy sexuality in their children. (Kelly, 1988, p. 153)*

Children learn to keep sex secretive and clandestine.

MALE

When I was about five, my cousin and I went into the basement and dropped our pants. We touched each other's penises, and that was it. I guess I didn't realize the total significance of the secrecy in which we carried out this act, for later on in the evening my parents questioned me about what went on in the basement; I told them exactly what we had done. They were horrified and told me that that was definitely forbidden.

I was never under any circumstances to do anything even remotely similar to that again. I can remember restaging this act with my cousin only once after that and, of course, this time I didn't tell my parents.

MALE

We got caught and punished several times for playing doctor. We played in the garage, quite a den of iniquity! Several kids were involved in this game because you can't play doctor without the proper staff present. This is most likely why we got caught. When five or six kids disappear into the garage, being very quiet, what parent isn't going to be curious?

MALE

One of my favorite pastimes was playing doctor with my little sister. During this doctor game we would both be nude and I would sit on her as if we were having intercourse. On one occasion, I was touching my sister's genital area and mother discovered us. We were sternly switched and told it was dirty and to never get caught again or we would be whipped twice as bad. So, we made sure we were never caught again. In general, I was raised with an attitude that sex was a dirty thing that should be hidden, and certainly never mentioned, so I learned to be secretive and silent.

Sometimes the child had a guilty or fearful sense about playing doctor, even though a parent had not discovered the activity.

FEMALE

My friend said to me, "If you show me yours, I'll show you mine." I said, "All right, but we should go into the garage where no one will see us." I knew or thought that if someone caught us, we'd both be in real trouble. I don't remember what brought on this fear, but he seemed to have the same idea. So we went into the garage, and that was the first time I ever remember seeing a boy's penis. He and I explored together many more times.

FEMALE

At about the age of six or seven I can recall going down the street and into a boy's tent. We took off our clothes and looked at each other's "private parts." I was very worried about being caught and felt guilty afterwards. I felt sure my parents knew what I had been doing, and all their wrath was going to fall on my head shortly, along with the end of my life as I presently knew it. But nothing ever happened and time washed away those uneasy feelings. But it didn't wash away the idea that sex was something to hide, and that it was in a way, evil.

For some people, an almost automatic connection has been made between the experience of pleasure and the feelings of guilt and fear.

MALE

In second grade, I remember exploring a little girl's body (to our mutual delight), but then later the teacher found out about it and told my parents. I remember feeling bad, as though I had done something most normal kids wouldn't do. My feelings of abnormality and inferiority that day have caused me lots of misery. The whole matter of what is sexually normal seems to be at the heart of lots of difficulty.

MALE

A neighbor girl, my female cousin and I used to show each other our sex organs. That was really thrilling, and also really frightening. These two sensations have seemed to go hand in hand in virtually every sexual experience I have had. I've always felt that to touch someone's penis or vulva was wrong, and was always sure I would be caught. But I kept on doing it because of the pleasure.

Parents reading adult meanings into children's play may be surprised if they take time to listen to the child:

FEMALE

My daughter was about four years old, and her friend Jimmy, also four, was lying on the living room floor with her. As I came in the room he sat on top of her rocking back and forth while holding her arms pinned down to the floor. They were laughing and giggling and rolling around a lot, and I felt uneasy, although they seemed to be having a great time. Finally, in my uneasiness, I said, "What are you doing?" He looked up at me with a broad smile and said, "We're playing motorcycle."

PRE-PUBERTAL PLEASURE

MALE

I recall some of the games we used to play when cousins came to stay. We would play a game of hide and seek till a female cousin and I could be alone to examine each other's body. She didn't have breast development yet and neither of us had pubic hair, but we sure had a good secret going in the hayloft. Girls became more and more interesting and I wanted to know everything about them and how and why they did all they did. Our playing ended at the time of menses, pubic hair, and acne. It all seemed innocent enough before then.

FEMALE

I remember when I was about 10 or 11, and used to play with my cousin after school. She and I would normally play with Barbies and stuff, but after a while we started to play with each other. Not really with our hands, it was mostly with other body parts, like a foot in between each other's legs or lying on top of each other and rubbing up and down. This didn't happen real long and we didn't do it a whole lot but I think I had my first orgasm that way. I just remember a warm, pleasurable feeling going from by abdomen to my toes. At first I was scared; I thought maybe I started my period or something, so I jumped up and ran to the bathroom. Since I discovered it wasn't my first period, I decided it must have been an orgasm. But that feeling was never repeated until just this past December.

Curiosity can lead to surprising results.

MALE

I had my first interpersonal sexual experience the summer when I was 11. I was visiting my uncle's farm and had to sleep with my cousin who was 18. I woke up in the middle of the night, noticing my cousin was sleeping soundly. I remember having the urge to touch him. I very slowly and carefully began feeling various places on him. He still seemed asleep when I felt his erect penis. Up to that time I thought that only I ever had erections; now I thought it must run in the family. When he said, "Now let me feel yours," I almost had a heart attack! I immediately pretended to be asleep and rolled to the other side of the bed. I was really scared, and when he tried to touch my penis, I warded him off by pretending to be loudly talking in my sleep. My experience of exploration with my cousin when I was 11 was my last "sexual" experience until I was 18. During that seven-year span, masturbation was my only form of sexual gratification.

SOME CONCLUSIONS

Interpretations of any given "sexual" activity may be quite different for children and adults. Adults often feel discomfort because of the widespread occurrence of experimentation and exploration and ask, "Why are our children doing this?"
    Curiosity and ignorance *seem to be prime motivators for children. They genuinely want to know whether and how their bodies are different from other chil-*

dren's. Many times, even with patient parental explanations and answers to questions, children still have questions which are often dealt with by direct observation or experimentation. Much childhood bodily exploration prior to parental intervention is matter-of-fact seeking for information. When parents discover the activity and judge it severely, the children may begin to experience guilt.

Fascination *with anatomical similarities and differences is often a factor in curiosity and exploration. Children learning about sex without adult negative judgment may experience the same amazement as they do when they learn why the wind blows or how the seasons change.*

Pleasure *discovered in the course of exploring is often a factor in the repetition of a given activity, even in the face of parental threats, punishments, or disapproval.*

Adults *need to be aware that they cannot assume that children are expressing the same complex emotional and relational factors as adults are in sexual activity. Adult motives, feelings, and intensity are inappropriately attributed to childhood genital exploration. It is quite appropriate and necessary, however, for adults, especially parents, to formulate guidelines to help children learn about genital behavior and exploration—as a means of facilitating children's healthy sexual attitudes.*

SOME SUGGESTIONS FOR PERSONAL REFLECTION

(These notes are not to be turned in or shared.)

1. As you read through the chapter, have your journal or notebook available. As you complete the excerpts on a given page, pay attention to feelings and memories that are triggered by the readings. At the end of each page of readings, take time to jot down some notes, feelings, or memories out of your own experience. Pay attention to what your real feelings are—not necessarily what you think you "ought" to be feeling.
2. When you have completed the chapter, look at your notes: What patterns do you see? Are there any surprises in what you have written? Anything you want to pursue further?
3. If it could have been different in your family of origin, what one change would you like?

SOME SUGGESTIONS FOR SMALL GROUP DISCUSSION

1. Remember that individuals are in charge of what they share in this group. For your group to function most effectively, each person needs to be free to share or remain silent without pressure. Since these are sensitive issues, it is important to let others know when you feel judged, pressed, or ridiculed in the group.
2. The following are descriptions of some situations that might be challenging to you. One member of the group will draw one of the slips which describes

a situation, then read it aloud. In the group, share how you would react in that situation. As group members speak, accept reactions that are different from your own, but feel free to ask them to say more if you do not understand their position. There is no need to come to a group consensus. The purpose is to explore with one another a range of personal responses. When you have finished with one situation, read another and repeat the process.

    a. You are the parent of a ten-year-old boy who has a very close boy friend who is 12. They often spend the night at one another's house. One morning, you find they have been sleeping in the same bed, and are embracing each other in their sleep. What will you do or say now or later, if anything? Why? What immediate feelings do you have?

    b. You are the parent of a five-year-old girl. You live in a neighborhood of older families, and are the only family with children. You look out the window and see your daughter and her best kindergarten friend walking nude hand in hand down the sidewalk. What will you do or say now or later, if anything? Why? What immediate feelings do you have?

    c. You are the parent of three children: six, eight, and nine years of age, the two oldest being boys. You come into your daughter's room and find all three nude, the oldest boy on top of the daughter, and the other son watching interestedly. What will you do or say then or later, if anything? Why? What are your immediate feelings?

When you have completed the activity, discuss generalizations you would make about parental reactions to sexual situations in childhood. Are there ways you hope to react differently than your parents did?

3. If you could create a society in which children would grow up sexually in the healthiest possible way, what would your society be like?

Chapter 4

Sex Roles and Expectations

INTRODUCTION

The process of identifying oneself as male or female and acting appropriately as girls or boys, men or women, results from a complex interaction between both biological and social factors (Money and Ehrhardt, 1972). "Biological influences do not work in isolation; children always develop within a social context, and thus nature and nurture inevitably interact" (Beal, 1994, p. 283). "There is now considerable evidence that gender roles are learned during late infancy and early childhood, rather than being an inborn part of our sense of self" (Beal, 1994, p. 114).

> In a modern complex society like ours, an adult has to be assertive, independent, and self-reliant, but traditional femininity makes many women unable to behave in these ways. On the other hand, an adult must also be able to relate to other people, to be sensitive to their needs and concerned about their welfare, as well as to be able to depend on them for emotional support. But traditional masculinity keeps men from responding in such supposedly feminine ways. (Bem, 1975, p. 62)

A concept in the literature today, rather than feminine or masculine, is androgyny—those most positive human qualities that legitimately belong in the repertoire of both men and women. Most of the evidence thus far collected suggests that people who are able to transcend traditional gender roles may be able to function more comfortably and effectively in a wider range of situations. Androgynous individuals can select from a broad repertoire of feminine and masculine behaviors. They may choose to be independent, assertive, nurturing, or tender, based not on gender role norms but rather on what provides them and others optimum personal satisfaction in a given situation (Crooks and Baur, 1993).

Most of the students who wrote these papers have been influenced by traditional gender role expectations in the United States. Because the excerpts came from a limited sample and were anonymous, viewpoints from many of the diverse ethnic groups in the United States today were not represented. Research indicates that, while human biology is a major determinant in sex roles of the genders, the varied circumstances in which cultural groups evolve also have great influence. For example, Margaret Mead described Tchambuli tribe gender roles in New Guinea: "The men spent most of their time caring for children, gossiping, bickering, primping and applying makeup, and haggling over catch. Fish was the staple diet of the Tchambuli, and women brought home the daily catch. Women kept their heads shaven, disdained ornaments, and were more highly sexed and aggressive than men" (Rathus, Nevid, and Fichner-Rathus, 1993, pp. 172–173). Our sample presents a problem in terms of being limited. However, the excerpts show that most of the students felt they had to learn (or rebel against) the family/peer/ community-approved sex roles.

As students wrote about their sexuality they reflected on their feelings about being male or female, about the expectations placed on them because of their gender, how they accepted or defied those expectations, and how their sex role identification affected their relationships with members of the other sex.

Physical appearance is part of what defines a person as masculine or feminine. For girls, this often meant dressing up, and receiving special attention. For boys, it often meant physical performance such as playing with certain toys and being active in sports.

FEMALE

I was given constant attention and was treated as my parents' most prized possession. I was my mother's little doll; she spent all of her time dressing me up and putting ribbons in my hair. A couple of years later my sister was born and we were dressed alike in little identical dresses of different colors. People always commented on how cute we were, and when we were a little older we were always asked if we were twins. So, as you can see, femininity and a cute little-girl look was always stressed when I was a child. From the age of 4 to 12 I took dance and ballet lessons every week to bring grace to my movements.

FEMALE

Every Sunday my mother would dress me up. I looked nice with my pillbox hat, white gloves, and black patent leather shoes. I was aware of being a girl, because I was the first girl born in our family and was given much attention because of that. As I grew up, I began to wonder what a girl really was; I needed to realize my uniqueness aside from being the first born of the four sisters.

FEMALE

Although I cannot recall when it began, I remember clearly separating masculine and feminine roles. Perhaps this was due to my rather traditional upbringing and a special influence from my Irish Catholic grandmother. There were just certain things girls did that boys didn't, and vice versa. I remember having very long blonde hair that was put in long spiral curls every morning before early Mass, and wearing dresses most of the time. My dolls were all feminine even though I repeatedly asked Santa for a "Dennis the Menace" doll and an electric train. Mother was going through a divorce, working to support me and my sister, and helping Grandmother with the house where we all lived. So I learned that being female necessitated martyrdom.

FEMALE

Growing up, I felt the intensity of the strict gender roles presented by the traditional values. Boys will be bouncy, aggressive, noisy, and naturally inquisitive. Girls will be well-mannered, assertive (but only with other females), and will naturally grow up to be accepting, nurturing people. The roles conflict with my personal ideal, I wanted to part of the group. I wanted to be like my brothers. I was bouncy, noisy, aggressive, and always questioning. My mother's understanding of my behavior ended about the age of 12. I was to be entering puberty soon, girls should be feminine, they should not be aggressive, and be in somewhat of the background. I did not understand.

FEMALE

One conviction I've always had is the feeling that a woman should be feminine. Even though the current trends indicate that women look more like men, I still enjoy putting on a fancy dress and getting dressed up for a special occasion. A lot of people I know can't stand to put a dress on and haven't worn one in years. It's kind of an ego boost to me to really feel and look like "a woman."

FEMALE

Between my parents and grandparents I learned I was "special" because I was a female, not a male. Being a woman was an important position. I almost expected to be pampered because I was part of that elite group. In school the dress codes were regimented, in contrast to today. I learned to sit in a "ladylike" way despite feeling that sitting "boylike" was so much more comfortable.

MALE

As a youngster I recall that my toys were "male." I had army men, guns, baseball gloves, bats, footballs, and boats; I was spoiled so their quantity was unlimited. Helping me along the way in my early endeavors was perhaps my most eager playmate, my father. He was extremely active with me and took me places with him as much as his work permitted. I identified with him very much, and at a preschool age I knew he and I were quite a bit alike.

MALE

Playtime from kindergarten through third grade often involved playing soldiers. One side would be the Americans, the other would be the current enemy. I had a huge assortment of toy weapons my father had made. Although I was by far the youngest kid in the neighborhood, since I had the guns, the bigger kids always invited me to play their "grown-up" games. We made a big deal of how many of the enemy could be mowed down at once, and how realistically we could be wounded or killed.

MALE

I participated in a string of sports to fulfill those athletic expectations of my peers. I tried out for the swim team one year, wrestling another year, played tennis another, and did poorly at each. Girls responded more positively to "I made the varsity squad this year," than to "I'm in the Honor Society."

> Boys are constrained to avoid the feminine role beginning at about two years, while many girls in early adolescence feel compelled to be feminine by internal and peer pressures that are as forceful as anything a parent could say. . . . Overall, however, the male role appears to be more restrictive, to the point of being so oppressive that some children refuse it . . . . Many more boys than girls actively resist conforming to the expected gender role. (Beal, 1994, pp. 282–283)

> Though more restrictive, the male sex role is rewarded more consistently in our society. A questionnaire regarding attitudes toward "sissies and tomboys" was given to 80 college students, 40 female and 40 male. The results indicated more acceptance from the females than the males, and "sissies" were expected to be less well adjusted than other children, including "tomboys" (Martin, 1990).

> Some women affirmed this in writing of their freedom to act either boylike or girllike while others encountered imposed restrictions or disapproving attitudes.

FEMALE

I knew I was a female, but it didn't seem congruent with what I believed or liked to do. I really wished that I had been born a boy. I was definitely a tomboy for as long as I can remember. Instead of helping in the house, I helped my dad in the yard; I identified with my dad and my brother and tried to copy them a lot. I always wanted to walk around the house without a shirt like they did, and couldn't understand why it was "wrong." It seemed that my goals and ambitions were all traditionally masculine. I enjoyed being like that, though as I grew older, my mother cautioned me about playing too hard with the boys because I was a girl and could get hurt. That only depressed me.

To carry this further, I fell into the same role as I grew older. Playing sports was important to me. I never really wanted the typical girl toys. Dressing up in dresses revolted me. Even in junior high, when the other girls started to dance and wear make-up, I never followed. Trying to impress boys with those things was out for me. I'd rather be playing baseball with them. To illustrate this further, I was still wearing an undershirt in eighth grade. I thought bras were dumb but my mother got me one anyway saying, "It is time." Despite being such a jock, I always seemed to have a boyfriend.

FEMALE

I was not really brought up to be a lady, do woman's work, or any such thing. If something needed doing, sex didn't matter. As a youngster I began house cleaning and doing the laundry on weekends when just in sixth grade; this was because my mother worked six days a week. However, I also did things with my father—painted the house, worked on the car, helped build a garage. In play, I also liked male activities. I was the only girl in the neighborhood, so my brother and I would play baseball, football, basketball, and other games with the boys. My parents never discouraged me from participating in these activities.

FEMALE

I really wanted to be a boy when I was young. One time, when I was about four, I tried to urinate on the tree in front of my house like my boy cousin had done. My mother saw this and spanked me for it.

FEMALE

My earliest memory that it made a difference in being a girl was when at age five, I couldn't camp out in the backyard with a five-year-old neighbor boy. Girls don't do that! No reason was ever given, just a negative answer. At least, this was a response as throughout my growing stages, I did not receive any sexual information or reasons. I have only one sibling, a sister who is 12 years older. I am like an only child, still without sisterly bonds. There was not a concentration on being a female. Even today, it is hard for me to understand the feminist movement. I was me—a person who had to remember that we were prominent people of society and I had to stand tall on my own feet.

FEMALE

I was a tomboy—the only girl in my family who was. My dad always seemed (and still does) so pleased when I showed him I could do things as the son he never had might have. I still get a real thrill when I show a man I can do something he may think only a man could do—even if it's only a show of strength. But, I also like to look and act feminine. I have long hair which makes me feel very feminine when it is just hanging down on my back over my shoulders.

FEMALE

I don't remember being treated differently than my two brothers (one older and one younger), until I got to be a teenager. At this time, it became obvious to me that my father had double standards for my brothers and myself. I was not allowed to drive, date, or do things with friends as early as my older brother. Although I believe that my father was doing his best to protect me, it felt very unfair and chauvinistic, and also affirmed to me that my father did not feel that I was as capable of taking care of myself or being able to be as responsible as my older brother was. Neither of my parents encouraged me to express my feelings, to challenge my abilities, or to take risks. Basically I think the reason was because they were not like that either. I grew up feeling very self-conscious and unsure of myself around people I didn't know well.

FEMALE

As we grew up, I do believe my parents did a good job of treating "the sexes" equally. My brother and I, from the earliest times shared equal responsibility for all types of chores. We both picked up, cleaned up, dusted, vacuumed, washed and dried dishes, cut grass, weeded flower beds and gardens (I still hate weeding!), and any number of other things around the house. We also played all the same games; baseball, football, swimming, jacks, dolls, whatever. This was just natural for us; we saw our parents sharing the same types of responsibilities all the time. My father worked for Fisher Body, as an engineer. My mother worked from the time I was in second grade until after I graduated from high school, as the cafeteria supervisor for the entire school district (23 schools). Maybe because Mom worked, or because that is the type of people they were, they always shared household chores and playtime activities, too. Theirs was a partnership marriage, not a despotic one.

Consequently, I grew up knowing I was the same as my brother, not sexually—I knew there was a difference, but the same in rights and responsibilities.

But when we got to high school, things changed. I got blamed for a lot more things than my brother did. My parents also assumed I'd do better in school, so they never gave me the credit I thought I deserved for the work I did. And still, to this day, I'm not sure if they are as proud of me as they are my brother. At that time, I also started to notice slight differences in their behavior toward us. I was required to do a lot more around the house while he was allowed a car and outside employment. My brother's curfews were less strict. It wasn't fair. There wasn't anything I could do about it. I just supposed it was my parents' problem, not the world's problem. I still felt the sexes were equal. Some people might be better than others, not sexes.

In general, according to a recent study (Etaugh and Liss, 1992), children from third through eighth grades increasingly prefer masculine toys and male friends. The toys children asked for and received were generally gender-typical.

FEMALE

I don't feel I was raised to "be a girl." We were always encouraged to develop our own interests and pursue those things which would best meet our needs. My fire truck was parked right next to my dolls and I spent most of my time playing traditional boy-type games. My childhood dream was to be the first professional woman baseball player in the Major League.

FEMALE

I adored my older brother. We played cars in the dirt and mud, romped in bathing trunks at the beach, and climbed sand-dirt banks. I remember taking my very own quarter and going to the dime store to get a metal pickup truck for our road games in our backyard. I had many doll things and played with these with my girlfriends. I had a large storybook doll collection and Mother got one for my brother once, but he didn't play with dolls so he gave it to me.

Men wrote of being limited in the range of choices they had for expressing emotions and other so-called "feminine" characteristics. There seemed to be no outlets for their feelings other than their internal confusions and frustrations of not fitting in with "what it means to be a man."

MALE

I often felt a great deal of pressure to be involved in a popular sport such as football or basketball. To like poetry, or to be involved with classical music were sissy activities. Band was an okay activity, but not orchestra.

MALE

I have a tendency to be gentle, warm, sensitive, affectionate, domestic, submissive, impulsive, and emotional—traits that are supposedly effeminate. As a man I ought to be powerful and dominant. I fought my natural gentle tendencies and attempted to be the dominant partner of all the dating relationships I experienced. The parts of me that were most me I sternly suppressed for fear someone would label me weak. I was so busy suppressing what I wanted to hide that I took no time to express the positive side of me. When I felt I was losing control of a situation I became very hard and refused to be sensitive to the needs of the other person. Because this was so much against my natural self, I experienced a tremendous amount of guilt and inner hostility. Rationally I could tell myself that it was all right for a man to have a large number of the personality traits of a woman, but to say, "I have a large number of traits that are womanly and I am glad of it," was a bit much to swallow. I am big and strong and I am a man. Even a fool knows that all men should be powerful and profoundly masculine. But since I do possess the gentle traits, could it be possible that I am gay? Well, I decided to just forget about the seeming contradiction so it wouldn't bother me anymore. Like hell, it wouldn't bother me! Then I began to realize that the most important thing I had to do was figure out who I was and be that person. If I was gentle then I'd better be gentle. I believe a person has only one being to be with and if he decides to reject that being then "he ain't got no being to be with no more." It's bad when people reject me, but that isn't half as bad as when I reject myself. Then I have nothing to offer anyone except some phony thing. Let me tell you, a person must be able to just let go and be.

Male relationships are severely restricted by codes that say, "Don't be feminine," which meant "No expression of any feelings but anger."

MALE

In grade school, although both boys and girls were taught that we should not show our emotions (crying), it was worse for boys in this area. Crying was discouraged by teachers through general disapproval and such classic lines as, "Big boys don't cry." I remember many times when I would desperately try to hold back my tears. A lot of kids would make fun of people who cried, so when I did cry I remember the feelings vividly. I felt stupid, embarrassed, weak, and inferior. Really, letting anyone see you cry was one of the worst things that could happen.

MALE

In the past I have denied most of my affectionate feelings towards males. I am aware that I have often wanted to show affection but have held back. Now I feel less fearful of those feelings.

MALE

Sex roles inhibit my relationships with other men; because of the role expectations, touching and any real closeness are off-limits or at least are pretty uncomfortable. I remember when a friend of mine moved to Texas; the girls kissed him and we boys shook hands. The teacher was delighted we were learning our roles so well.

MALE

At school and with my playmates a firm handshake or a slap on the back was all that could be shown to reveal affection for another guy. At school one day, in seventh grade, I walked hand in hand with a very close buddy. The ridicule we got from both boys and girls made certain I'd never do that again.

Sometimes a child learns that what is acceptable at home is ridiculed at school.

MALE

I recall my father crying several times, but at school one of the greatest humiliations was crying. I remember fighting a bully and bloodying his nose, but I "lost" because the emotional upheaval left me crying. Even during high school when I flunked an important exam, crying afterwards was much worse than failure. Covering up with jokes or silence was much more acceptable. I envied the guys who could think quickly enough to cover up any personal discomfort with a wisecrack.

MALE

Dealing with emotions was a complex thing. However, my father's behavior showed me it was okay to be gentle (holding, cuddling), angry (swearing, blowing off steam), and spontaneous (sad at one time, happy the next). But I couldn't show my gentleness at school.

Parents, by their own behavior as well as by explicit instructions, provide training in what it means to be masculine or feminine. According to Hoyenga and Hoyenga (1993), parent interactions with their children affect the style of interactions with the children's peers with the more directive fathers having less popular children and directive mothers having more popular daughters but no significant impact on their son's popularity.

FEMALE

I was born in 1953, the third child in a family of six children: four girls and two boys. I am female. I was always quite feminine and felt happy and secure about my femininity. I was as proud of my naturally curly long blonde hair as my mother was. My parents often made remarks to us kids like: "Act like a man" or "That's not very ladylike."

FEMALE

My mother was very influential in forming my ideas about roles and sexuality because my father traveled a great deal when I was young. She was an excellent homemaker and loved to cook and sew. She never worked outside the home after my oldest brother was born, and looked down on working mothers.

FEMALE

I learned my sex role from my mother. She taught me that a woman's place was in the home, and that there was no greater joy or duty than to be home with the children. She even refused a trip to Europe with my father since she didn't want to leave us. Recently, when I returned to school, the first term was disastrous. For six weeks I was sick to my stomach every morning before class, until I realized that the children were fine and my husband still loved me even though I was "working outside the home." My own experience finally contradicted an old "mother" expectation.

MALE

From watching my parents I learned that men were more violent, less warm and affectionate, and that they dominated women. My father was the chief disciplinarian and the authority figure in our family.

MALE

When my father was away, as he often was on business trips, I was "the little man of the house." I had to take care of my sisters and mother: fixing things that needed repairing, protecting the girls, bandaging skinned knees, helping with the heavy housework, taking care of the yard, locking up the house at night, being a peacemaker, and making sure that the kids didn't fight. (My father was the main disciplinarian in our house.)

> School represents the first major step away from home for most children, giving them an initial glimpse at what will be expected of them as adult men and women, expectations that are conveyed through the hidden curriculum.... Although boys and girls sit in the same classroom, they have quite different experiences. Boys receive more attention and instruction from teachers in response to the belief that girls get by through being conscientious students, while boys are bright but need extra encouragement and attention to do their best. As a result, girls become increasingly discouraged about their ability the longer they are in school, and their discouragement is exacerbated by the growing problems of harassment by their male peers. (Beal, 1994, pp. 154–55)
>
> We sort through the standards and scripts for behavior that our society has identified as "feminine," or "masculine," struggling to live up to the expectations of others while feeling comfortable with ourselves. The expressions of masculinity and femininity come in clothing styles, ways of walking and talking, mannerisms, hobbies, and all sorts of behaviors. (Kelly, 1988), p. 131

This reality makes excellence difficult for women, and some women in our sample wrote about the conflict they felt between their own desire for academic and business success, and societal pressures to the contrary.

FEMALE

For a long time I have had to deal with the idea that a woman should not be too intelligent. I am very intelligent and have come under a great deal of pressure because of it. My father encouraged me in my academic pursuits but my mother and the rest of the family felt that I should study less. I've had a number of people encourage me to play dumb while professors told me to prepare for my Ph.D.

FEMALE

I like being a girl and I like acting feminine, but I refuse to play the "dumb blonde" role. I am a business major and frequently the only girl in a class of 30 guys. My biggest gripe is being evaluated as somewhat less intelligent because I am a girl in a man's field. I feel I have to prove myself more than guys do, which makes me work even harder. Within the course of a term I am usually able to gain the respect of my fellow classmates, which is very important to me.

FEMALE

I am a very career-oriented person but sometimes feel I should not pursue it but rather fall back into raising a family, doing the washing, cooking, and ironing. I dated a guy who was a business major like me; he really didn't want to go out into the business world, which he pictured as one of politics and exploitation. He loves kids, likes to cook, and doesn't mind washing clothes, and doing other kinds of chores. I think he possesses more of the feminine role attributes and I more of the male—but can we really express ourselves and be accepted in today's society?

Because of the effects of sex role stereotyping, it is difficult even in an intimate relationship to go beyond the male-female stereotype to find the human being.

FEMALE

In a sexual relationship I always feel the need to have the male make the first moves. I try to reason with myself saying that this is not rationally necessary; however, I cannot actually act differently. I fear his thinking I am too aggressive—that it is not the "right" image. However, I do enjoy sex as much as he. Cues given to a partner in sex are so subtle that it is hard to understand what is being said. I constantly fear his losing respect for me or thinking I am dumb, oversexed, or undersexed.

FEMALE

My mother taught me that a woman's sexual pleasure is just as important as a man's. I have not been able to find any men who sincerely believe that. As a prime example, I lived for a month this summer with a guy who I sincerely believed loved me. I thought he would understand my needs, if anyone would. We had long talks about each other's sexual needs and desires. He said he understood, then tried to make me feel guilty because I wanted some things he didn't, and didn't want some things he did. When I confronted him with this, he said it was because he was frustrated. How did he think I felt?

FEMALE

My sister and I were enrolled in a very small Catholic school where male-female and child-adult roles were strictly observed. I went there from kindergarten through eighth grade. I remember constant competition between boys and girls academically and athletically, but the nuns "guilted" those of us who were "tomboys and ruffians."

FEMALE

Most of my life I've felt that men carried the world's burdens and women were created to serve and help them. I can't remember trusting any male, but feeling that I, as a female, had to depend on them for the answers to crucial problems and decisions. The fear of being hit by the strong male was overpowering so whatever was said might as well have been indisputable law. Surprisingly enough I vied for adult male attention a great deal.

MALE

The only girl I have ever really had a good friendly relationship with was a "tomboy" who played baseball and other sports with us. She wasn't a girlfriend, just a friend. I related to her as if she were a boy. I don't think I have ever had another relationship like that with a girl. Usually I treat females differently than males. I related to them in a different way, even when I was a little kid and had no idea of what sex was all about. This still inhibits my relationships with women. I seem unable to relate to women in a way that allows us to become friends. Instead, I view women as potential sex partners, so either I get involved with them sexually or not at all. So I feel like the lack of integration of my sexuality with my humanity really inhibits my relationship with the other half of the human race.

MALE

I'm afraid of being inadequate. One way to maintain a successful masculine role is to dominate women. If I feel myself slipping into a subordinate position with a woman, then I have failed as a man. This fear is motivated by my home situation where I saw my father bring home his paycheck from the shop, turn it over to my mother who decided how to use it, including the minimal allowance she gave him.

MALE

Although I grew up with two younger sisters, I've always felt at a loss to know how to react to girls. I have a very platonic view of love, and I feel very uncomfortable with the "conquest" approach. Yet it seems impossible to speak freely of uncertainty and fears, or to admit ignorance to a girl. Even being really excited and showing it seems out of place—"flighty" or "gushy."

MALE

I was very hesitant to ask out a very impressive woman I met at lunch last week—partly because I didn't want her to misunderstand my intentions and partly because I did not have as much trust in myself as I should have had. She had said that she wasn't dating, so I knew that I was not making a risky decision in that respect. But she had also said that she was happy not dating which added to my hesitation in asking her out. I really only wanted to get to know her better and felt that we could discuss "going out" or dating once we got to know each other. When I asked her out I made it clear that what I really wanted to do was to get to know her because she struck me as a neat person. She said, "That's really nice. But we don't have to go out. Just come on up to my room and we can talk if you want to." That really impressed me: she trusted me! And she wasn't bound by social convention to date or to go out when that was only a means to an end—and not the end in itself. I finally did make it up to her room and felt most relaxed.

And sometimes individuals find the stereotypic sex role useful and/or comfortable.

MALE

I don't allow myself to get involved with girls in any kind of meaningful relationship. I see girls as a softening agent to guys like me who can't afford to soften up in a love thing. The reason I can't afford to soften up is that I'm in sports and a degree of meanness and toughness is needed for me to excel. To have a girl would possibly jeopardize my chances to excel. If everything was going real smooth with a girl, how could I psych myself up to be tough? When I have been rejected by girls, I have displaced my rejection and anger in a manner which is positive and beneficial to me, i.e., pushing myself in workouts and punishing myself in order to be better in sports. So by feeling rejected and bummed-out when girls quit on me, I better myself in different ways. This whole way of functioning is only a temporary arrangement I have made for myself, and hopefully will not last too long. I may never get another chance to push myself to my limits in sports. I have to do it alone, with no outsider going the long road with me. Don't get me wrong, I don't hate girls; they're the right thing for me but it's the wrong time and place for me to get involved with them. For now, my shadow comes in line before them.

FEMALE

I have never felt any need to change my feelings about being a woman. The only thing that I ever felt was a good cause in the women's movement was equality in the job market. A lot of my friends have condemned me for not taking a strong stand in the movement but I have always felt happy with most female stereotypes and lived comfortably with them.

Students reflecting on their experiences in the course expressed relief at their new insight. It's OK for people to freely choose and express human traits that fit themselves, rather than being limited to only characteristically masculine or feminine traits.

FEMALE

Because of this course, I have thought about my sex role more than I had before. I have come to the conclusion that I like the so-called feminine traits in me, but gentleness doesn't have to mean weakness, and sweetness doesn't have to mean that you're dumb and naive. I'm glad I don't have to feel pressured into being aggressive and unemotional. I like guys best who don't give in to society's expectations of a "macho" man. I am most comfortable around people who don't expect me to play a role. I'm uncomfortable around my mother who is constantly bitching about my unladylike clothes and the fact that I don't set my hair and wear makeup. She thinks I'm rebelling if I wear clothes she thinks are masculine.

MALE

The day we broke into an all male group in class to talk about sex roles was great. I never realized that I feel masculine when I stroke by beard, drive my car, and fix or build something. How can I distinguish between what is an undesirable sex role identity, and what is a "me" identity? The two are more integrated than I thought, I guess. In this course I have become more firmly convinced that sex roles are mostly (entirely?) artificial and undesirable. I have really been able to conceive of the possibility of completely getting out of my male sex role, but I'm not sure if I want to.

FEMALE

I was really afraid of some personal traits or characteristics I had which I considered to be "masculine." I guess one thing that really came across to me in this class was that that was OK and I didn't necessarily have to have all those traits which society defines as "feminine" in order to be a woman. This was really a hard thing for me to come to and

I can't say I'm all the way there but I feel a lot better about myself as a woman. I really can't say I'm a feminist, but I now see the importance of looking at people as people first and not necessarily just as male or female.

SOME CONCLUSIONS

Although more men and women rationally accept the need to move beyond the stereotypic masculine and feminine roles, they are assaulted daily with the affirmations of traditional roles. While it is difficult to move gracefully from one role to another, each with conflicting expectations, people do have the freedom to choose those behaviors which will allow them to be creative and spontaneous men and women.

SUGGESTED ISSUES FOR PERSONAL REFLECTION, GROUP DISCUSSION AND INTERACTION, PERSONAL JOURNAL

1. In a class situation, divide into men's and women's groups of five to six people in each group. The task for the group is to brainstorm all the "shoulds" or "oughts" received as little boys or little girls. Include those messages that are still current. Select one person to be the recorder. When all lists are completed post the lists and allow time for everyone to move around the room and read the lists.
   When people return to the small group, they discuss the following:
   a. Which "shoulds" do I believe are appropriate for children?
   b. What expectations do I still maintain for myself?
   c. What do I think is appropriate for members of the opposite sex?
2. Group members should then form heterosexual couples. Each person replicates the following diagram and writes:

1 My expectations for myself	3 What I think my partner's expectations are for him or herself
2 My expectations for my partner	4 What I think my partner's expectations are for me

When completed, pairs share their papers and discuss:
a. Where are the areas of conflict? Of congruence?
b. Are there some expectations I would like to change for myself? For my partner?

Chapter 5

Sex Education, Formal and Informal

INTRODUCTION

*P*arents are the first and by far the most influential and important of the sex educators during a person's growing up. The information given is important but so are behaviors that show parents' feelings about being male or female and about their children's gender. Parents teach by example about roles expected of each gender, touch, privacy, relationships and sex (Calderone and Johnson, 1989). Parents give many messages, often unknowingly. For instance, many parents while playing with their toddlers, point to body parts, asking the child to name them: nose, arm, toe, eye. Interestingly, genitals are usually ignored completely or given "nursery" names such as wee-wee, etc. The message to the child is that genitals are not like the other parts of the body (Lansdown and Walker, 1991). When parents choose a positive approach that encourages their child's healthy sexual development, the child is much less likely to internalize confusing, inaccurate, and shameful beliefs about sexuality. The following are examples of messages that will enhance the child's knowledge, self-esteem, and decision-making process:

- Sexuality is a natural and positive part of your life.
- Your body and your genitals are beautiful and good. . . .
- It is very normal for you to experience sexual feelings. . . .
- Use knowledge and your values to make decisions about whether to act on your sexual feelings. You will not always want to act on your sexual feelings. Sometimes it is just nice to have them as feelings. Other times you might decide to find a private place to touch and pleasure your own body. (Wilson, 1994, p. 2)

It is difficult in our diverse culture to find consensus regarding sexuality education: Who should teach what, when it should be taught, and to whom. Whether the subject of sex is introduced intentionally by parents and/or by educators, human beings will learn about it because sexuality is innate, as is hunger. It is interesting that we deal so differently with two aspects of our humanness. We teach children how to deal with their hunger; almost all children are taught table manners, for instance. It is equally important for parents to talk with their children about their family values, sexual behaviors, and relationships. Such teaching is most effectively done before children reach puberty when their need to make decisions about sexual behaviors is complicated by newly emerging, unfamiliar, and strong feelings. According to Kelly (1988), children learn gradually from birth onward about their bodies and sexuality, but around 10 or 11 a spurt of knowledge and comprehension occurs. This is the opportune time for parents to review sexual information with their children in order to ensure real understanding.

All human beings have as part of their development the task of discovering what sexuality is all about—how they were conceived and born and what part they, personally, will play in the reproductive cycle. As evidence in previous chapters suggests, learning happens in many ways: some will engage in reading, observing, self-stimulation or masturbation, and sex play with their peers, and most will have questions before anyone thinks to give them the answers. But these questions are not always asked. Therefore information should be provided whether or not it is directly requested by the child. There is continuing controversy and uncertainty in our society about who should teach what, when, and how. Teaching about the emotions that go with the experiences seems to be almost entirely omitted. This may be due to the controversy about whose values should be imparted to children and in what kind of setting.

It is probably a truism that children learn their values and attitudes about sexuality at home, and their information from peers—or at least away from home. The students in this sample reflected the fact that their families did communicate indirectly, if not directly, their value positions about various sexuality matters but often did not communicate factual information effectively.

Children begin to wonder, and that wonderment prompts them to ask questions, experiment with peers, and/or figure it out for themselves. Children's answers, arising from the variety of ways they cope with this wonderment, are amazing. Here are some of the things our students said they once believed.

FEMALE

I remember for the longest time I thought when a woman was pregnant the skin wore away on her stomach and the baby just came through the wall. That was about the same time I thought french kissing made you pregnant.

FEMALE

I believed the stories about if you sat on a man's lap you got pregnant because older kids had told me.

FEMALE

In my early childhood I can remember thinking that babies just automatically "happened" when two people got married. It was just some magical thing that after a woman was married her stomach popped out every once in a while, and when it did she knew she was about to have another baby. It was as simple as that!

MALE

I remember one time specifically when I asked my mother where babies come from. Her retort was that they occur when people get married. At all weddings I went to for the next several years, I would follow all details of the ceremony, waiting to see the part that caused the babies. I imagined all sorts of bizarre procedures such as cutting wrists and placing them together.

FEMALE

When I was 13, I still believed that a man and a woman lay side by side together in bed and magically something would come from him and go through her navel. This was all very confusing and I thought about it a lot. I couldn't figure out how a woman could have an unwanted pregnancy. I never asked anyone about it.

FEMALE

The boy next door was two years older than I. Good old Kenny told me where babies came from. Here's how he explained it: "OK. Your mom just gets pregnant. You know the baby just starts growing in her stomach. Then when it is time for the baby to be delivered, your dad takes her to the hospital. (Here's where the good part comes.) She lies down on a table at the hospital and takes off her pants. The doctor does the same, only he doesn't lie down. He sticks his "thing" inside your mom and the baby grabs on. As soon as the baby's got a good grip, the doctor pulls the baby out of your mom and BINGO—a baby!" I remember thinking, "Gosh, I guess the doctor who helps babies be born can't be a woman!"

FEMALE

You know, as a kid I thought this whole sex thing was pretty sick when I thought about my very own parents doing it. So I said to my friend, "Man, your mom and dad must have sex an awful lot to have so many kids!" This, of course, threw her into a fit. She explained her theory to me in no time. You see, according to her, a mom and dad only had to have sex once when they were first get married. That one roll in the hay was enough to produce a lifetime of children. I listened rather suspiciously, although I had to keep my mouth shut seeing as my statement seemed to really flip her out. If her theory was true, I wondered, why in the heck my mom and dad continued to share a bed.

When information was provided, it was often vague and did not encourage any kind of questioning or interaction.

FEMALE

I was born the fourth of seven children to a Catholic farm couple. I was raised by a strict father who felt the pressure of having to feed and clothe such a big family, and a quiet, docile mother from whom I received unconditional love. I have two older sisters and one older brother, one younger sister and two younger brothers. Growing up on a farm with dairy cattle I had the opportunity to view the mating and birthing process at an early age. Recognizing that act as being similar to the one performed by human beings did not immediately register. In fact, I cannot remember when I realized that sex between a man and a woman would often times result in a baby being born. My parents did not have a standard speech to give any of us kids regarding the issue of sex. In recent conversations with my siblings I discovered that none of us was told by either parent about "the birds and the bees." I remember hearing my oldest sister argue with my parents when she began dating. This usually centered on staying out past her curfew. My parents would want to know why she needed to stay out past eleven o'clock at night. Her answer was that all of the kids her age were allowed to stay out past eleven o'clock at night. Her curfew remained the same until she was older. I recall certain phrases that my parents used to say to "be good, don't do anything you will regret in the morning, and don't do anything to embarrass the family name." I was ten years old at the time and these rules made an impression on me. What the phrases meant to me were to not have sex and get pregnant or you will ruin the family name. I recalled these when I began to date.

FEMALE

When I was eight, my mother bought me a book from church on reproduction. She told me, "Read it and then hide it so that no one will know." The book didn't tell me very much except some technical things about ovulation that were way above my head. It did have two pictures of statues, one of a naked woman and one of a naked man. They were not well defined at all.

Some students didn't receive any information and didn't recall being inquisitive about sex.

FEMALE

I had little sex education. In fact, I had no sex education at school and was never told the facts of life by either of my parents. I don't believe I finally pieced together all the facts on where a baby comes from until eighth grade. I don't recall ever having asked any questions or even being interested in sex information so it may be just as much my fault as my parents' for not telling me.

FEMALE

Development and sex itself—both subjects were taboo. I think my parents were—and in many ways still are—totally ignorant of much of the information themselves. I guess I was not a very curious child because I never even tried to get info on my own; what little information I got was obtained from my peers and overheard adult conversation. About 80 percent of what I now know about sex and about myself physically, I learned from my husband.

Even when parents offered to answer any questions they might have, students felt it wasn't enough to counteract the nonverbal messages of parental embarrassment.

FEMALE

I came from a very large Catholic family where sex was never discussed. Everyone seemed too embarrassed to talk about it, and it wasn't long before I caught this feeling. It's still hard for me to talk about sex, even in the most vague terms, without feeling silly and embarrassed. There was never anyone who I could ask my questions of and I started sneaking library books home. There was nothing wrong with the books; a librarian helped me pick them out. I just didn't want to have my mom know. From these books I learned a lot but I never could understand about sexual intercourse or how a woman became pregnant.

MALE

An invisible veil has always surrounded sex in my family. The deep fears and disgust communicated by my mother were balanced somewhat by my father's directness and naturalness about sexuality. Often sexual matters were discussed in the context of "dirty" jokes, which made my father laugh, my mother get embarrassed, and I got more confused. In those rare moments when "the facts of life" were discussed, there was a solemnity that labeled this as an area of fear and guilt.

Many students said it was hard to be ignorant, but even more difficult and embarrassing to ask questions. Their ignorance was compounded by fear and embarrassment.

FEMALE

If I did manage to screw up my courage to ask, my mother always tried to answer me truthfully and openly. The problem was that I did not know what questions to ask, and I was embarrassed to ask the questions that I did have.

FEMALE

When I was in fifth grade, our parents gave us kids two short books to read and said if we had any questions, to ask. I read the first book, which really didn't teach me anything new, but did not read the second one. I'm not sure whether it was embarrassment or disgust with what I thought was such a dirty thing that kept me from reading. My older brother and I felt embarrassed about asking questions, but my younger sister asked lots of them.

FEMALE

My formal sex education began at age nine when my mother gave me two books to read. After I finished them she asked if I had any questions. Because I knew she'd be embarrassed to answer them, I was too embarrassed to ask. So, I saved my questions for my best friend even though she wasn't always the most reliable source.

FEMALE

I can't remember ever thinking about sex until I was about ten years old and we learned about menstruation in school. There was one question the teacher wouldn't answer and said to ask our mothers. That was "How does the sperm get into the vagina?" I wouldn't even talk about it to my mother. She sat me down one day and asked if I had any questions; I said, "No," nervously awaiting the time I could leave. I told her I already knew everything—that I'd learned it in school. Then my dad came in and said that if I had any questions he'd be glad to answer them. I was shocked to think that men knew about these matters!

FEMALE

My family was very unemotional. I felt all we shared was a house and the same last name. I don't remember kissing my parents good-bye or saying "I love you" for years. Sex, babies, or anything to do with producing life was not, I repeat, was *not* discussed in our house.

I finally learned something when I entered sixth grade. My best girl friend who had a sexually educated brother in high school told me what the word "fuck" meant. I still couldn't figure out how a man could get a woman pregnant by putting his penis in her. Not wanting to appear totally ignorant to my peers, I went along with anything they said. I knew I could never ask my parents about this. They would wonder about my friends, so I had to keep all my questions inside me.

FEMALE

Quite often I act as if I know all about sex and anything that has to do with it, even saying that I've done it—which is a pure lie. I pretend so people won't think I'm naive and dumb concerning sex. Through my imagination and my fantasies, I see myself as a "real woman" and want others to see me that way also. Actually, I know practically nothing about the actual steps of intercourse. I've heard many things but often wonder what little thing is being left out in the description. Is there something else to it that I don't know about? And at this age in my life, I'd be too afraid or embarrassed to ask a friend. I can just see me now, the night before my wedding, asking Mom those last few questions. At least she will know I'm still a virgin.

Unwillingness to ask questions may also occur because of unpleasant experiences in relation to questions asked in the past.

FEMALE

When I questioned why boys had parts I didn't, I was told "because." That was all. As I grew older, I found my parents to be reluctant to answer questions that dealt with any sexual matter. This led me to believe that sex was "bad" or "nasty."

FEMALE

I remember asking my older sister, "Do you have to go to college to be a mother?" She laughed when she told me, "No, you don't have to." She thought it was such a cute thing to ask and had me repeat the question to others so they could laugh too.

MALE

I was pretty sheltered 'til far into my high school career—many times I wonder how I got along with the few bits of knowledge I could actually be sure were true. I didn't know many things but would not ask, often because of my pride. I was sure I'd be seen as dumb by everyone else in the world. Little did I know that my sinking ship was a common craft in common waters.

FEMALE

My parents are very old fashioned in their ways of thinking and in their values. "No dating until you're 16. A girl never calls a boy." These are familiar phrases from my high school days. The one I still hear today that is loaded is "Be good." I think my parents expected me to learn about sexuality from my brothers and sisters and their examples, because nothing was ever explained to me except for menstruation. I never asked questions for fear of being embarrassed or getting laughed at. I can remember asking my sister something personal and having her laugh at me. Then she called her friends and told them about it. So much for asking questions!

FEMALE

I do not remember how old I was, but I do remember asking my mother what having sex was like. She explained that having sex was not exciting for women. Men were the only ones who got any satisfaction from it. She explained that it was merely a wifely duty and it was nothing to look forward to. At that point I feared the pain and the chore of it. It was only when I was older and Mom told me that she and dad had always had a wonderful sex life that I realized how deceptive her story had been; I now understand this was a way to prevent me from believing sex was enjoyable. The only message I got was that sex is something you ought to do for someone you love. If I had been told that it was something wonderful and special that can be shared between two people that care about one another, I think that my adolescence would have been much different.

Some people asked and had positive experiences as a result of their questions.

FEMALE

About the age of three or four, I remember being curious about Dad and Mom's physical body. I recall walking in on Dad as he was standing up going to the bathroom. I can remember making some remark about his genitals, and asked why I didn't look like that when I went "pee." I thought he was unique! I remember wanting to see that again for a few weeks after that experience. I remember asking Mom (several times a day) if Dad was going to the bathroom so I could watch. Needless to say, I never saw Dad again with his pants down.

MALE

As I recall, my unending questions about my body, my mother's body, and my father's body, and so forth, all seemed to take place in the evening. I would get tucked into bed for the night, and my mother would sit on the edge of the bed, talking to me before I went to sleep. I was usually the one who would begin the conversation, and she would answer my numerous questions. To the best of my knowledge, her answers and discussions were always frank and factual. I never got any stories about cabbage leaves or storks. My penis was always called just that, not a ding-a-ling, or other cute name. The female organs were also referred to by their proper names.

FEMALE

At about 11, I started to have more questions like: "Where do babies come from? There's more to life than God planting a seed in Mommy's stomach for a baby to be born." Mom was prepared; she had bought a book on sex named *Where Do Babies Come From.* It was in very simple language. She explained intercourse as something very beautiful between two people who were married and in love. She named the parts of both the male's and female's body for me and encouraged me to read the book and ask questions.

FEMALE

I was brought up in a family that was fairly open about sexuality. As long as I can remember, there was always a book called *The Meaning of Life* on the bookshelf, with lots of pictures and diagrams of how I came to be me and what I was going to become. I don't remember a session where I learned the "facts of life." My sex education was, I believe, an ongoing process. I believe my questions were answered as honestly as possible, including the scientific terms for the various parts of the anatomy. My mother is a court reporter, and she would tell us about her court cases, including those dealing with sex. I knew that people got raped and that people such as exhibitionists existed. These subjects were never talked about with disgust, but with sympathy for people who had to look for an outlet for their sexuality in that way.

Traditions from their religious community had a strong impact for some students.

FEMALE

The orthodox Jewish community was surprisingly open about sex. Judaism does not regard sex as a sin; in fact, prolonged abstinence is discouraged. Boys are taught it is not allowed for a man to have sex with his wife against her will. He has to ask explicitly for permission to begin love-making, and has to wait for an explicit answer. He is not to act on the assumption that if he did ask she would say yes. Moreover, sex is forbidden when the wife is asleep, drunk, or ill because one cannot be sure of how assertive she can be under these conditions. Although in the religious seminars there is no sex education in the way we define it, students are instructed to follow these rules.

MALE

I grew up in a strict Catholic family in the suburbs. My parents were both devout in their religious beliefs and practices. We regularly attended church as a family. All of my brothers and I attended catechism until we were in the eighth grade. We were told that sex before marriage was a sin, and so was masturbation. Sexuality was never brought up except in terms of what was inappropriate behavior. Pornography and things which portrayed women in a sexual or degrading manner were forbidden in the house. We were also told not to look at those type of materials. I cannot recall ever being told about the "birds and the bees." My parents did show affection for us and one another in front of us. They were not embarrassed to be found kissing. I believe the demonstration of affection was normal in our home. Our growth as sexual beings was definitely retarded and repressed.

MALE

It has taken a lot of personal thought to determine my own set of beliefs and attitudes toward sex. The reason for this, well, let's start when I was going to Catholic grade school. Everything was dictated to me and questions were left unanswered or always put off for someone else to answer which never happened. Classes were situated in such a fashion that the girls were always split apart from the boys; when you came in contact with a girl, by now you had an inferiority complex. This type of atmosphere went on for eight years, with no sex education whatsoever. If you think this doesn't warp your mind, try it sometime. It's like walking in a big circle with no one to turn to.

FEMALE

One thing that has really affected my sexual development was the fact that I have gone to a Catholic school for 12 years. I can remember learning that soft kisses were okay but anything more passionate is a sin unless you are married. In ninth grade, a layman in our parish set up a sex education program for one week in which we learned about anatomy of both sexes and discussed dating, and how far one could go before committing a sin. Well he was pretty liberal compared to some of the nuns, and he said that up until heavy petting was all right, assuming you weren't intending to go all the way. I thought the program was pretty well done, considering our school, and I learned quite a bit. In my senior year I had a marriage class, but we didn't really get into the sexual aspect of it at all, most likely because it was taught by a nun who was quite conservative. I left for college vowing that I would be a virgin till I got married. It is sort of funny when I think that so much was considered a sin till you get married but after that it is all right.

When given no information, these students reported trying to find out for themselves; they didn't remain innocent.

MALE

My sexual education came in the form of "hands-on" experience. A practicum if you will, except that the only over-seeing I received was my father's grin and later my brothers' teasing as to whether I "got lucky." I think I was lucky. I went with beautiful girls who were sensitive and kind, particularly through high school. But then I was sensitive and kind as well. When I moved out on my own I attempted to meet more of my emotional needs through my sexual relationships. Sex became a way for me to feel loved, not a way for me to love a woman.

FEMALE

My education in the area of sex as a child was nil. My parents never said words like "intercourse," "make love," "penis," "vagina," and so forth. Because of this sexual rigidity, I was forced to read my own books, talk to my own friends, and get my own sexual information. I resent the fact that I was never given any sex education at home.

FEMALE

I was interested in anatomy and wanted to know the whys and wherefores of it. My mother avoided the question of "How are babies made?" with an "I'll tell you when you're older." So naturally this anatomy question became a mystery to solve, and before she ever got around to telling me about the convenience of the penis and vagina I was well on my way to finding out for myself.

FEMALE

As a child, I was very curious about the opposite sex—I had virtually no exposure to the male physiology for the first 13 or 14 years of life. I had no brothers and I saw my father only fully clothed. Consequently, as an eighth grader, I jumped at the chance to "go steady" with a boy and readily agreed to "pet" and "neck" with him because it partially satisfied 13 years of curiosity. I did have exposure to other young girls as a child—mostly "playing doctor" and trying to find out via examining my playmates' bodies what my body was all about.

Peer or sibling information often substituted for or supplemented information given by parents.

FEMALE

When I was seven my brother was born and I got to see his tiny penis! I thought it was really cute and was quite intrigued by it. My grandmother, aunts, and mom got a real kick out of changing his diaper and watching him pee straight up in the air. They all acted very natural and matter of fact about his male anatomy. My mom taught me to change his diaper and once when I was alone with him I was playing with his penis and he got a tiny erection. It was like having a doll that responded; I thought it looked like a flower. My feelings about my brother's penis were *a lot* more positive than about my dad's. My dad's was too big and scary and as I got older I began to worry that sex was going to hurt.

MALE

No discussions about sex took place at my house with my parents. I learned everything at school or in the streets. I had some sex ed in school in fifth, seventh, and tenth grade, but mostly I listened to the street instructors—usually older peers, who were easy to approach with "silly" questions because they were more down to earth in their answers.

MALE

I am the youngest of four boys. When I had questions related to sex, I usually asked one of my brothers. Before I reached puberty I had heard them talk about masturbation, pornographic magazines, kissing, and fondling girls. When I reached puberty, they told me about what girls had done to them, like oral sex. They also told me what they had done to girls: oral sex, sucking on breasts, and using their fingers to bring a girl to orgasm. They never mentioned having intercourse until after I had already engaged in it.

FEMALE

At about age nine, Ruth, a neighborhood friend, told me how moms and dads make babies. I was shocked and didn't really believe her. I remember looking in the baby book that we had at home for supporting information, but I never found anything concerning this matter. I did not ask my parents or older sister about this.

FEMALE

The girl who lives behind us was a year older than I, and one day I asked her if she knew how sperm got into the woman. She told me point blank that a man stuck his organ into the woman. I couldn't believe it. It seemed so strange. I could just imagine a man and woman saying, "Let's have a baby," sitting down, taking off their pants and "doing it." She said it was supposed to be enjoyable, but I couldn't imagine how anything like that would be.

MALE

At age seven I started asking one of my older brothers questions and he told me the answers pretty accurately. He gave me a complete lecture on intercourse, conception, and birth.

FEMALE

Something I found quite difficult was to explain to my younger sister about how a girl got pregnant. Fortunately, we were in our beds with the lights out so I didn't have to look at her as I talked. She didn't say much but I think she took the news very similarly to the way I did: "You're kidding! . . . It's done like that?"

MALE

At the age of 12, the facts began to roll in. My sister had just begun having menstrual cycles and new terms were being used around the house, which sent waves of pleasure radiating out from a fully erect penis. My friends and I would hide and swap knowledge. An older friend explained that girls had a "hole" that guys like to stick their "wong" into. This puzzled me because I had seen naked girls and never noticed any apparent "hole." Anyway, I derived great pleasure in thinking of such seemingly impossible facts. Something about the way I picked up these facts made me feel as though I had done something bad. I felt very guilty and often would consider giving up such discussion with my peers, but never did.

FEMALE

I found out the facts of life in sixth grade. With one particular girl friend I'd make up sexy stories; we'd talk about where people did it and how it felt, and we'd picture our mom and dad. I always wanted to go with my big sister (seventh grader) to the trees where she and her two friends would go to discuss the "birds and the bees" but they said I couldn't come until I knew about the B & B. So that afternoon I asked my mom about it. She told me but said not to tell anyone. So next day, I went down by my own tree and told all my friends. One girl went home and told her mother what I said, to see if it was true. Her mother got all upset and called me a "poor child." I always felt funny in front of her after that.

FEMALE

It's a weird and rather ironic story of how I first heard the shocking news about the "birds and the bees!" I happened to be in bed with a boy when I found out! The catch is, the boy was a playmate of mine and we were only around seven or eight years old. Our parents were close friends and many times when the families would visit each other, they'd put us to bed at each other's houses so they wouldn't have to go home early. Anyway, Nick and I were such good friends that one night I asked him if we could get married when we grew up. He said that he couldn't marry me because I wasn't Catholic and he was. We would have a problem raising the kids. I don't know exactly how the conversation drifted from this point to him telling me what guys do to girls in bed, but anyhow he told me right straight about sexual intercourse. Knowing little kids, I think he told me because he just learned it and it's hard to keep things to yourself when you're little. Besides, why shouldn't he tell me! I was one of his best friends, his best girl friend for sure! I can remember how shocked I was. I really didn't believe him at all.

MALE

One day one of us boys, who was a little bit older than the rest of us, called us into the shed. He said he had something to show us. He took his cock out and started to "jack off." He rubbed it for a while and then he "came." Man, was that something. He told us that's what makes girls get "knocked up." Yeah, we knew all those big words. From then on, we would get him to jack off to see how far he could make it squirt. Needless to say we were disappointed when we couldn't make ours "come" too. We kept working at it.

Some people learned about sex through dirty jokes their peers told.

FEMALE

"A fly on his back under the Mackinac Bridge had such a hard-on he couldn't get under." This triggered my first question to my mother: "What is a hard-on?"

FEMALE

One day when I was 11, some girl told a joke and I got the idea of how intercourse really took place. I was shocked and horrified. I went home from school and asked mother about it. I remember crying when she told me. She explained it really nicely and gently but it was such a shock.

Others got their information from reading and films.

FEMALE

My father is a doctor; consequently he has many medical books. During late elementary and early junior high I secretly used to look through them finding such terms as "fellatio," "masturbation," and "anal intercourse." Although I didn't know exactly what they meant, it was still exciting to sit hidden in the corner of our living room, and read case studies of people with sexual problems. It made me tingle and was the first time I remember being sexually stimulated. I was afraid to talk to my parents about it for fear of being punished. I shared my discoveries with peers and we figured it all out together.

FEMALE

I really found out about the mechanics of intercourse from a sex manual I found tucked on the bookshelf. It was dated in the 1930s or 1940s. I was about 12 years old. The manual showed various positions along with stating possible problems. It made no reference to sex being a pleasurable experience. I shared the manual with my girlfriends and we resigned ourselves to the fact that we would probably endure this disgusting act if we were going to have children, but no one thought it looked pleasant.

FEMALE

I got most of my early sexual knowledge reading books. They weren't pornographic (in my opinion) but did go into some detail. *The Story of Jean Harlow, Peyton Place, Fanny Hill* and encyclopedias were the extent of it. I still remember bits and pieces from them but never really understood what was going on. I was a studious young girl and one of the smartest in my class, so naturally I'd go to books for my information instead of asking people. I remember getting a funny feeling in my abdomen when I read about the actions of intercourse, but never related it to being "turned on."

FEMALE

I can remember that I could not wait to either pick up a so-called "dirty" book or see a movie in which a nude love scene was presented. The people in the movies always looked so relaxed, happy, and fulfilled. Sex looked like such fun between two people, a rare and beautiful experience. "Dirty" books were passed from friend to friend. After everyone had read the book we discussed it, and if any girl had interesting stories or experiences she would share them and allow us to relive those exciting moments with her. This was my only opportunity to discuss sex with "reliable and knowledgeable" sources. There were no sex education classes at my school and candid discussions with my parents seemed impossible at the time.

FEMALE

High school brought new learnings. Guys talked about "fucking" and "screwing" girls. Most of my sexual information came from girlfriends' *True Stories*. Around tenth and eleventh grade we started reading *Playgirl* and *Playboy* and other such magazines. It was in high school that I decided I'd be a virgin till I was married.

MALE

I got the majority of my information during my freshman year on campus when I picked up a copy of Masters and Johnson's book. It was a very explicit and informative paperback. The rest of my knowledge came from porno flicks.

When nothing else worked, children often found unique sources of information.

FEMALE

I have always been very shy so I have had very little contact with boys. When passing a statue or viewing a picture of a male, I paid special attention because of my limited knowledge and curiosity. But I tried not to show any interest to others for fear of what they might think or say.

MALE

What I had learned of myself and women through my readings was beginning to cause an itch to explore at the age of 14. The thoughts of performing intercourse never occurred to me because it still was not three dimensional in my mind. I craved the sight of a naked female. If I could only see the pubic region, maybe sex would seem more logical. I had evil thoughts like hiding under my sister's bed or window-peeking to satisfy my curiosity. Thoughts like this continually interfered with my concentration. I was troubled because it seemed so impossible to satisfy my visual curiosity without getting into trouble.

FEMALE

I was raised in an all-girl family and therefore had very little knowledge about the "opposite" sex when I was growing up. Of course I played with boys, but I never knew that their genital parts were any different than my own. As I grew older, I heard that boys were somehow different; I think it took me until I baby-sat for a little boy, to finally be exposed to a boy's genitals. Even now I am unsure about many aspects concerning them.

Some students reported experiences that were frightening because of their lack of information and preparation.

MALE

I had masturbated often over a period of years. Then one day a whitish, sticky substance came out. I was far too embarrassed to ask anyone about it.

FEMALE

I remember necking with my boyfriend at the drive-in when I was seventeen. When I went to the bathroom, my pants were kind of wet. That seemed really odd. Honestly, I thought something was wrong with me.

"The talk" about menstruation was reported often in student papers and the kind of parental response to the onset of menstruation often seemed to affect subsequent communication regarding sexual matters.

FEMALE

I remember walking in on Mom and seeing a soiled sanitary napkin. I asked her about it, and she explained that women who were able to have babies bled every month. I didn't think about that experience again until I had to see the "female" film in fifth grade. And after seeing the film, I wanted to reject that those things would happen to me.

FEMALE

My mother had a pretty hard time talking about the little she did talk about. The only reason she did at all was because my Girl Scout troop was showing a movie talking about menstruation and the mothers were told to talk it over first with their daughters. This lack of communication exists even today when it comes to the topic of sexuality.

FEMALE

In fifth grade, a few of my friends began to menstruate and my mother and I began to have big talk sessions about the facts of life. I remember those times as very relaxed and helpful sessions. My mother must have purchased at least $20 worth of pamphlets and books for me to read. She went through most of them with me to tell me what she thought and answer any questions I had. Even so, I remember being afraid to ask her some things (i.e., definitions to unfamiliar words, exactly how intercourse was performed, and so forth) because I didn't want to embarrass her.

FEMALE

At the age of 11, my mother told me about menstrual periods, informing me accurately and with finesse. Her manner helped to alleviate my fears of the "curse." Mom and Dad explained most body related information in a matter-of-fact manner and regarded the body functions as a fact of life. But at the same time, they never really got around to telling me about the "birds and bees" facts of life.

FEMALE

At age ten, my mother told me the facts of life so when I started my period I would know what it was. One of her girl friends had started, had not known what was happening, and had been frightened. My mom didn't want this to happen to me. She had sent for a whole Kotex kit so I had all the equipment plus my own booklet. I always felt free to ask her any questions I wanted, and still do to this day. She has been very open and very honest.

One common source of information about menstruation is the movies that are shown at many schools and are seen by most girls and many boys.

FEMALE

About this time we began to see movies about menstruation at school (one a year). My mother never told me about menstruation until I brought the note home from school asking her permission for me to see the movies. Even then, all she said was that when girls got to be my age they started to bleed and that I would understand it all after I saw the movies. Even after the movies though, I was still confused. I thought that when a girl started her period, it went on every day until she got to be around 40.

FEMALE

The movie on menstruation was pretty confusing—all those hormones, etc.—but I felt like I knew what was going to happen to me. Sometime later I started my period. Wearing that sanitary napkin for only one day didn't sound so bad. I couldn't believe it when I discovered I was still flowing the second, third, and fourth days. I ruined a lot of underwear. I figured something must be wrong with me because I was sure the movie had said the flow would last only one day.

Some of the students reported parental resistance to having them see these films or having them participate in sex education at school at all.

FEMALE

Toward the end of sixth grade, all the girls were sent home with a note requesting permission to see *the movie* on menstruation. I thought, "At last I'll find out what a period really is!" I gave my mother the note and waited three days for an answer. Nothing was said until the day it had to be returned, signed. "Are you going to let me see the movie?" I asked. "Well, I don't know . . . I'll have to ask your father," she said. How would I tell her it had to be returned by this afternoon or I would be the only girl in the whole class who couldn't see the movie!

Surprisingly, I did get to see it. After my parents' reticence, the film's information met a real need of mine, and I was very excited about becoming a woman.

FEMALE

For some reason unknown to me, my mother felt I should not see *the movie.* I remember several of my friends talking about sex when I was in seventh grade. I was confused because I did not understand what was being said. I questioned my parents about this, and they talked to me in our living room behind closed doors so my younger brother could not hear what was being said. They explained briefly about sexual intercourse and then they gave me a paperback book to read. This was to explain and clarify everything for me. They said I could come to them with any questions, but I was hesitant. I could not understand everything in the book and I resented them for not explaining the facts to me in greater depth.

Feelings triggered by the movie tended to vary depending on a student's previous experience and upon how the film and subsequent discussion were presented.

FEMALE

My first conscious and significant awareness of my sexuality came in sixth grade when the girls were shown *the movie* on menstruation at school. I can remember my mother calling me into the kitchen while she was doing the dishes and telling me that I was to see a movie about growing up and becoming a woman. The next day at school all the girls were whispering about "the movie." In the afternoon I can remember all the guys being ushered out of the room and taken to the gym. All the doors were closed in the classroom and our teacher asked if anyone knew how to spell menstruation. Some proud girl blurted out the spelling and the teacher wrote it on the board. Then one of the boys in the class, returning from some appointment late, opened the door. Our teacher ran to the back of the room and told him he must go to the gym immediately. I couldn't then and still can't understand the secrecy. I think menstruation is an important concept for boys to learn about to help them understand women, and I don't think sixth grade is too young an age.

Although many women report that the only sexual information they received from adults was about menstruation, some reported that their parents dealt with more than these facts.

FEMALE

My relationship with my mother has had a great effect on my attitudes toward sex and my own sexuality. I can talk with her about virtually anything. It used to surprise me to have friends say that I'm lucky to have a mom I can talk with. I remember sitting on the edge of the tub one time, listening to Mom explain about the tampon she was inserting into her vagina. I was in fourth grade. Her approach was direct, reassuring and informative; she's very matter-of-fact about sex, nudity, contraceptives, and so forth. This directness with us kids, along with her proper usage of terms for explaining our bodies and bodily functions, laid a foundation for my present attitudes about sex. I am comfortable in discussing sex (my feelings, experiences, and so forth) with others in a direct way; I don't like referring to my own sexual experiences in a vulgar manner.

FEMALE

My mother told me to make a guy work for a kiss, and that once a guy stuck his tongue in her mouth and she bit it. So, I never let a boy kiss me in high school. I was scared to death of them. It was almost as if a kiss would make me pregnant. I had heard some talk about "frenching" and didn't connect it with my mother's story.

FEMALE

The only time I remember my mother telling me anything about sex was the summer I went to camp; she read me a chapter out of a church-published book. I can remember trying to figure out why she was reading to me about Mary and Joseph and telling me that the older girls would want to tell "nasty" stories and talk about things I wouldn't understand.

FEMALE

When I asked a group of grown-ups what Midol was, I guess my mother decided it was time for me to be lectured on where babies come from; she provided me with *What Every Teenager Must Know* and a question and answer period. The information I had gained from my friends was surprisingly accurate, but my mother was able to give me a good understanding of female functioning from menstruation to pap tests.

Several students reported parents and teachers imparting strong attitudes along with information about sexuality.

FEMALE

My only knowledge of the biological parts of sex were from jokes and stories I'd heard, until my sophomore biology class. There we were told that sexual intercourse was a wife's duty and even though it hurt, a wife should give in to her husband's wishes since a man was a sexually oriented being and he couldn't help himself.

FEMALE

In my family, we were always open about sexual matters and would have a lot of family discussions around the dinner table. My Dad was more strict on the subject than Mom and would say, "If you girls get pregnant you can pack your things, and if you boys get a girl pregnant it is your responsibility so wear a condom and protect yourself." I know though if one of us girls had come home pregnant he wouldn't have kicked us out. He was using his scare tactics! It worked.

FEMALE

I remember my friends and I repeating to each other the admonition our teacher had given: "If petting goes too far (touching anything below the head) you won't be able to stop; intercourse will be the inevitable result." It made me think something was wrong with me when a boy first touched my breast and we didn't end up having intercourse.

FEMALE

The school did show the usual films about "first womanhood" and the boys saw a similar film designed for boys. We were segregated so that the biology of the other sex remained a mystery to us. Also, the films were shown in seventh or eighth grade and for many of the girls, including myself, the information came too late. We'd already experienced the "miracle" of menstruation first hand. In later science classes I learned a great deal about the reproductive cycle of the frog and the starfish but the chapter about human reproduction was skipped until upper biology (eleventh or twelfth grade). At that time the female reproductive system was briefly covered and the process of fertilization was discussed. The major portion of my sex education received within the school consisted of one statement made by my biology teacher at this time. "The egg is many times larger than the sperm and as there are millions of sperm released to travel down the reproductive system the egg makes a very big target for all those little arrows. One is bound to hit the target." Those few sentences did a lot to cause me to keep my curiosity and any desire to experiment very far under control for at least the next few years.

treating it as something that doesn't exist. I don't want my child to go through the same fears and anxieties that I experienced.

MALE

Sex was taboo at our house; you couldn't say that "dirty" three letter word without somebody blushing, trying to hush it up, or giggling. If you'll pardon the pun, you could say that sex was kept under the blankets at our house. My parents never really told me about the "facts of life"—my mother made a vain attempt by asking my older brother to read a book about sex, but that's as far as it went with us kids. Just recently I got into a bit of an argument with my mom when she expressed her negative feelings about sex education in the public school system. I got angry and told her she was being hypocritical because neither she nor my Dad had educated any of us kids about sex. It is important that kids learn about sex in school because some parents don't do it at all.

Many parents do remember having given information although their children often do not recall it. This may be the result of early input which was not supplemented or expanded as the child grew older. Perhaps the information was not important to the child when it was given. A child will probably comprehend and remember only the sexual information that makes sense in terms of his or her own experience. For instance, if a child asks what the word 'fuck' means, a possible response might be: "'Fuck' is a word a lot of people don't like; it really offends them. Another term that means the same thing is 'sexual intercourse'—two people holding each other very close with the man's penis in the woman's vagina. This is one way for adults to express their love for each other." Saying this to a ten-year-old may enable him or her to understand intimacy a little better. To a five-year-old it communicates a fact that may or may not be remembered, but it probably would also say to the child that the parent feels positive about sex and it is okay to ask questions.

FEMALE

My mom was really cool in teaching me about menstruation. When I finally got my period she and I celebrated and it was treated as a happy, natural event. I felt real close to my mom then because I felt we had something important in common. I never dreaded my period or call it the "curse" or spent two days in bed with cramps like a lot of my friends. After the menstruation and very basic "birds and bees" education my mom must have thought that pretty much covered it because there was no ongoing discussions about sexuality. This made it difficult later in the world of dating and relationships because all I had to go on was these fanatical directives from my dad and the hearts and flowers version from my mother.

MALE

Although I was taught when I was ten that I should wait until marriage to enjoy sex, puberty struck, and I discovered pleasure in my body. It did not seem wrong or inappropriate to enjoy it.

FEMALE

The Girl Scout movie I watched only served to scare me to death. It showed only the uterus (or "womb" as it was referred to), the fallopian tubes, and the ovaries, all of which were located "somewhere inside of a woman." It talked about how "if an egg is met by the sperm (heaven only knows how they got in there), then a baby will develop in the womb. When I saw the sperm "swimming" around, I thought for sure that a girl could get pregnant if she was swimming and there was a boy around her in the water. It wasn't until the summer before seventh grade that I found out what intercourse was. I was visiting my best friend one day and her cat had just had kittens. She told me that she has asked her mother how it all came about and her mother had told her. She then asked, "If that is how cats had kittens, is it the same with people?" When she told me her mother's reply, I was astounded and I thought that it was really weird and so unnatural. Anyway, I wasn't afraid to swim with boys anymore.

Many students reported a feeling of repulsion when they first learn about the physical act of intercourse.

FEMALE

Although we did see a movie in fifth grade on menstruation we were never taught about sex in any other way. I remember learning the real way one becomes pregnant in fifth grade (up till then I thought you prayed to God for a child) and I was repelled by the idea of a guy putting his penis in me. I was not looking forward to my wedding night at all!

FEMALE

My initial reaction to learning the "facts of life" was confusion, embarrassment, and almost repulsion. Man, how do you do it?! Standing, sitting, or what? I was frightened by the idea of having a man's penis inside me (wouldn't that hurt?). Besides, I'd be so embarrassed to be naked in front of a man. I never knew about the feeling of closeness, or intimacy, or satisfaction; no one told me about them. Instead, sex was introduced merely as a means of reproduction.

Learning about sex is ongoing and complex. Information comes from many sources, and needs to be continually modified and integrated.

FEMALE

I learned about sex from an older cousin. She told me what I wanted to know. She answered all the questions I could create. I was about eight years old when I wanted to know what sex meant. My cousin explained it meant sharing love between two people, and sexy meant short skirts, makeup, and beautiful hair. I was satisfied. My Barbie dolls were sexy. My parents had sex. I made the crucial mistake of repeating the word "sex" when I heard it on the Bionic Woman. My mother dragged me out into the kitchen and grilled me. Who told me, what did I think it meant, and never, to ever, say that word again. I was terrified. Why was love between two people so evil? Why were my Barbies so bad—after all, I should not say that word again. I probably should not even think it— God would know and punish me. Well, I survived that night. But I was confused.

A year later I learned about the stamen and the pistil; I understood. Then, I learned about chickens; okay, I understood. I knew the egg was fertilized by the sperm, and a beautiful chick developed inside the hen. I was completely amazed. Sex education, or better labeled the female menstrual cycle presentation, was given when I was in the fifth grade. Boys and girls had separate classes that day, and the sixth grade girls came into our room. I was in awe because the instructor talked about periods, breasts, and personal hygiene so openly. Some girls asked questions, some giggled; I was silently embarrassed. I remember my brother (who is a grade ahead of me) asking me what the girls talked about during physical education that day. I tried to be honest, but he wanted to know everything. I gave him the pamphlets I had received from class, and ran. How embarrassing! Telling my brother about the menstrual cycle was humiliating.

Some students were concerned about what, when, and how to teach their children about sexuality. It is interesting that they omitted the subject of emotional responses to sexual experience, reflecting the continuing cultural ambivalence between avoidance and fascination with sex education.

FEMALE

I'm learning more about my sexual attitudes as we raise our two and one-half year old daughter. She's asked what my breasts are and I've felt pretty open and comfortable in talking with her about my breasts and her breasts. But the day she sat naked on the floor and spread her legs and said, "Look, Mommy! What's that?" Well, that day I was very uncomfortable and replied, "That's part of you." Inside me, I was scared and nervous and embarrassed—but I also wanted to be open and honest and positive. She seemed to accept my reply; I guess I'm not sure just how much information a two and one-half year old wants or how to give her the information in the most helpful, healthy way.

FEMALE

I really regret that my parents did not feel more comfortable talking to me about personal matters and feelings that I would have to deal with in my teenage years. I still am not sure how and when I figured out what sexual intercourse was. I was too embarrassed to ask my friends because I didn't want them to think that I was as ignorant as I was. As close as I can remember I was probably a junior or senior in high school before I understood this life process.

FEMALE

Perhaps the secrecy and perversion I grew up with has had some positive effect. It certainly made me doubly determined to do all in my power to stop the cycle—to ensure that my children and even their children's children know what's healthy and what's not.

Our papers seem to support the following general guidelines about what information is appropriate and when (Leight, 1988):

18 MONTHS TO 3 YEARS OLD

1. Anatomical gender similarities and differences—i.e., "Why does he have a penis and I don't?"
2. Names of all body parts including genitals—scientific terms, special family or ethnic terms, and terms used by peers for genitals might all be appropriate.

4 TO 6 YEARS OLD

1. Information picked up from inadequate sources can be dealt with in conversation—i.e., a TV news report about a rape and murder victim.
2. Vocabulary—accurate definitions for terms heard with parental interpretations.
3. Discussion with the child about the matter of deriving pleasure from touching one's genitals—masturbating.

4. How babies are conceived.
5. Appropriate and inappropriate touch, and rules about privacy for self and others.

7 TO 9 YEARS OLD

1. Personal development, changing body and new emotions.
2. Information about the development of the other sex.
3. Timing should be related to the individual's development. When a girl's breasts begin to develop or any of her friends' breasts begin to develop (even as early as seven or eight years) she should have information on menstruation.
4. Clarification of information: correcting faulty beliefs.

9 TO 12 YEARS OLD—PREPUBERTY

1. Arousal—same and opposite sex.
2. Menstruation and wet dreams.
3. Contraception.
4. Sexually transmitted diseases.
5. Family values about sex and relationship.
6. Homosexuality.

12 TO 15 YEARS OLD—EARLY ADOLESCENCE

During these years, information given should be more specific, enabling students to integrate information they have already gained. The kind of information these young people may want is suggested by the following questions asked of a middle school teacher:

1. What is "come"?
2. Can a doctor tell if you are a virgin?
3. Is it true that the first time a female has sex she might bleed? If so, why?
4. Why do some girls have harder and longer periods than others?
5. Can a girl have a wet dream?
6. What happens when you have an abortion?
7. Do babies go to the bathroom when they are in the uterus?
8. How old should you be to use a tampon?
9. What causes cramps during menstruation?
10. Why does a boy have wet dreams?
11. Does a male have just so much sperm to use up in his lifetime?

12. What is that milky white or yellowish stuff that comes out on girls' underwear?
13. After you have just had one period, can you be pregnant if you had intercourse?
14. (Asked by a boy) Are periods a very messy routine? Are girls embarrassed by them? Does it gross girls out?
15. Is it normal for one testicle to hang lower than the other?
16. How does a girl urinate when she still has a hymen?
17. Is it hard to have sex when the man has a super huge penis?
18. Does it hurt during sexual intercourse?
19. What does it feel like when a girl or guy reaches orgasm (or comes)?
20. Is it possible to get pregnant without the girl and guy having sexual intercourse?
21. How many times can a couple have sex before getting pregnant?
22. What's wrong with a woman smoking when she is pregnant?
23. Can a girl get pregnant when a guy uses a condom?
24. Can drinking alcohol cause birth defects or other problems to a fetus?
25. What benefit is the father's presence at birth?
26. What is oral sex?
27. Can a girl get a sexually transmitted disease if a boy puts sperm in her mouth?
28. If you're sexually active, how can you keep from getting AIDS?
29. Is it legal for a girl of 14 to buy contraceptives?
30. Does a girl have to "come" before she can get pregnant?
31. How can you tell if someone is gay?
32. Will close friendships between people of the same sex usually lead to homosexuality?
33. How do gay men and lesbians have sex?

16 TO 18 YEARS OLD

1. Knowledge of ways to pleasure self and another.
2. Communication in relationship.
3. Negotiating skills.
4. Realistic expectations and commitment.
5. Family planning.
6. Parenting.

In conclusion, "Sexuality education is a life-long process of acquiring information and forming attitudes, beliefs, and values about identity, relationships, and intimacy" (Kantor, 1994). The journey to sexual maturity is often difficult but is eased, according to many students, when significant adults (parents, teachers, and others) are comfortable with their own sexuality and communicate information in a clear and direct manner throughout the stages of the young person's development.

SUGGESTED ISSUES FOR PERSONAL REFLECTION, GROUP DISCUSSION, PERSONAL JOURNAL

1. What do you remember believing about conception and birth when you were quite young?
2. Where or from whom did you learn the "facts of life?" How did you feel about the information?
3. What was your experience of sex education in school?
4. What did you want to know, but never asked?

Chapter 6
Variations in Sexual Orientation

INTRODUCTION

*I*n recent decades, there has been a shift in language used to refer to people whose bonds are with same-sex people. Previously, "homosexual" was the common term in popular as well as scholarly usage. Currently, the preferred term for males is "gay men," and for females "lesbian." Actually, lesbian came into usage in the late nineteenth century (Money, 1991).

The complexity of human sexual response is being clarified by differentiating between sexual orientation, sexual identity, and sex role (Stein, 1993).

Sexual identity is an inner awareness or knowledge of oneself as male or female. With very few exceptions, sexual identity corresponds to the biological sex of the person. Research indicates that this sense is in place very early—between 18 and 36 months of age—and there is no evidence that it changes.

Sex role is the term given to the way a person enacts her or his sexual identity. Long before mature sexual behavior occurs, children are learning about sex roles. At an early age, they internalize how girls and boys and men and women are supposed to act. Every culture and every era has particular behaviors and characteristics that are considered appropriate to a given gender. These roles are shaped by the prevailing cultural, social, and religious norms. Sex roles, then, vary from culture to culture and can change within an individual's lifetime. For example, some behaviors that were considered unacceptable for women 50 years ago—smoking, wearing slacks, asking a man for a date—have become commonplace today.

Sexual orientation is different from sexual identity and sex role. It refers to a person's erotic response tendency. Distinctions between sexual identity, sex role, and orientation are crucial because of popular misconceptions about the nature of homosexual orientation (Money, 1991). Gay men and lesbian women are oriented (attracted) to people of their own sex. They are not confused about their identity as male or female, nor, in most current relationships are they assuming the role of the other sex. Gay men are men whose erotic response is to men, and lesbians are women whose erotic response is to women.

In the late nineteenth and early twentieth century, heterosexuality was generally assumed to be the outcome of normal development; therefore, the explanations of origins of homosexuality were identified as arrested development, or early experiences of a traumatic nature with the other sex or perverted character. However, current studies indicate that sexual orientation cannot be explained by incidence of early sexual trauma or negative heterosexual experiences (Peters and Cantrell, 1991). According to Stein (1993, p. 19), "Most theoreticians believe that the factors determining adult sexual orientation are established very early, probably by age two or three, but the manner in which these factors interact with opportunities and influences throughout the course of a lifetime can lead to a great variation in the expression of sexual orientation by the individual (Klein, 1990; Shuster, 1987).

"Marmor's (1965) statement that homosexuality is 'multiply determined by psychodynamic, sociocultural, biological, and situational factors' (p. 5) has been strongly supported by subsequent research and so continues to describe in general terms the current understandings of the origins of homosexuality and, indeed, of any sexual orientation."

The American Psychiatric Association removed homosexuality from the category of mental illness in 1973 because of the consensus in the growing body of research (Kinsey, 1953; Ford and Beach, 1951; Hooker, 1957; Marmor, 1965 and others) that there is no correlation between sexual orientation and mental illness. This landmark action called into question any therapeutic attempts to change the orientation of gay or lesbian clients. When efforts have been made to help people change their orientation, they have been signally ineffectual and ethically questionable. They have resulted in somewhat lessening same-sex behavior, but also in the lowering of self esteem (SIECUS Report, 1993, p. 19).

Some gay men and lesbian women have a sense in childhood—before any sexual activity—that they are "different" from their peers. Others have no awareness of such internal indicators and begin to realize it only when they fall in love with a person of the same gender.

MALE

My sexuality is something that I have struggled with for many years. Sometimes I think I do not truly know the impact of what it means to be gay in a homophobic society. Other times, my homosexuality, along with other personal struggles, have brought me to my knees in despair. I've known for as long as I can remember that I was gay. Often times, one reads about case histories that have quoted people as saying, "I knew that I was different but I didn't have a name to put on it until I was old enough to realize that the name of what I was, was gay." In my case, for whatever reasons, I know that I was gay by as early as age five or six—and that it was very different, maybe even wrong, as my family, society and church would later teach me. I have no idea of what it is like to grow up straight. I feel that I have a strong idea of the concept of the straight lifestyle. I know for a fact that I have no idea of what it is like to grow up and live free of fear of "having people find out" or having family members tell "fag jokes," and though at the time they may not have known of my sexual orientation, I was a "fag" and therefore felt complete rejection.

MALE

Last fall I had an experience during residence hall staff training which was both exciting and troubling to me. We saw a film of two homosexual males who were living together. The film portrayed their love for each other and explicitly depicted their lovemaking. While the scenes excited me sexually, that excitement made me feel very anxious. For the first time in my life I faced my own homosexual feelings, and the fear and terror they elicited. Since that experience, I have felt a certain disappointment that my fears have continued to prevent exploration in this area.

FEMALE

Marianne was quite a trip, to say the least. She taught me how to masturbate. We'd masturbate together and see who could reach orgasm first. I'll admit it: I faked it the first couple times till I went home and figured out just the right spot to rub. It's strange, I was hanging out with Marianne throughout high school, playing around with her sexually, but never found myself "in love" with her. Not to mention I never even thought what we were doing might be dirty or abnormal in our society's eyes, or put a label like lesbian on our activities. Marianne was a good friend about whom I have a lot of memories.

FEMALE

All through high school I had been in a theater and arts crowd and I could easily accept homosexuality. I never felt that it was wrong or abnormal, because I felt (and still feel) that everyone has homosexual feelings to a certain extent. However, a guy I was very much in love with began having more and more homosexual feelings. He had sexual relations with a couple of guys, and finally decided he needed to get out of the relationship with me so that he could try the gay life. I felt angry that he broke up with me, and that everything seemed good about our relationship, except that he had these nagging feelings of wanting to be gay. I started to have doubts about my sexual attractiveness, and I wondered if I could ever find anyone else.

FEMALE

My partner told me that during her adolescence, she was driven to find information on homosexuality, and read widely. She also collected everything she could find on Martina Navratilova. Terrified but curious, she kept searching.

Kinsey's research (1948, 1953) documented sexual orientation as not simply homosexual, heterosexual, or bisexual. He developed a continuum to describe the range of orientation. The continuum begins at 0 which represents exclusive response to the other sex; 3 represents relatively equal response to each sex; and 6 indicates exclusive response to the same sex. Location on the continuum is determined by the incidence of fantasies, dreams, and erotic responses to the same or other sex. Therefore, a person described as a 5 would have minimal incidence of erotic response to the other sex, and a 1 would have minimal incidence of response to the same sex. The experiences described in the following pages represent homosexual and bisexual orientations which could be identified on the Kinsey scale from 2 to 6.

MALE

I am 20 years old. I masturbate and have wet dreams without guilt and I have never been interested in having intercourse with a woman. I have concerns about not being attracted to the female body, but have avoided useless worrying about it. I am not sure I have faith that this attraction will develop.

FEMALE

One thing that scares me is my dreams of making love (kissing, fondling) with another girl. I often felt this was a sign that I was lesbian or something. But I have figured out that I am dreaming of what I would like a boy to do to me. Through my caressing of another female, I am expressing my desires, and how I wish these desires would be fulfilled by a male.

FEMALE

I worked on Mackinac Island the summer following my freshman year. I was caught off guard. All through high school I was never asked out once. Now four or five young men had their sights on me. This was kind of neat. One man caught my eye too. Charlie. Charlie was a great guy. He was the first man I made love with. One year into our relationship I realized I was attracted to women. I even explained this to Charlie. He sort of thought I'd get over it I guess. Our relationship lasted for another three years, and not another word was said about my attraction to women.

MALE

I am attracted to women but also have some attraction to men. So, I don't think it makes sense to limit myself to being sexual with women only. I feel bisexual. Society is very afraid of homosexual relationships, regarding them as threats and corruptors of the morals of this country. Why is it so terrible to love another man so deeply that words cannot express it?

FEMALE

I have found out that I have a very keen interest in homosexuality, and I think I have more homosexual feelings than I admit to. The idea of lesbianism used to threaten me, possibly because of my own feelings. Now I can understand lesbianism in a whole different way. I can understand why a woman might prefer another woman as a partner, and in a way it sounds neat to me. I can accept my feelings more easily now, and admit that there are some aspects of loving women that appeal to me. I am happy being heterosexual, but if society hadn't forced me into that role so much, I might have been free to love anyone I cared to, man or woman. And I wish I had had that freedom!

FEMALE

I am bisexual. It has been hard to get to the place where I can admit that even to myself, let alone put it on paper. Intensity was not "cool" in my family, and even as a small child, I recall feeling guilty about intense feelings about some very special older women. I suppose these were crushes. I never had any sexual fantasies, but if they touched me in a caring way, it felt powerful. As I began to mature physically, I got interested in boys and fell in love twice. I never had a crush on a girl my own age or younger. I dated pretty steadily in high school and college, and it was during college that I met and married my husband. I love him very much, and we have a great sex life. After a year of marriage, I met a woman for whom I gradually developed very strong feelings. Nothing changed with my husband, but she and I shared many interests and deep understanding. That depth of feeling and strong sense of connection seemed to lead us naturally toward physical and then sexual expression. But gradually we became aware that such a relationship might hurt many people important to us if it were known, and she and I terminated the sexual part of our relationship. I continue to love her and to love him. To me, these loves don't seem competitive; they are different. Sex with him has tremendous variety—from intense emotional expression to just fun or pleasing him. With her, it was always an expression of intense caring. In many ways, I wish this weren't the way I am. It's hard and it hurts to have to hide such strong feelings. But it is also very deep and beautiful. I wish it were OK for everyone to love a person of the same sex or/and the other sex intensely, including sexual expression of that intensity if there is real respect for commitments and to the well-being of all people concerned.

Crushes may or may not be indicative of lesbian or gay orientation.

FEMALE

There was one particular friend I had in high school, Kelley. WOW! She was beautiful! Now, we never did anything sexual, but I thought she was the greatest. I had a crush on her. She often wasn't very nice to me, and many of my other friends would ask, "Why do you hang out with that bitch?" I didn't have an answer for them. All I knew was I couldn't wait to spend time over at her house on the weekends.

FEMALE

At the age of 13, I was extraordinarily infatuated with Anne, one of my camp counselors. When summer ended, Anne left camp the day before I did. She had given me a picture which, that night, I cradled as I mourned. The woman who was my cabin counselor ridiculed me. "You're not one of *those,* are you?" she asked. I had no idea what she was talking about, but her tone of voice made me feel deeply ashamed. My connection with that counselor was an important experience. In spite of that crush, I know I am not lesbian.

Judgmental teachings of some religious groups can cause shame, isolation, and terrible pain.

FEMALE

I had two brief relationships in my late teens which I felt were shameful. My fear prevented me from exploring my own identity for many years.

My pious nature and submission to religious authority may have contributed to my fear. The adults who were important to me at that time did not know how to talk about sexual orientation with me.

MALE

Homosexuality went against everything my mother's religion taught. So, we made a verbal agreement not to talk about my homosexuality. Our arguments had led nowhere but to hurtful tears and angry words. It was hard for her to hear that I wanted nothing to do with religion and that I doubted God (just where was He when I had all my pain? After all, I was His creation, and now the church tells me that God thinks that homosexuality is a sin and I'm bound for hell). According to her and my brother Chris, I was doomed to hell until I changed from gay to straight.

I will never forget telling my first therapist about a story I heard in a fundamentalist Christian church when I was a kid. It had haunted me for years. The story went like this:

> There was this boy who was asked to clean his bedroom. His parents were trying to sell their house and some prospective buyers would be coming over to tour the house in a couple of days. Well, the boy put things off and never cleaned his room. The parents showed the house, but to their embarrassment, their son had not cleaned his room. They confronted the boy, and told him that he would have to beg God for forgiveness or he would to go hell for not obeying his parents.

After hearing this story, my therapist asked if I knew I was gay at the time I heard it. I said "Yes," not giving it a second thought. "And if a boy who doesn't clean his room and obey his parents will go to hell, what will happen to a gay boy?" Then I realized the full impact of the judgment of the fundamentalist church on me.

When my brother first found out I was gay, he wrote me saying I was "doomed to hell and loneliness." He challenged me to explain several Bible verses condemning homosexuality. But, when I came out to the rest of my family, my brother seemed to have changed his mind. He sent me another letter explaining that he had been doing some reading about homosexuality, about some of the pain that gays go through, and about some of the roots and possible explanations of homosexuality. He said that no matter what, he would not judge me. I was on cloud nine. Finally, I had gotten some much-needed support from my brother. Though he did not approve of my homosexuality, at least he was making an effort to understand. On his thirtieth birthday, I bought him a birthday card that said "Thanks for being my brother and loving me for who I am" type of message. I wrote a note thanking him for caring enough to do some reading on homosexuality and that I would love to talk with him. His acceptance came at a time in my life when I was losing hope for life in general, and the letter helped to reaffirm that there is good in the world and that I might be accepted as I am rather than judged. After receiving the "accepting" letter, however, I was stunned to receive another letter from him two days later, analyzing the "causes" of homosexuality and suggesting I could be "cured."

I should have known better than to trust his support. The loss of his support impacted me terribly, and death seemed to be the only way out, the only way to escape the pain. Once again, I sought healing in therapy.

In a society which does not legitimize talking about nor teaching about sexuality, gay and lesbian people grow up without adequate information about their sexual orientation.

FEMALE

I did not even know what homosexuality was. I had never heard the term, although I had read extensively. One day at a friend's house, we were listening to music in her bedroom, she came on to me in a very surprising way. We were good friends and spent much time together, but this particular night was different. Her eyes had a new sparkle, she got very close to me, her touch lingered; she was different than she ever had been before. I was 16 and she was 15. I did not understand, but I knew that I was aroused. We were good church-going kids who had never heard anything about this. She is now out as a lesbian, and continues to be one of my best friends.

FEMALE

I really felt many of my feelings were abnormal, especially for a woman. I used to see pictures of nude women or would see them in movies and get sexually excited. I was always told that only men could be sexually aroused by a visual stimulus. It is good now to find out that other women also have similar feelings, and that it is OK.

Homophobia is a term used to describe beliefs and behaviors of those who fear, are revolted by, and hate gay men and lesbians. Homophobia is also motivated by the need to deny any homosexual feelings or desire in oneself (Weinberg, 1973). It can result in a variety of negative and hostile actions, including judgment, hostility, harassment, and overt violence. It can lead to unrealistic beliefs that orientation can and must be changed.

Although there were no excerpts about overt violence, antigay violence is a reality in our society (Vasbinder, 1993). One scholar (Harry, 1990) suggests that it may be caused by immature males needing to prove their heterosexuality to peers. Antigay offenders may (1) actively seek out gay and lesbian victims, (2) victimize gay men and lesbians as occasions arise, and (3) fail to intervene when faced with such violence perpetrated by others. Violence seems to be carried out against gay men or lesbians who fit the stereotypes of "butch" or "femme" appearance and behavior.

As young men and women are beginning to know their identity as gay or lesbian, the results of a homophobic society result in what has been called "internalized homophobia," and they believe about themselves the negative judgments that society makes about homosexuality in general. If such young people do not have support and accurate information, they may internalize the homophobia all around them, resulting in self-devaluation and self-contempt. A significant number of gay and lesbian young people experience severe anxiety and depression, and become suicidal. This tragedy indicates faults in society, not emotional problems in the young people themselves.

Therefore, coming out to self and others is often a painful process. Parents and family may have difficulty supporting a gay or lesbian family member. They are forced to deal with their own issues and prejudices, and may not immediately have the resources to affirm the person coming out.

FEMALE

While being honest with myself is important, being honest with those around me has been the most difficult part of my life as a lesbian. I am not able to be out at work. I am out to my sister (limitedly), but not with my parents. I realize I may never to able to be out with the entire world, but I'm moving closer to that.

MALE

I grew up the youngest child of four. My three older siblings were bossy and whatever they said was law. Because I was so young, I had no way to defend myself against their teasing. In later years (before they found out I was gay) I was hurt by their homophobic jokes. While I have let go of most of my resentment, the memories remain. One of these is the time my great uncle was visiting at Christmas and my oldest brother told me all "fags" should be shot or shipped off to an island. My great uncle agreed strongly with my brother. After that one incident, the meaning of family and Christmas was changed for me. As a child, I was neat about my person and belongings. My other brother teased me and said I would "grow up and make somebody a good little housewife." While I was in high school, my sister had a talk with me about the fact that I had mostly all female friends (I felt more comfortable and accepted by females back then). At one point she said, "If you don't have any male friends, people might think you're gay." Another time, my father and I delivered a load of lumber to a woman who was a known lesbian. My father's advice to me before we went in was to "stay away from them (lesbians)." Then there was the time my mother came home and told an "incredibly funny joke" that she had heard at work. The joke was "What do you call a gay man in a wheelchair? Roll AIDS!" A joke that was so funny to her was about something that is now killing millions of gay men, gay men just like her son.

FEMALE

There are pictures of a somber baby, stories about her being the watchful one, always staring, seriously considering the faces and conversations of adults. Though I do not remember much of her, that child was me, the oldest of five Catholic children. At the age of seven or eight, after hearing my parents quarreling, I realized that I would never be able to talk to them. They had too many things and people to take care of, and seemed so full of worry. I grew up choosing silence, responsibility, unquestioned obedience. As expected, I married and had my own children, but was sad and tormented. After 19 years of marriage, I finally acknowledged the real me—a lesbian woman—and am finally capable of feeling joy. I am peaceful—and silent no more!

MALE

Society, friends, the church and media had told me that gay is wrong—that I am wrong, sick, and immoral. Now as an adult, I know my sexual orientation just is. It is a part of me I didn't choose, any more than I chose my brown eyes and hair. My sexual orientation is a part that is okay but seen by many people as wrong, sick, diseased, and morally corrupt. In 1986 I started my coming out process. In earlier years, it was easier for me to keep my secret within myself and too painful to even think about coming out. Eventually, it was becoming too painful not to come out.

Telling my family that I was gay was very difficult for me. I told my sister before I told my mother. When I said the words "I'm gay" my sister responded: "I was afraid that was what you were going to say." The look on her face broke my heart. Several months later when I came out to my mom, her first words were, "No you're not!" Our conversation ended in hostility. She was in shock and I was highly stressed. "What are you going to do now?" she asked. "Probably go and kill myself," I said. She let me leave, not saying another word.

My mother proceeded to come out for me to my two brothers and my father. She viewed this situation as a family problem and felt that the immediate family members should be informed. When I found out, I was angry. She had disclosed and risked something so dear, so deeply personal of mine without my permission. I felt violated.

I was, however, curious as to how the rest of the family took it. My oldest brother wanted to know "what the hell was wrong with me"; my other brother cried; my father, with whom I have never shared a close relationship, said he had suspected for a while, that I was still his son and he still loved me. He went on to say that I would always be welcomed home anytime. Out of all the darkness in my life at the time, this one incident of acceptance from the man who gave me life meant more than anyone will ever know. Through all the pain I felt growing up, this one incident allowed the birth of a new relationship between me and my father.

MALE

Rejection of a Family

I opened my soul
For you to hear
And share with you
My inner fears
I finally told you
I finally could show
A part of me
I wanted you to know
I trusted you
And opened up
To finally let you see
An important part of me
Instead you turned
And shut me out
You wouldn't accept me
And what my life's about
But you must understand
That I had to let you know
In order for me
To let myself grow.

Many straight people fear that they night be approached by a gay or lesbian person. What they do not know is that gay and lesbian people are not interested in approaching them. In our society gay men and lesbians have to depend on what they call "gaydar"—a "sense," though fallible, about a person's orientation.

FEMALE

One of the women I taught with caught my eye. Not that I wanted to go out with her, but I thought she might be able to introduce me to some of her friends. She asked me to go out for drinks with some of her friends.

And that was when I met my present partner. It's an interesting thing, "gaydar." Gaydar is that radar, that way of somehow "knowing" who is lesbian and who isn't. Thank goodness it doesn't fail us too often.

Societal devaluation of homosexuality leads some gay and lesbian people to try to be heterosexual by getting married.

FEMALE

When I found out I was pregnant, I gave in and agreed to get married. I had to give up a college scholarship. I tried to be happy, but what I wanted most was missing. I spent my entire pregnancy without ever making love with my husband again. I knew the night of our wedding something was really wrong. I cried all the time and I did not have anyone to talk to. Things got a little better after my daughter was born. He occasionally would surrender to my desires, but it was always after I begged. Twenty months later I delivered a son. My husband still did not show any sexual interest in me and my ego was shattered. He started not coming home after work. After four years I had an affair with a friend of his. For the first time ever I had sex with a man that really desired me. When my husband found out about the affair he told me he was gay. He left soon, saying he did not want to hurt me any more. I was 23 with two small children and was having an affair with a married man. This relationship was purely sexual and had no future. I ended the affair, got a job, started college and became promiscuous. It was fun at first, but I knew I wanted a stable relationship and eventually, I found a man who loved me and my children.

All too often, the self-image of the gay or lesbian young person reflects the devaluation and denigration of the world around them which defines them as deviants who deserve to be ostracized and punished in various ways.

MALE

I wish that kids who feel they are gay could have role models so they could see that there are well-adjusted gay people. This might cut down on the high suicide rate among gay teens. AIDS has only made it harder for both young and old gays to be themselves. It has again become okay to engage in fag-bashing and to push us back into the closet. I can see areas that I need to grow in, one of which is to become more comfortable with my sexual orientation. Because of past experiences, I have had to hide this side of myself. I was even drawn to the Mormon Church, but when I joined, I had to hide my sexual orientation. Doing this has made me feel like I am cheating the gay community and living a lie.

FEMALE

As a teenager, I spent days on the beach watching straight couples walk hand in hand down the beach, occasionally stopping to embrace and kiss. Then I realized what a heterosexist world we live in. I got really pissed. I didn't understand why a gay couple couldn't walk down the beach in the same way without fear. I do now. I'm not so angry anymore. It just is. I can influence people around me, but may not always be able to change them. I do have the power to put myself in safe places.

MALE

Since physical and verbal endearments are impossible in public, our social life takes on a ghetto nature. We have only bars, steam baths, parks, and a few other assorted locations where we know we can locate each other. The action *rarely* occurs before 11 at night. The psychological effect of relegating all communal and private social activity to the middle of the night is destructive. Even if I consciously deny it, having to sneak around in the night gives me the feeling of being dirty. How can I *really* respect myself when the world respects me so little that I must wait until it sleeps before I can live as myself? I feel so envious of straight people's freedom. They assume they can approach a person they are attracted to at any time. Because my social life has to be carried on during the late night hours, I find my daytime performance both physically and mentally diminished. All of this is a potentially inexhaustible source of guilt and self-hatred.

One male student writes about the circumstances that led to disillusionment and fleeting sexual encounters.

MALE

When I first became active in the gay world, I was full of self-confidence. I felt physically attractive, mentally capable and industrious, and that I was an incorrigible "nice guy." I figured that, as a matter of mathematical certainty, there would be others like myself in the gay world. I thought everyone wanted to settle down with one person just as I did. My plan, therefore, was simple—just make myself available, pick one out, and let chemistry clinch it. I was almost disastrously naive. I wanted to settle down, but it seemed that I was the only guy that did. Everyone that I wanted to settle down with got gypsy-feet soon enough, and some were downright crude about it. I have been active for a year and two months now, and my longest relationship has been a week-and-one-half duration.

The solution to the problem seemed to be a change in my plan of operations. Since sex came too cheap to others, I mustn't value it too highly myself or I will get hurt. Instead I should have sex with those I am sexually attracted to and hope that among them, I will accidentally run across a lover. Do you see how promiscuity is self-perpetuating? If the culture devalues relationship, the individual must either devalue it also or get hurt.

There is another reality that can lead to promiscuity. If the person is aware that he is involved in what society considers to be "immoral" sexual activity, why should he take pains to be "moral" in his conduct? The gay culture has had to operate outside traditional morality, and will continue so until society recognizes its validity, or until enough individual homosexuals extricate themselves from the merry-go-round. Unfortunately neither is likely. In the face of this it is difficult for me to avoid complete despair. I can only hope that I keep my own sanity and bump into someone who feels the same way before I grow too old.

The same student comments about his perception of the necessity of being youthful. [Although he sees this as a reality only in the gay world, it is equally so in the heterosexual one. Eds.]

MALE

I am very afraid of losing my youth to the merry-go-round. Each wrinkle that appears on my face will represent an irreversible defeat, along with a reduced capacity to lure what I want. I can think of nothing more pitiable than two aged faggots clinging to each other because no one younger will have them. A real loving relationship in older years seems very difficult to achieve. This gives me a sense of desperation which I feel is unhealthy, counterproductive, and almost unshakable. I have found difficulty coping with many aspects of gay life: society's official attitude, the concept of masculinity, the effect of being a nocturnal creature, the degradation of having to go to sleazy bars, the necessity of secrecy, the inability to trust straights, the lack of emotional support from parents, the psychological effects of promiscuity, the separation of sex and love, and the effects of age. If I could change these, or my orientation, you can be sure that I would. The temptation is either to indulge in a lot of wishful thinking or to give up. I hope I succumb to neither.

When society as a whole can erase some of the deeply ingrained prejudice against homosexuality, gay and lesbian people will have the opportunity to fulfill their richest human potential (Rubin, 1970).

MALE

I hope the heterosexuals learn about and accept gay men. Societal prejudice emotionally destroys many good people and/or holds them back from full development as persons. As a gay man, I find it very difficult to maintain self-respect. It is probably obvious to many people that society's attitude toward gay people is devastating in a rather direct way. I, along with most of my friends, claim to be free of guilt about our actions with other men. My guilt manifests itself in subtle and pernicious ways. It is, for instance, almost pathologically important to me that I am seen as masculine in appearance and mannerisms. Society has convinced me that I am less of a man than most, so I must guard the vestiges of manhood zealously. Whenever I notice myself making what seems to be an effeminate gesture, I get depressed. I eventually dispel the gloom by making a firm resolve never to repeat the "offense."

MALE

Since society supports the straight couple and discourages and rejects the gay couple, everyday romantic gestures are judged as inappropriate. It has probably not occurred to most straights what it is like not to be able to touch the one you love (of whom you are unspeakably proud) and to have to pretend you're nothing but friends. Instead, you find some secret place in the middle of the night where you can express your real feelings. What a hell of a place to have to be to show you care!

MALE

Straight people can help by making sure never to look down on gay people. Chances are that someone you know is gay. If you ever find out that your brother is a homosexual, don't tell him that it's all the same to you. Instead, invite him and his lover to dinner. And don't kiss your wife in front of them unless you are prepared to see them kiss.

SOME CONCLUSIONS

Most of the students writing of their growing up experiences had not yet had the opportunity to know same-sex couples who were in long-term committed relationships. Stein (1993, p. 25) quotes Peplau and Cochran (1990) as follows: "Research has demonstrated repeatedly that, despite the sanctions against them, more than half of gay men and lesbians participate in enduring close relationships with another member of the same sex. Surveys of gay men have shown that 40 percent to 60 percent of the men are involved in steady relationships, and studies of lesbians have shown that between 45 percent and 80 percent of women are in relationships." The lifestyles of gay men and lesbian women are as varied as those of heterosexual men and women. The research of Bell and Weinberg (1978) was a comprehensive examination of homosexual lifestyles. Crooks and Baur (1993, p. 43) comment on that research: "It is an important contribution to the literature, in an often sensationalized and misunderstood area of human experience."

SUGGESTED ISSUES FOR PERSONAL REFLECTION, GROUP DISCUSSION, PERSONAL JOURNAL

Note: In your discussion, remember that there may be gay men or lesbian women in your small group or in the class who have not come out. Seeking to "bring people out" is inappropriate.

1. What and how did you first learn about gay and lesbian people?
2. What strikes you most about the anecdotes in this chapter?
3. If a friend were to "come out" to you, how would you react? or like to react?
4. If someone belittles gay men or lesbians with humor, how do you feel? What do you do? Or what would you like to do?

Chapter 7

Adolescence: Emerging Sexuality

INTRODUCTION

The onset of puberty demands of young people a radical reorganization in their behavior. Adolescents must cope with their own physical changes and with variations in the rate of development that they and their peers have reached at any given age. As maturing sexual beings, they also must learn how to deal with new reactions to them from family and friends. Puberty arrives at different ages for different youth, ranging from ages 9 to 16 for girls and from 11 to 18 for boys. The average age is about one and a half to two years earlier for girls than boys. According to Lansdown and Walker (1991), there is a definite physical maturation sequence.

In girls the order is as follows:

1. Initial growth spurt.
2. Initial enlargement of the breasts.
3. Appearance of straight, pigmented pubic hair.
4. Period of maximum growth.
5. Kinky pubic hair.
6. Menarche: usually about two and one half years after initial breast development. (Growth spurt slows and only rarely does the girl grow more than an additional three inches after menarche.)
7. Growth of axillary hair.
8. Ovulation: 12 to 18 months after first menstruation.

9. Increased underarm sweating and adult body odor.
10. Pimples and acne.

In boys the corresponding order of pubescent phenomena is as follows:

1. Beginning growth of testes.
2. Appearance of straight, pigmented pubic hair.
3. Slight breast enlargement in about 30 percent of males, lasting up to 18 months before disappearing.
4. Initial growth spurt.
5. Beginning of penis lengthening.
6. First ejaculation: about one year after penis begins to lengthen.
7. Kinky pubic hair.
8. Period of maximum growth.
9. Axillary hair, sweating, and adult body odor.
10. Facial hair begins to develop.
11. Marked voice changes.
12. Development of beard and often pimples/acne.
13. Sperm mature.

"Adolescence . . . is that period of social and emotional development that moves young people toward adulthood and is mostly a social and cultural phenomenon. Puberty is that time when youngsters become capable of reproducing and their bodies begin to take on distinctly male or female secondary sex characteristics" (Kelly, 1988, p. 154–55). It is an exciting and difficult time.

PART I—PHYSICAL CHANGES AT PUBERTY

Physical changes bring with them a variety of concerns. "For girls, breast development, menstruation, vaginal lubrication and discharges . . . may be a source of worry. For boys, concerns may focus on genital size, spontaneous erections, ejaculation, and masturbation (Diamond and Diamond, 1986).

MALE

Junior high was a rather awful time in the life of most guys I know, myself readily included. What a drag puberty was. I really wish my parents would have given me some type of sex talk and filled me in on what was going on with me. Once in a great while my mother or father would say something like, "Don't worry, son," with regard to my acne. That didn't help a whole lot. I had greater questions: for instance, one that had plagued me earlier was, "When am I to get pubic hair on my genitalia?" Junior high locker rooms were particularly grotesque, especially when some of the more physically mature dudes, who were not always the most intelligent, made fun of the younger less physically mature guys. I thought I'd always be singing first tenor in the choir—until the change came and wrecked my voice. Suddenly I had pubic hair, was six feet tall, and shaving once or twice a week. This rapid change was hard for me to integrate.

FEMALE

When I was 11 to 14 or so, things changed. I can remember being extremely sensitive about *everything.* If someone looked at me wrong I'd cry. The tension seemed almost unbearable at the time. I felt too old to play with dolls but too young to act like a teenager. I wanted to grow up but it was fun doing things that kids did. My body started to change and that kind of scared me. I wasn't really interested in boys yet and no one was really interested in me; but that was OK.

Spontaneous erections were disconcerting and often unpredictable.

MALE

When I was about ten years old, I was making sand castles on the beach with my uncle and his fiancee. I was wondering how she looked under her bathing suit and I soon noticed that for an unknown reason I had an erection. I didn't think much of it, so I kept building my castle and it soon went away. About seventh grade these impromptu erections became more frequent, and I dreaded having to get out of my seat in class when I had one. Erections usually occurred when the class was boring, and they would sometimes last the whole hour. I was afraid that everyone would notice. Luckily nobody did. Or if they did, I didn't know it.

MALE

I remember leafing through magazines like *Life* to look at pictures of girls in bathing suits or underwear. I was especially fond of advertisements about bras, like: "I dreamed I was a knockout in my living bra!" It would show the picture of a healthy young woman in a boxing ring wearing boxing gloves, boxing trunks, and of course a bra. I used to fantasize, something like—she sprained her ankle and I had to go over and help her. I think I used to daydream a lot about helping some girl who was getting a hard time from everyone else. I guess I wanted to picture myself as the savior of pretty girls in trouble. I do believe that I would get an erection when I looked at these pictures. I did not know what an erection was all about, but I enjoyed it.

MALE

Frequent erections at inappropriate times and places were embarrassing. I didn't talk to my friends about them. This stemmed from being informed by my parents that it was a pleasure for later in life.

MALE

In junior high I remember two guys had a *Playboy* foldout and when this one guy was in the shower, they taped this foldout to the inside of his locker door. When he returned from the shower, and opened the door, he saw the picture and immediately tried to conceal his midsection. I was shocked to see his penis erect! It was a phenomenon of which I had been totally unaware.

A boy's first ejaculation signals the onset of puberty.

MALE

The most traumatic experience of my life came when I experienced ejaculation for the first time. Since it didn't take place during a nocturnal emission, I was able to figure out what had happened. I was overwhelmed by fear, guilt, shame, and worry. You see, my parents had felt that it would be in my best interest to discontinue our discussions on sexuality when I was 13. Instead, they suggested I read a book on the subject. The text they handed me was aimed at parents. I got only a few pages into it before it turned me off. As a result, I was totally unprepared to experience daydreams about girls, desires for masturbation, and of course orgasm.

After keeping all of these emotions inside for what seemed like forever, I finally broke and, in tears from shame, explained to my parents what had happened. They reassured me that what I had done and felt was perfectly normal.

MALE

I remember reaching puberty earlier than the average boy. I had my first ejaculation during the summer when I was ten years old. This first ejaculation was from masturbation. I didn't know anything at all about what was happening until I was in junior high a couple of years later.

MALE

I had my first ejaculation when I was 13, and it was a shock since I knew nothing about sex.

When ejaculation first occurs in a "wet dream" it may also be disconcerting.

MALE

My first nocturnal emission really put me on a trip. I had remembered something that had puzzled me in my Boy Scout handbook on this subject. I looked it up, read it about one hundred times and was relieved to find that it was a perfectly natural thing that had happened to me.

MALE

I first felt attracted to girls when I was in the sixth grade. I felt very shy around them, a shyness that lasted about six years. It was then that I first remember having thoughts and dreams that were semierotic. For the first time in my life, I did not mind going to bed! I had my first orgasm during one of my pre-sleep erotic thought sessions that I found somewhat scary, but at the same time pleasurable and wondrous.

When pubic and body hair began to grow, it was often a milestone.

MALE

I will always remember seventh and eighth grade as traumatic. It was in seventh grade that I started to grow body hair. At first I would shave it off, only to watch it grow back.

MALE

The only early feeling about my body of any significance is one concerning pubic hair. I was under the impression that it only grew on girls. You can imagine my shock when I discovered it on my own body. No one else in the locker room had any. I was so embarrassed that I cut my few strands off with shears. Even when I realized that there was nothing wrong with me and that all guys grew it, it was still hard for me to accept.

FEMALE

Around age 12, I became interested in my body and discovered some things. My breasts were getting bigger and pubic hair was beginning to grow. I shared a bedroom with my younger sister and we compared our bodies. We looked at each other and talked about our changes. It was exciting yet scary.

Many women students wrote about their reactions to their developing breasts. That first bra was a milestone though not always a welcome one.

FEMALE

I could say that all through my teens and even now I share many of the same physical characteristics as that of a telephone pole. All through junior high and high school I was almost a head taller than everyone else. All of my friends began to develop in the sixth and seventh grades but I had to wait until the ninth grade. I wondered if my body was ever going to develop. I was pretty self-conscious about my lanky figure and was sure this was the reason no one I liked ever liked me. About the eleventh grade I finally started getting over my self-consciousness and began accepting my skinny figure. I made myself believe that "Thin is in."

FEMALE

I was very self-conscious about developing. I never wanted to get breasts and I never wanted to start menstruation. I even cringed at the word "woman" because I never wanted to be one. I'd cry at night about growing up. It was supposed to be a big deal that I was growing to be a woman, but I didn't see anything exciting about it. I didn't start wearing a bra until seventh grade and that was only because my mother made me. After a while I got used to the idea and by November of seventh grade it seemed natural. I liked boys, but knew I'd never kiss one for a long, long time. There were big parties in junior high where people would play spin the bottle, post office, and so forth, but never in the world would I go.

FEMALE

I was very excited about my breast development. It was a big competition to see who was wearing a bra in elementary school. When I began wearing one, I also liked wearing see-through blouses so everyone would know. And, with increases in cup size, I felt very attractive and pleased.

FEMALE

Starting to wear a bra was humiliating for me. A lot of girls couldn't wait, and began to wear bras before they needed them. But I was embarrassed and avoided it as long as possible by wearing heavy sweaters. I was sure everyone would notice the first time I wore one. But once the embarrassment subsided, I felt like a woman and was proud.

Developing earlier or later than one's friends can be uncomfortable.

FEMALE

Being one of those unlucky girls who develops later in life than all her friends, I was worried at times that I would never develop! My friends were getting big breasts and I was still as flat as a pancake with skinny legs besides. It was really important to look good for those junior high boys though, so I even tried stuffing my bra a few times. That was too scary though because someone might find out in gym class and that would have been *terribly embarrassing.* I never did get very big in the boob department, but I've learned to live with it (or *them,* whatever!).

FEMALE

As I grew and entered high school, I became increasingly aware of my lack of physical development, that I hadn't begun to menstruate yet and that guys didn't find me attractive. I demanded that mother buy me a bra and I got a doctor's excuse to never take gym. I couldn't stand the thought of dressing in front of other girls when I was so undeveloped. At one point I even used to "stuff" my bra with toilet paper, but I was always so self-conscious that it was lumpy, or one was bigger than the other, that I soon abandoned the practice.

Breast size is a concern—to be neither over- nor underendowed.

FEMALE

About the time I was ten, my body started to change shape. I noticed I was starting to "jiggle" when I ran or jumped, so I started making sure my blouses and skirts were not too tight. By the end of fifth grade, I really needed a bra. I never wore training bras, my first was a full fledged 34B. I quickly filled a 34C. I can remember my mom asking me if I was stuffing my bra with Kleenex. I was shocked! Of course not, there was enough of me as there was. My "chest" was almost my claim to fame. I was never embarrassed by it. In fact, it brought me some attention that I was really in need of.

FEMALE

I remember becoming aware, in junior high school, that I was flat-chested. I used to be so ashamed because I didn't wear a bra. Maybe if I hadn't been the oldest child my mother would have been more aware of my sensitivity about my nondevelopment, and because I was extremely sensitive about my body shape, I was too embarrassed to talk with her.

FEMALE

All through junior high and high school I felt unhappy about being "overendowed." I felt just too uncomfortable in sweaters—there was so much to reveal and I was always sure that the only reason boys liked me was because of my bustline.

FEMALE

In junior high I was in water ballet. We had to wear tank suits that neither hid nor enhanced any part of one's body. I was a very skinny and flat-chested kid, the kind people might joke about—when she stands sideways and sticks out her tongue, she looks like a zipper! Or a carpenter's delight, flat as a board—you know the type. I was a little self-conscious that I had nothing in the "boob" department but I had not yet started my period so I had faith that someday I would develop.

Parents' comments about their daughter's breast development makes an impact.

FEMALE

In junior high I was uptight about my sexuality, especially my femininity. I started developing very early. By the time I was 11, I needed a bra and I had started my periods. The girls in my gym class in sixth grade laughed at me because my breasts were pretty big and I still didn't have a bra. I tried to cover myself up when I dressed and undressed. On my eleventh birthday my mom gave me a sailor blouse and inside was my first bra. It was the best present I could have received. The bra made me feel a lot better about myself, but I was still unsure of my femininity for a long time. I wanted to be attractive to the boys, but I had always been sort of a tomboy and I was big and chunky. Until I was about 15 I felt that the boys would never like me as anything but "one of the guys," and I didn't date.

FEMALE

One time my father talked to me about my slow physical development and told me not to worry. He pointed out that I would just become mature sexually about the age I would be getting married just like Mom had, and since she still looked young, I too would probably stay young-looking as I grew older. His comments helped.

Nudity in the shower rooms is embarrassing to many boys. Breast development (or lack of it) causes embarrassment for girls in many situations. Teasing from the boys is common.

FEMALE

In eighth grade I finally started my period. I also got somewhat of a shape, but not much to speak of. I was pretty little, with very little breasts. I was often the butt of jokes about my small breasts. I learned to laugh it off, but I do remember a lot of hurt feelings. I still get the jokes today, but I've finally accepted that I'm no cover girl.

FEMALE

My breasts developed very late. This brought me a lot of grief from my male peers. I dreaded situations like going to the beach. In junior high when I made the cheerleading squad, they announced the girls who had made it over the public address system. When they said my name, one of the boys in the back of the room shouted, "Oh no, we can't have a flat-chested cheerleader like her!" Those junior high years were awful!

FEMALE

At the same time of getting used to my period I was adjusting to the idea of wearing a bra, something which was a big bother and embarrassment to me. I was one of the first in my class to get one and it embarrassed me to wear it. It was the big thing for the boy who sat behind me to snap my bra strap during class, causing me to turn shades of scarlet.

The onset of menstruation is an unforgettable time for most women.

FEMALE

My first real sense of loss of innocence was when I started my first period. I was in fifth grade (just starting). I was really upset because my breasts were enlarging and that next summer I would have to wear a bra. My first period started the day before I went to two-week resident camp. I was really hit hard by puberty because I realized that I had to be a cheerleader and not a football player. That is pretty hard for a football player to accept.

FEMALE

I was nine on the eve of my first slumber party invitation. Before the party, I suddenly was very sick, had a stomachache, and started to bleed between my legs. I was horrified!! My mom came in and went to get me a large Kotex pad. Her only statement was that I had my period and I couldn't go to the party. I was upset, sick, and scared. I had no knowledge of the menstrual cycle and how it affected me. I didn't learn until a year later from my peers.

FEMALE

I'll never forget seventh grade when it seemed all my friends were menstruating but me. At first I was thinking of coming to school one day and telling them I had gotten my first period but I was afraid that they'd know I was lying so I didn't. Pretty soon no one talked about it much so by the time I did get my first period no one really cared—except my mother who told me I was now a woman. I didn't feel uncomfortable at all with the event and I suppose most of that is due to the fact that I'd heard so much about it.

FEMALE

Finally, when I was 17 and still had not begun to menstruate, Mom got worried and took me to a specialist. He said nothing was wrong and just to be patient. If when I was 18 it still hadn't started, he would try to induce it artificially. By some miracle I started menstruating the summer before I was a senior. I was away at camp at the time but I was prepared (I'd been waiting for years), and that day was very happy for me. I didn't tell Mom until I'd had two or three periods and when she found out and asked when it had happened, I replied casually, "Oh, a while ago." I was just so embarrassed that it had taken so long and was still sensitive about her interest and discussion. In rereading this, I realize that I haven't begun to express adequately my shame and suffering about the long delay. I only hope that I shall be able to help my daughter work out this problem so she won't be as alone as I was.

Instruction and conversation, or the lack of it, impacts the experience of menarche.

FEMALE

My period started the summer before sixth grade. I was 11. What a bummer! I knew what was happening to me because of a movie I had seen in fifth grade. It was called "Polly grows up." My mother was not good on information giving. In fact, the only thing I can ever remember my mother saying to me was, "Don't let anybody touch you until you're married!" Not why, or what might happen, just don't! Back to my period. It was a pain. Now with a bra and my period I was really different from the boys. I still didn't feel anymore attractive or special. Teasing from my family members about my body really started to hurt. I was so self-conscious.

FEMALE

The only thing I knew about sex was intercourse, and then I started my period at school one day. It was shocking and disturbing. I remember sitting in music class when I started to feel ill. When I went into the bathroom, I was horrified to find my underpants bloodsoaked. Then I was really sick, mostly from fear, because I didn't know what was happening to me. I was really afraid I was going to die or something. I told no one about this but requested that I be able to go home for I didn't feel well. Once home, I debated for a long time on what to do. I was afraid to tell my mother for fear of what she would do but I knew there was nothing else I could do. She explained that it was a natural function and that she should have told me sooner. She had been waiting to use the program they present in the schools as a basis on which to found her explanation. Unfortunately, that didn't happen soon enough in my cycle.

FEMALE

I began menstruating when I was 12. I remember feeling great ambivalence about it. I was a little frightened by the blood and resented having to wear a "diaper." I was sure everyone would be able to tell I had a pad and belt on! On the other hand, I was excited to know that I could become pregnant—that I had become a woman. My mother got very excited about it, and I really couldn't understand why. She told my dad about it when he came home, and I felt very awkward. Sex was never really discussed in my home. I felt like it was a very private thing—certainly not to be talked over with my father—a man!

Embarrassment seems to be a nearly universal accompaniment to the first menstrual period.

FEMALE

I was glad when my period finally started since my girl friends had all started—or had said they did. Somehow I got the impression that I'd have it only once and that was it. When I went back to school, a friend of mine yelled at me after lunch, "What's wrong with you, you on the rag?" Well, he was just teasing but I couldn't figure out how he knew except maybe I was walking funny. I was embarrassed and mad. I hated having my period!

FEMALE

Well, eighth grade came along and I was hoping I'd start to menstruate soon. It finally happened April 1st; I'll never forget that day. My mother had *never* told me what to expect or how to prepare for it. My only information was from the movie in sixth grade. My older sister and I didn't communicate at all. Who should I turn to? It happened in school, so I told my girlfriend and went into the bathroom and bought a Kotex from the machine. I wore it until the next day and bought another at school. I didn't have the courage to tell my mother until the fourth day. She said, "Oh you kids, you're so much trouble," and proceeded to march into the bathroom and show me where everything was; then she went back to bed. I was so hurt, I silently cried to myself.

FEMALE

In the seventh grade when I was having my period, I would sometimes fake illness so I wouldn't have to go to gym. I was so ashamed and afraid that someone might find out it was "that time of the month." Also when I went to the bathroom I waited till no one was around and then put the nickel in, pulled the handle, and ran into the nearest john.

Women have a variety of attitudes toward menstruation. The slang synonyms used for it ("on the rag," "fall off the roof," "come sick," "time of the month," "coming around," "the curse," "period," "Herbie," and so forth) are examples.

FEMALE

I had been informed about menstruation, so when it finally happened, I took it calmly. I thought "Well, it's finally happened; no big deal!" When I told my mother, she was excited, but acted calmly and told me calmly what to do. By her not making a big fuss over me, I learned to just accept it and not go into a major production each month.

FEMALE

At ten my mother explained the "facts of life" to me. I can remember not really understanding what it was all about but figured once that first period came I would begin to understand. I remember wondering when that first period came, "Why do women have to put up with this?" I thought cramps were the end of the world for awhile. My friends and I envied the girls who didn't get their periods till they were older, and they envied us. I remember a sort of fear that all the girls in school had—that the boys would discover their sanitary napkins in their purses. One thing that surprises a lot of my friends now is that even in junior high we talked with other girls about our periods quite freely. We had coined the word "Herbie" to mean our periods so we could talk quite openly about them without the boys knowing what we were talking about: "Herbie came today" or "I'm getting sick of Herbie" meant nothing to anyone who happened to overhear us.

FEMALE

I started menstruating later than most girls my age, but I was just as glad not to have to fuss with it any sooner. It wasn't until right before it came that I started feeling peer pressure. My mom had told me all about it, so I was not shocked or scared when my period began. It took a while before it came regularly each month. I never had a bad experience with my period like staining a white dress. I did leave school a couple of times though, because "I didn't feel good." I really felt fine, but it was a good excuse for me to miss some school because my dad condoned it. He thought it was a valid excuse because God unfairly created women to have cramps and suffer each month. So all I had to say was, "Dad, I have cramps," and he'd let me off.

Many women experience menstrual discomfort (dysmenorrhea). This may involve cramps, headache, backache, and nausea. The cramps are probably caused by spasms of the muscles of the uterus or cervix (Calderone and Johnson, 1990). Lynn Leight (1988) suggests moderate exercise, and a balanced diet and that some nutritional supplements may help. If all else fails, she suggests antipostiglandin medications, which must be prescribed by a physician.

FEMALE

Menstruation was a sign that I had finally started maturing. I did not have the cramps, backaches, or other physical problems often associated with menstruation that often sent my friends home from school. Those girls seemed to look at their period as an illness; to me, it was just a hassle to be taken care of for a few days a month.

FEMALE

I finally started my period the summer between eighth and ninth grades and I was furious. I hated it! A Kotex was so uncomfortable and I couldn't go swimming. I was so afraid people would know I was having my period. Had they known, I would have been embarrassed to death. I really felt like it was a curse because I usually got cramps. I would not go into a store and buy Kotex—too embarrassed. I was always afraid that if people knew they would not want to get near me and especially not touch me.

Knowledge about sanitary napkins usually precedes finding out about tampons.

FEMALE

I asked my mother what sanitary napkins looked like. She replied—standing with her back to me—that when the time came I would know. Her voice was sarcastic and cold, prohibiting further questions. Later I examined a napkin (which I had previously found and looked at anyway), pulled it apart, and tried to see if there was anything unusually secretive or wonderful inside it. There wasn't!

FEMALE

I was a cheerleader in high school and I was always super afraid people would be able to tell I had a Kotex on under my cheering uniform. I didn't know how to use a Tampax but I knew I hated Kotex. I once asked Mother about using Tampax. She said that only older girls do. So, I was afraid to ask permission and went ahead on my own. I found it very difficult to insert one but, determined to rid myself of Kotex, I managed.

FEMALE

I wanted to be one of the "in-group" that had started menstruating, and it finally happened on a Saturday when my mother was shopping. I used Kleenex as a pad until she got home since I wasn't supposed to know where the napkins were. I told my sister (four years younger) what happened; she started crying and I told her I was just fibbing so she would stop.

PART II—SOCIOSEXUAL EXPERIENCES IN ADOLESCENCE

One of the important ways gender identity is confirmed in adolescence is through imagery and fantasy. Adolescents begin to imagine sexual acts and fantasize about desirable romantic partners and sexual experiences (Kelly, 1988). Fantasies and crushes (which are also usually based in fantasy) are pleasant for some and guilt-producing for others.

FEMALE

I remember feeling so guilty even thinking about sex.

MALE

When I became older, I began to notice the shape of women's breasts. At the Catholic school I went to, the nuns wore habits that hid the contours of the breast. This stimulated my curiosity and I continually tried for a glimpse of a curve.

MALE

From about second through seventh grade, I was often sexually attracted to the nuns who were my teachers. I would look at these nuns and wonder what they looked like in the nude. I enjoyed the times I got a glimpse of the outline of their breasts or saw their legs. The nuns wore long robes and it was a treat to even occasionally get a look at their black nylons.

FEMALE

When I was in seventh grade, I became interested in boys and dreamed about having boyfriends. A boy touching my body never occurred to me, and when I saw a girl and boy making out, I got "grossed out." Even so, throughout junior high I progressed from one crush to another but never told anyone.

MALE

My religious hang-up shaped my sexual daydreams. If I voluntarily daydreamed about something sexual I was committing a grievous sin. I cleverly devised a form of daydream to get around it. Here is an example (approximately, an age 11 daydream): A pretty girl and I are going for a hike and picnic. We come across this nice cave and decide to go in there to eat. While in there a rockslide occurred, blocking us in the cave. We had enough food and light but could not get out. Our clothes soon rotted away, so we were both naked. There was nowhere to hide in the cave and nothing that could be used as clothing so we were forced to look at each other's naked body (no sin because all of this was not willed). Then the girl would get cold and I would have to come over and rub her naked body, in order to warm her up. I was just a victim of sweet circumstance.

Young adolescents often choose to interact in small groups, avoiding situations where couples are alone or where sex is expected. In these group situations, they may have the opportunity, with feedback from peers, to learn to negotiate, to communicate, and to resolve conflicts.

FEMALE

I recall many discussions about how to talk to boys on a date. Nothing helped, and I could never do it right. The artificial setting of dating left me tongue-tied, and was agony for me.

FEMALE

In the summer after seventh grade I had a mad crush on my friend's brother. He finally began to notice me. We had mutual friends and hung around in the same crowd, so we spent a good deal of time together. Sexually, our relationship was quite innocent. The boldest thing we ever did was to hold hands, and we didn't even do that until we had been a couple for a year. I've always thought that it was pretty neat that we didn't feel any pressure to become sexually involved until we were both ready for it. I knew I wasn't ready for it then.

FEMALE

At this time all my friends were boy crazy; I wasn't. I was more scared of them than uninterested. I was very shy and found it extremely hard to talk to boys. Whenever a boy would call I would hardly say anything to him or, most of the time I would beg my mother to tell them I wasn't home. I remember in sixth grade I went steady for a long time with a boy I never talked to. It was arranged by friends who found out we both liked each other. Whenever either of us wanted to break up we would give one of our friends the ring that would end the relationship. Talk about being shy! Finally, I began to develop crushes on boys, but none that ever liked me.

Although many parents in the United States disapprove of any expression by young adolescents of their sexuality, there is encouragement from other sources: the social pressure to have a boy/girlfriend in junior high, TV, popular songs, movies, magazines, the examples set by older teens and active encouragement by some parents. All or some of these may create conflict for some adolescents who do not feel ready for such experience (Kelly, 1988).

FEMALE

I was really scared of the thought of being asked out for a date. When the eighth grade May Dance came around I was asked. I accepted because I didn't know how to say no. I got so nervous and worked up over it—to the point where I was physically sick, so my mother gave me permission not to go. The next year I was asked to the same dance and I forced myself to go. I thought maybe if I went through with it, it would be easier next time and I wouldn't feel so uneasy. I actually had to have medicine to calm my stomach down so I could eat the whole week before my first date. The big night came and my date brought me three yellow roses but I was so nervous all night that I had an awful time. I spent the whole evening wondering what I should do if he tried to kiss me. To my relief he didn't try.

FEMALE

A guy who was 17 took me out on my first date when I was 14. He took me to the beach. He kept hanging on to me and kissing me and I was frightened to death that I was going to get pregnant. (I suddenly understood about unwanted pregnancies.) All I wanted was to get away from him.

FEMALE

I always had crushes and fantasies about boys I liked, and couldn't wait to really make out; yet in early high school if I'd go out I was panicky and afraid of "parking."

Although girls mature physically about two years earlier than boys, boys precede girls in interest in sexual activity by about two years. Girls seem to like the status of having a boyfriend; the relationship comes first, then interest in sex. This difference can create misunderstanding in early relationships.

MALE

It's strange, long before I knew anything at all about sex I was attracted to girls. I really enjoyed dancing with them (the only time I touched them), feeling their hands, and their breasts.

FEMALE

Those first few clumsy attempts at kissing and touching left me embarrassed and somewhat afraid of boys because of the sudden passion that sometimes seemed to overwhelm them. I was afraid of myself for feeling that passion too. I learned from my friends at school that "nice girls" didn't let the boys go too far. A quiz on sexual experiences that, as I recall, came from Ann Landers, was circulated at one time. We girls all took the quiz and rated ourselves on a scale from nuns to nymphomaniacs. Of course no one wanted to be at either end of the scale; we had to "protect our reputations."

FEMALE

The first time I "made out," I had a lot of mixed feelings about it. The boy started breathing heavily and I later learned that meant he was turned on; I felt weird about that, almost bad about it, and wondered—if I can turn him on, then how can I turn him off? I didn't like the way he kissed me either. My teeth hurt the next morning.

FEMALE

In ninth grade, a boy seemed to like me and I liked him very much. But I soon found out all he wanted was to get it (kissing) as easy as he could, from me or anyone else. Of course, he found someone who would kiss him more often than I would, so he dropped me. Years later, at a fraternity party, I had a blind date and right off he tried to french kiss me. Later in the evening when we were alone I told him to cool it. He replied, "Well, what did you expect when you came here?" Just from these two experiences, I became afraid of boys, unsure what they wanted from me—friendship and love or only sex. I want to be accepted for myself as a person, not a sex object, and I want to fall into love, not into bed. When I do finally fall in love, then I will be willing (I hope) to give as much of myself as I possibly can.

MALE

I was a flirt in fifth and sixth grades. But in junior high, I really got a chance to operate—a lot more girls. In seventh grade I went to a few dances, though I spent more time standing around with the guys than dancing. In eighth grade I started going to dances at the other high schools. This was a good cheap way to take a girl out. Slow dancing was my favorite as I really didn't have the coordination for fast dancing. Besides, slow dancing gave me a chance to rub up against the female body. I had my first "steady" girlfriend in the eighth grade. She was from another school and I had met her through a friend. She was very attractive and very "bosomy." We enjoyed the new relationship for a while. I was content to kiss and french now and then.

MALE

At the age of 13, I started to pursue girls and went steady with the first one that would let me. Of course, if you went steady, heavy petting was expected. Even though I was "liberated" from the direct surveillance of my mother, a certain degree of guilt checked any thoughts of attempting intercourse. By age 16, the heavy petting was not satisfying. My friends talked about some of the girls with bad reputations, but I was afraid to take them out. So I decided the thing to do was go steady, because the guys who did always had the best stories to tell. Well, they didn't actually tell me anything, but the way they would laugh when I would ask the right questions told me all I wanted to know.

Middle school parties afforded initial opportunities to experience kissing and petting in safe, temporary one-to-one relationships.

FEMALE

My first "sexual" experience was a boy kissing me on the cheek when playing post office. I can remember the dread as well as the excitement of being called into the other room for "stamps."

FEMALE

My friends had parties on the weekends in middle school, and I sure learned a lot. Many kids started going steady and exchanging I.D. bracelets. These parties were a good chance for girls to get together with their boyfriends and "make out." The parties turned into a room with a mass of bodies lying around. In seventh grade I had a very aggressive boyfriend, so I became a part of this whole new experience. This guy taught me how to french kiss which was a big deal then. I remember feeling a little scared, but I went along with it.

FEMALE

In middle school I can remember finally looking like a girl in a pullover sweater, and being pleased when the boys noticed it too. That was the era of "make out" parties where you went to a party and spent the evening kissing your boyfriend-of-the-week. The sexual question was "Should I french kiss or not?" At that time the thought of frenching completely disgusted me.

Peer pressure and teasing are powerful and not to be ignored. Some adolescents do what their peers are doing; others rebel. All are influenced.

MALE

Around my senior year, I started discovering that I was popular for one reason or another and for the first time started dating. (It was also, not coincidentally, the first time I had access to a car.) I am sorry to say that I conformed to my peers' expectations and each date became an attempt to get as far as I could sexually. This surprisingly didn't turn off too many girls and it wasn't until after graduation that I stopped using girls.

MALE

None of us knew a lot about sex, so we had to pool our information. Sex quickly became the main topic of discussion among our small group of male friends. We even joked about playing an imaginary football game; yards gained were on the ground or by a pass. Everyone knew what a touchdown meant but wouldn't tell if he'd made one with his girl. Even though it was a joke, I could feel the competition to get more.

FEMALE

I remember being teased because the boy next door liked me and I liked him, but the teasing got to us so we stayed away from each other. I never went though the "boy crazy" stage in middle school like a lot of my friends did, feeling they needed to "go steady" to be with the "in crowd." I never felt I needed a boyfriend to feel secure.

FEMALE

In ninth grade, I had my first boyfriend. I was extremely scared to tell my parents that I was "going" with a guy, so we used to sneak out of basketball games and dances to hold hands. Because of this fear, holding hands was the extent of our intimacy. None of my friends had boyfriends and they constantly teased and ridiculed me for having one. When I finally got the nerve to invite him over, my parents were kind of cold toward him. Finally, the pressures were more than I could handle, so I broke it off completely.

MALE

I did not follow the typical masculine behavior of the jock. One of my most disquieting times during early adolescence was the usual bull session telling about sexual exploits. Even then I knew, as I suspect most of us did, that the stories were just so much bull, and I resented the need to impress my friends. I also rejected the idea of using women to enhance men.

MALE

The first time I kissed someone was at summer camp. I didn't know what I was supposed to do and was really afraid. Kissing a girl seemed the criterion to be in the "in-group." It was a real ego boosting event. What happened was that this girl and I wandered out to a field and leaned up against a tree. I sort of kissed her on the mouth (our mouths were, of course, closed) and then we just stood and hugged each other. It was exciting but not particularly pleasurable. Later that summer, I kissed another girl and it wasn't exciting at all. The kiss was closed mouth and I couldn't figure out why kissing should be so popular. It seemed a waste of time to me. She and I talked about our sexual experiences. We both said we had been "to second" which meant that I'd been in a girl's shirt and she'd had some boy in hers. I lied. She probably did too.

FEMALE

I had wanted to have more boyfriends, I just wouldn't "chase" them. "After all, once I catch a boy then he may want to do such things as kiss, hold hands, or even touch my gradually developing bosom, and who knows what else!" It is not that I didn't want the attention, but I think, looking back, I just didn't want to knuckle under to the pressures from the other kids. So I stuck my flag in the ground proclaiming my individuality, with my parents, parents' friends, and friends' parents applauding while I stood my rather lonely ground. I watched my peer group grow up having boyfriends, parties, and cliques. And I wondered when I would be strong enough and old enough to be able to be my own person capable of feeling I didn't have to fight the peer group.

Girls are concerned about counteracting an undeserved bad reputation or preserving a good one.

FEMALE

Middle school has to be the worst time for sex rumors! I hate it when people gossip about sex or spread things around about what other people have done. This happened to me once. When I was in eighth grade another girl and I had a crush on Brad. Well, Brad asked me to go to a party. While we were there we went outside and talked and when we got back in, Delores had told everyone that she saw me give Brad a hand-job. Every guy I was ever with later claimed that he got a hand-job from me, because he had to live up to the rumor. Of course I had never done it at all. I was really reserved and afraid to ever do anything physical when I really liked someone. This rumor stuck with me for so long! It still really bothers me because I'm sure that some people still think I'm a slut.

FEMALE

When I was 15 I dated a boy who was much older. We engaged in petting, but he wasn't satisfied with that since his friends were already "going all the way." Though we never did, he told his friends that we had. We lived in a small town and such gossip spread quickly. I spent the rest of my high school years trying to prove to subsequent boyfriends that I wasn't easy. Yet, I liked sex play; I guess I unconsciously solved the problem by engaging in heavy petting and then expressing to the guy how guilty I felt. This sequence of petting and then crying was repeated time after time and must have been trying to my boyfriends.

FEMALE

I had so many questions, but couldn't ask my friends because of the games we played with one another. I can remember experiencing immense frustration because I always denied to my friends that I went any further than kissing on a date. Only "loose" women got "felt up." Even when I went away to college and sex was discussed more honestly, I still had difficulties opening up and sharing with my peers. Consequently, I often wondered if I was functioning "normally" or not—but I was too afraid to risk asking someone.

Most adolescents in the United States are beginning to engage in some kind of heterosexual expression by the early teens. Katchadourian (1989) suggests that the kinds of sexual expression follow a rather predictable progression from the less intimate to more intense interactions. The pattern seems ordinarily to follow the sequence: holding hands, embracing, kissing, light caressing, fondling, breast and genital stimulation, and finally intercourse. Many adolescents (more males than females) go through the entire sequence; a few never begin until marriage. A positive experience was often reported when the sexual activity was an expression of the total relationship or when it was mutually desired.

FEMALE

Barry and I had a good relationship. We were quite open with each other and before long we petted. These were my first sexual experiences and I really enjoyed them. I really was quite uninhibited. Our relationship continued for a year and a half and it really gave me a good outlook on sex. We petted but never went as far as intercourse. I enjoyed it and don't remember feeling any guilt about it. I then started dating another guy who wanted to have a heavy sexual relationship and I didn't. He tried to force it. He tried to make me feel bad for not doing anything with him sexually. I would have felt bad if I had. We fought about it a lot and finally broke up after two years of conflict. I was very relieved. I finally felt I could be my own person again.

MALE

My high school girl friend and I were more friends than lovers. As children, we had never explored our playmates' bodies, so we were both afraid to do very much sexually. We did pet lightly but mostly just kissed and held each other (and took walks in the cool night air!).

MALE

When I was 15 I met a friend's 16-year-old cousin who had very large breasts and liked it when I touched them. While she was visiting at my friend's home, I used to go there early in the morning so I could feel her in her nightgown with no bra on. We were "saved" when she returned to her home in another state.

FEMALE

My first sexual desires started when I was 14. A guy I liked a whole lot put his arm around me, and I thought there was not a neater thing in the world than that and to hold hands with him. That really turned me on. At 15, I got my first kiss and thought it was the greatest. I loved to kiss my boyfriends at that age, but that was the limit. I thought that petting was just too gross for me and I never wanted to even try it. Everything changed though, when I met Dick. He was a year older, and my first "real" boyfriend and I was his first girlfriend. At first he was shy; I even walked him half way home just in hopes of getting a kiss, but it took him three months to screw up his courage. A few months later he touched my breast and I almost fainted. After a while I really loved him to touch me. About a year later he tried getting down my pants and I said no. He must have tried 50 times but it was always the same answer. One night, his hand went too fast and I almost died. After I relaxed, I just couldn't believe that great feeling. Everything that was gross and dirty before, now turned into something beautiful when it was between the two of us. He was very gentle. He always wanted me to touch his penis, but I never would.

Prolonged sexual arousal may cause a severe testicular ache, commonly called lover's nuts (or blue balls). This is temporary and causes only temporary discomfort.

MALE

The summer before ninth grade I went to a marching band camp. It was my first coed camp. My parents warned me not to mess around with any of the girls while at camp. In ninth grade I wanted to kiss, pet, and neck but I was afraid of rejection. It was more of the same. In eleventh grade, I took an old friend to the homecoming dance. Then we dated steadily for the next two years. She was the first girl I ever kissed. It was also my first date where I had the use of the car. We continued to date and our kissing and necking got serious. That year after the Spring Prom I got my first "blue balls" or "lover's nuts!" My senior year I was developing a desire for sexual intercourse with her, but petting was still too scary for me.

In conclusion, adolescence provides time and space in which young people can progressively explore the sexual and emotional parameters of relationships.

SUGGESTED ISSUES FOR PERSONAL REFLECTION, GROUP DISCUSSION AND PERSONAL JOURNAL

1. Which were the excerpts that triggered strong memories for you?
2. Recall the circumstances and your feelings when you experienced your first ejaculation or first menstrual period.

3. What about peer interaction—did you conform, rebel, lead, follow, or retreat?
4. What were your first boy-girl parties like?
5. What was your relationship with your parents during your early and later adolescence?
6. Were you early, average, or slow in your physical development? How did you feel about that?
7. What was your reaction to having to disrobe in the school shower room?

Chapter 8

Intimacy: Sexual and Emotional

INTRODUCTION

As adolescents begin to experience intense sexual feelings and move toward relationships, they are learning about intensity and intimacy. It takes time to learn that intimacy is not the same as intensity but intense feelings cannot predict lasting closeness; instead they can block an accurate perception or development of the relationship. Intimacy, on the other hand, includes feelings of intensity but is more demanding of those involved. True intimacy happens in relationships where there is ongoing, respectful communication of feelings between equals who are committed to understanding self and other (Giddens, 1992).

Judy Blume in *Forever* (1976), Norma Klein in *It's OK If You Don't Love Me* (1977), and Ursula K. LeGuin in *Very Far Away From Anywhere Else* (N.D.) capture in their respective novels the nuances in relationships of couples who "fall in love" for the first time and experience the joy and closeness along with the trauma and confusion of becoming intimately involved. Many of the depicted experiences and emotions have a universal quality which readers can easily understand if they think back to their own experience of "first love."

Expressing this "first love" sexually is a powerful new experience, whether it be by holding hands, kissing, necking, petting, or having intercourse, and it brings with it new emotions that range from fear and confusion to wonder and sheer delight. Often the intensity of combining sexual expression with emotional involvement takes people by surprise, is unexpected, and triggers excitement and anxiety.

MALE

The sun was still very high in the sky. It would have been a very hot afternoon if there was no breeze blowing over the pond, rustling the leaves of the maples and oaks and whistling through the pines. I felt my tennis shoes ooze into the mud and I began to worry that the wetness of the grass would soak through our jeans. I already held her hand in mine. That was nothing new. We had spent many evenings that summer roller skating together. And now, as the horseflies and mosquitoes began to draw back, I began to draw nearer to her. Even though we were talking, I remember I took a deep breath as if to gather up the strength of the wind as I moved my left arm from my side and positioned it behind her back. Our blue jeans touched. We sat closer to each other, laughing at how we were quickly sinking in the mud. I couldn't help but think, "Oh my God—is this really happening to me?" We both stopped talking to watch the loons swoop down on the pond crying out in their haunting, lonely, and shrill voices. I soon tired of watching the loons and turned to watch her hair blowing in the wind; I reached out to stroke her beautiful long blond hair. Then my arm maneuvered itself past her hair somehow and made it to her left shoulder.

    I guess she didn't feel like watching the loons either as she leaned her body against mine. I felt a surge of hope and promise inside me. At that moment in time I felt that nothing could go wrong. So there in the mud, I decided to take a risk. What would she think of me if I kissed her? What a painful and yet beautiful moment. But I couldn't pause in mid-air forever. I must either continue toward her and gently take her in my arms or pull myself away from her until I could be more sure. My love for her and my desire to have her love me was suddenly overwhelming and we held on to each other so tightly that it seemed as if we would never again be two separate physical beings.

    I had taken the risk and our friendship survived. We once again looked out on the pond and noticed how calm the water was. The loons were gone and the only noise was made by the breeze brushing leaves against each other. We looked at each other and were drawn together. I can remember that it was the best kiss I ever had. We didn't care that our blue jeans were covered with mud. The sun was getting a little lower in the sky and she had to be back soon. It had been a nice weekend, but now it was time to go home. We walked back slowly holding hands all the way.

FEMALE

When we got to my house he walked with me to my door and I stood there very nervous because I knew this would be a first in my life—the kiss. I remember feeling like I would faint from being so anxious. Well, he did kiss me and asked me to go out that weekend on a date. It was wonderful being able to say yes as I now was old enough.

I was a freshman and Hal was a junior then and our relationship lasted for three years. We sat together in study hall and held hands in the hall. We even shared a locker which was a big deal in those days. I wore his varsity jacket and we exchanged class rings. Once, when I returned from a week long trip, Hal surprised me with a pearl ring. I was overwhelmed with joy and totally in love with this man. Looking back, it was the most romantic and exciting time of my life.

For many people, their first or significant sexual experience was an exploratory one—one which involved looking or touching.

FEMALE

I had been going "steady" with a boy since eighth grade and in tenth grade he moved to another town. One weekend I went to visit him at his house. We had been swimming and decided to take a shower together in his basement. I couldn't bring myself to take my swimsuit off so we took the shower with them on. I remember being really turned on and thought that we were doing a very sexy and daring thing. Later that night I went to my room and he came with me. We started to watch TV and then started kissing. We were on the bed lying down and it felt very nice. I remember him putting his hands under my shirt and I liked it. I felt like a woman for the first time in my life. I had been into the tomboy role for so long that I almost forgot what I was. I thought of that weekend for the rest of the summer, redreaming that one moment.

MALE

My first kiss was special to me and it reminded me a lot of the television shows that you watch when the kid gets his/her first kiss. I saw all kinds of fireworks and heard sirens and felt a warm tingle in my body. I never told anyone that that was my first kiss, but I think my girlfriend knew. I'd had all my friends believing that I had been kissing girls since I was in third grade because I was scared of what they would think if they knew the truth. Now that I look back I am sure that a lot of them had been lying like I was for fear of what the other guys would think.

MALE

I recall a warm summer afternoon when I was 18. I was out at the beach with a special little 16-year-old young lady. She was the first girl who seemed to reciprocate my feelings. We really had fun together. We went to my house one day when no one was home. Still in bathing suits we ended up in bed kissing and holding each other. She became so flushed, breathed so hard and made sounds that I was not familiar with. I certainly couldn't remove her suit and do as she wanted because I "respected" her. I was sure she would think less of me if I took advantage of her. I was trying to be good. After all, I had years of association with a strict Wesleyan Methodist family and church members. I was still wondering if I would go to hell for some act. I wasn't sure that somehow some superior being wasn't watching. We got up and dressed and left. Because of my restraint, I felt that she would see me as more honest, honorable, and trustworthy but she just seemed less interested. We stopped seeing each other and I found out later that she had become pregnant and married someone in the following months.

Several people reported learning from their early encounters with other people and so their sexual activity had a kind of "educational" dimension.

MALE

In seventh grade I was shy and my only contact with girls was at school. I remember having a crush on quite a few girls that year but they never knew it. Eighth grade was more of the same, but things began to change during the following summer. I started to experience success relating to girls during our annual family vacation. I met girls my age at the campgrounds and I found it pretty easy to talk with them; I felt new confidence and began to feel bolder. That summer I had my first french kiss. She was as inexperienced as I; the kiss was rather awkward, but it didn't matter to either of us. Maybe it was easier that summer because the girls didn't know me, and my friends weren't there to apply any pressure. Anyway, I returned home a changed person.

MALE

I thought about sex a lot but I was very shy. Though I dated quite a bit my junior year, I was afraid to kiss. I was sure I wouldn't do it right. I was embarrassed to be a junior in high school and still not have kissed a girl. I dated a few "nice" girls, but they always waited for me to make the first move. I never did and it became quite depressing and frustrating. During my senior year, I was selected president of the student council. That meant that every girl in the school knew who I was; the majority of them wanted to date me. At a pool party a friend of mine had, I met a girl who was a little below average, looks-wise, but very nice. She had a somewhat tainted reputation. I figured maybe this was my big chance to break out of my rut. The next weekend we went to a movie. I had my hand on her leg through the whole thing. In the car on the way back, I was rubbing the side of her blouse while gradually moving my hand toward her breast. She made the first move when it came to the kiss goodnight. We genuinely enjoyed each other and I was so freaked out about it, I gave her my ring about three or four weeks later. We went steady for a year and a half. The relationship progressed in the following manner: touching her chest through her blouse; getting under the bra; then sliding my hand down the front of her pants; lying nude on the bed and petting; and then to coitus. This transpired all in a matter of months. I learned most of my basics from her.

MALE

My sophomore year in high school my girlfriend was two years older than I was. She was also a varsity cheerleader and one of the prettiest girls in her senior class. A lot of my friends used to look up to me because I was going with her. She taught me a lot about how girls liked to be touched and what they did and did not like. She was the first girl that I ever got to "explore." We did just about everything except have sex.

FEMALE

I felt that we were so close and that everything was OK. With him I experienced my first orgasm which seemed to be a fantastic feeling that I never knew existed. I also got used to him being erect and kind of learned what that was all about. It was all very exciting for me.

MALE

My sex life had been entirely limited to masturbation with only two exceptions. When I was 19 and home on leave from the Air Force, I was invited by a chick to spend the night with her. I told her I was a virgin but she didn't believe me until we got into bed. I began shaking so violently that she said, "Wow, you really are a virgin, aren't you?" I managed somehow to say yes. Here, I realize now, was a turning point in my life. She could have devastated me at that point. Instead she very carefully, very sweetly and quietly showed me her body, allowing me to explore it with my hands while explaining what was what. It was beautiful and I know now that I owe a lot to her understanding. It was not a very good night for her own satisfaction but it was a landmark for me. It helped very much to remove the fears I had harbored about my being homosexual. Here I was, 19, and I had never been with a girl before—only males. I had had no proof that I wasn't gay. That night certainly reassured me.

A few students described experiences in terms of sexual interaction without any emotional intimacy. These reports are echoed by Hajcak and Garwood (1988) who suggest that adolescents' nonsexual needs may well create an artificially high sex drive, an overwhelming intensity greater than just the libido or biological phenomenon would explain. Goff (1990) suggests that many young males are unable to deal with intimacy issues. However, Crooks and Baur (1993) suggests this may be changing and that now adolescent males are more often choosing to have sex with a girl they feel affection or love for rather than with an acquaintance or stranger.

MALE

My first steady, an older, wiser girl, introduced me to oral sex at the age of 15. I was appalled. How could she do such a disgusting thing? In a matter of minutes, she had converted me. Looking back, I recognize that she was seeking love by being attentive to my sexual response, and I was responding sexually to her seeking love. And always there was the guilt of having let her do something incredibly wrong just to please me. Maybe even as a juvenile, I knew I was selfishly satisfying myself physically, while not being available to her emotionally. Maybe that was all I was capable of. It was pure fear, not respect for her that allowed me to resist her repeated requests to engage in sexual intercourse.

MALE

My first sexual relationship occurred when I was 13 years old. I had just started going to boy/girl parties when I noticed some of my friends pairing off and going into the dark part of the room to make out. In order to make out and maintain a good reputation, one first had to ask their prospective partner if they wanted to "go around." The term "go around" was an appropriate one, for that was exactly what it meant. It was actually a license to join the make out bunch at the parties. I decided I wanted to join the action. I became determined to ask a girl to "go around" at the next party. There was only one problem; I had to decide who I should ask. This was a difficult decision, for on my first attempt at asking a girl to "go around" I wanted to make sure she was one of the more popular "in" girls, while at the same time being reasonably sure she would say "yes." This was cause for much thought and I was greatly relieved when a friend of one of the "in" girls told me that girl had a crush on me. Within an hour I had my first real girlfriend. "Going around" didn't involve much sexual investigation ("copping a feel") or time (usually a couple of months). Breaking up a "heavy" relationship was quickly followed by starting another! By the time I was 15 I had had enough of the licensed making-out. I was looking forward to high school and dating.

MALE

Tenth grade brought many changes in my life. I started dating the same girl on a steady basis, earned my driver's license, got my first job, and started meeting and hanging out with more people. To the adults who knew me or came into contact with me, I was a parent's dream. I showed them my "all American" side. Their daughters and my friends knew both sides of my personality. They were the only ones who knew the real me. It was during the time in my first steady relationship that I started to fondle girls' genitals and breasts directly, not over their clothing. Soon I began dating a lot of different girls simultaneously. There were four high schools in the city I grew up in, and I had a girlfriend at each of them. I was amazed how my sex life had changed in two short years. Eventually it became sexually frustrating to not have an orgasm during the heavy "petting" sessions with my girlfriends. I would often come home and masturbate, while looking at *Playboy*, to relieve the tension and pressure. I felt and acted like an adult sexually, but didn't realize I was immature and far from being an adult emotionally.

FEMALE

In eleventh grade I had my first experience with oral sex. A friend and I were out driving around; we had gotten some wine and were having fun. We drove through a Burger King parking lot (a local hangout) where she saw some guys she knew. We stopped and talked to them. One said his parents weren't home and invited us to his house to party. We went. In fact, there were about ten of us that went. It was wild. We bounced quarters, ate chips, and smoked cigars (I don't smoke—it was just one of those things), and had a great time. This guy and I began hitting on each other and we ended up making out right there at the table. We then progressed to an upstairs bedroom and undressed. I had never had oral sex before and felt kind of pressured. But he went down on me and then more or less forced himself on me. We ended up in a "69" position. He tried to push me into intercourse but I said no. I always believed (probably from my 12 years of Catholic schools) that intercourse should wait until marriage. The next day I had so many hickeys that I wore turtlenecks for a week.

MALE

When I finally decided that sexual intercourse prior to marriage was something I could handle I was 20 years old. I determined that I was "in love" with the person and willing to marry if pregnancy resulted. Our first experience was a first for both of us. Penetration was uncomfortable for her so we reconvened a couple of weeks later and consummated our relationship. As I recall it was orgasms for both of us and we were sexually active through our 18-month relationship. Because I really wasn't ready to make a commitment, our relationship waned and finally ended with her giving me the heave-ho. As I look back, I can see that sex was the number one factor contributing to the demise of the relationship. Too much self-gratification through too-soon sex without any hand-holding or strolls on the beach. After all, when was the last time you saw a Holstein cow and a bull romantically watching the sunset over the bay?

FEMALE

Following high school, I dated and was engaged to five different men. I enjoyed the sexual activity very much but found fault with each man after receiving a ring. Sometimes I was dating several men at one time. I rated sex as *Number One* in importance! I did extensive traveling world-wide at this time and had no reservations about picking up men. It was a game! Once a girlfriend and I pretended we were hookers to see if we could get $200 each. We could have, but chickened out at the last moment. I went through this period convinced that I had successfully separated love and sex. I needed sex a lot but not the love part. Sad and scary story, but true!

Exploration and leisurely learning about one's own body and that of one's partner without any pressure toward intercourse can be a significant sexual experience.

FEMALE

When I was 18, I started dating a boy who eventually became my husband. He was raised in an orthodox, religious family who sent him to study in a Yeshiva, the Jewish equivalent to a Catholic Seminary. Although he was several years older than, I he had virtually no sexual experience. I was his first girl. Our lack of sexual experience and education proved to be a wonderful asset. We discovered sex in our own way at our own pace. We did what we enjoyed rather than what someone had told us we should do. We had a chance to discover what gave us pleasure and what did not. Therefore, when we actually had intercourse, it was after a year of mutual exploration of our bodies and sexual responses.

FEMALE

I had one boyfriend in high school. I was a senior and he was 21. He had married young, fathered a child, and divorced within a year. My parents forbade us to see each other even though they liked him and knew his family. We continued a clandestine relationship until I went away to college. We engaged in "necking" and "petting" in parked cars and at my parents' house when they were out. He was kind and patient and did not push me to have sex with him.

FEMALE

The summer before ninth grade, I "fell in love" with a guy who was three years older than I. My parents restricted the kinds of dates I could go on with him, but even that didn't stop us from parking on country roads and having some pretty exciting petting experiences. My memory of that time was that my mom's idea of waiting for marriage was crazy—petting and orgasms were just too much fun to say no to.

FEMALE

Here at college it seems as though everyone has intercourse with their boyfriends. I've felt like a minority, but I've still held fast to my values. A boyfriend of mine from home used to come down to visit often. At first he would stay with some other guys, but then he started staying in my room. We would usually sleep in the same bed with our clothes on. Nothing much happened but the idea of sleeping with some guy really excited me. It did something for my general feeling as a woman. As time went on, more happened with this guy but we never had intercourse. I am still a virgin and imagine I will be for quite a while.

MALE

My girl and I began sexual exploration together from the common starting point of zero. We progressed from kissing, to petting, to heavy petting in a long and unhurried process. Even now, we are both "virgin" in the technical sense, though we do practice "femoral intercourse." [Note: "Femoral intercourse" refers to intercourse where the man places his penis between the woman's thighs rather than in her vagina.] I am satisfied with this relationship and feel no pressure to engage in full sexual intercourse for its own sake.

For many people, there seemed to be an experience that was especially significant, possibly because it was a "first" experience or because it had special meaning for the person.

THE "FIRST KISS"

MALE

One of the nicest things that ever happened to me was the first time I kissed a girl. She was the first girl I had ever been in love with, and there was a feeling of closeness and euphoria; it was a peak experience and really beautiful. This was the point at which I first comprehended what sex was all about; I became aware of a whole new world I'd never guessed existed.

FEMALE

Before my first real boyfriend in tenth grade, I had secretly admired a certain guy but he never asked me out. I had gone out on dates with others who asked, but cringed at the thought of any one of them kissing me for over one-half second. It wasn't until I met Don that I actually enjoyed kissing. Then it was so natural and I liked it.

NECKING OR PETTING TO ORGASM

FEMALE

In the late spring of my sophomore year I began to date another boy. We liked each other a lot and that relationship lasted two and one-half years. For a long time we stuck to necking or "making out." I would fight further advances for a long time, but eventually we progressed to petting. We never did french kiss. I had been taught somewhere along the line that french kissing was a sin. Of course, I had also been taught that petting was wrong and I felt guilty at first; gradually that went away. It was during this petting that I experienced my first orgasm. I was rather startled by the feeling, but also pleased. We never had sexual intercourse.

FIRST EXPOSURE TO THE BODY OF THE OPPOSITE SEX

FEMALE

When I first started messing around with guys I didn't want to be touched under my blouse. I would always touch the boy to keep him happy but I was afraid that he would be disappointed at the size of my breasts and he'd lose interest in me. I can remember the first time that I touched a guy's penis and how shocked I was to feel all that hair! I was totally freaked. I guess the only nude males I'd seen up to that point had been children. I thought only girls had pubic hair!

MALE

I started going steady with a girl in my junior year and by my senior year I was getting tired of just looking. The girl with whom I was going steady had the same moods and was as straight as I was. She was getting tired of it too—her curiosity was beginning to overtake her moral stand. So after hinting around about it one night, we decided to let each other discover the other's body. It was an experience we'll never forget. Her breasts were the greatest, most sensuous thing I had ever touched. Sex was a very important aspect of our relationship. There was only one limitation to it though. We had agreed we wouldn't have sexual intercourse until after we got married. We felt that we couldn't handle the responsibility if she did become pregnant, and we wanted to leave something for marriage.

REHEARSING INTERCOURSE

FEMALE

I remember what it felt like and how impressed I was the first time a guy lay down on top of me and we went through the motions of having sex (with our clothes on). What a new feeling that was and how anxious I was to do the real thing, but, of course, not until the proper time—marriage.

MALE

I spent the summer between eleventh and twelfth grade with my brother who was caretaker for an old Boy Scout Camp. One day I met a girl on the beach across the lake. I invited her back to the cabin that night and she said OK. I paddled my canoe across the lake to get her and took her into the cabin. We drank some wine and beer and before too long we were drunk. I led her into the bedroom and laid on top of her. This was my first sexual experience with a girl and was I ever naive. I couldn't figure out how to get her bra off. She finally unhooked it and I remember "dry fucking" (as we called it then). It was very pleasing to me and I felt very happy. [Note: "Dry fucking" refers to the motions of intercourse while both partners are clothed.]

Virginity was defined by many students as simply a lack of having been penetrated; a woman could thus participate in oral and manual stimulation and still be perceived as a virgin.

FEMALE

I was at a party two years ago with all my friends. We were all home for the weekend and getting high. One of them asked me to dance and while we were dancing, he kept running his hand over my buttocks. It was really making me horny. Somehow we danced into a room (not a bedroom) and he put his hands down my pants. I didn't fight it—I liked it. He asked if he could "eat me" and I guess I said yes. It was wonderful and I had an orgasm. I wouldn't let him go any further though and I remained a virgin because I had never had a penis in me.

FEMALE

After some minor petting, a boyfriend suggested oral sex. I didn't want it because I didn't like it, but agreed because I wouldn't have intercourse with him. He finally broke up with me because, "If I loved him, then I would have sex with him." I really began to worry that there was something wrong with me. Finally I decided that if I had performed better fellatio, he would have stayed with me. With that reasoning I kept my virginity but still satisfied most of the boys I turned on. Actually, It gave me a sense of power, and control.

Some people described a first or significant experience that involved sexual intercourse. For some, this sexual experience was in the context of a casual or ongoing relationship; for others, no relationship existed previously.

MALE

I remember one girl I had sex with the first night we met. She called me after that but I really didn't want a relationship with her. I don't know if I felt guilty about balling her or not. Somehow I felt she was a slut because I had balled her so easily. I felt kind of bad about not calling her or seeing her anymore. I felt that I had used her to some extent, but I didn't want a relationship that I couldn't extract myself from easily. I liked her as a good lay but I didn't really want her as a girlfriend.

FEMALE

About a year ago I was home and some old friends were getting together. Somehow we were all talking about sex (guys and girls). Kevin was horny and everyone was teasing him and encouraging him to go find a woman. Somehow they started suggesting me and everyone was urging us on. Later, when Kevin didn't have a ride home, I offered to take him. We got to his driveway and I said goodbye; he kissed me, then kissed me again a little more passionately. Soon we were getting into serious petting. That was the first time I ever saw an erect penis (a penis of any kind). Well, he petted me enough so that I had an orgasm and then he said he wanted me to help him. He asked me to take his penis and kiss it, then take it in my mouth. Well, this certainly turned him on, but I was definitely not experienced at fellatio and ended up with bruised lips and he was not satisfied. We moved into the house and onto the couch and were still petting each other. He tried to put his penis in me but it hurt so bad (I was so tight) that we just gave up and I went home. I really had mixed emotions about this; I felt Kevin would never look at me again and I don't think he would have if it hadn't been for one thing. Somehow during the time in the house I had said that I was scared, and he had said he was too and that it was also his first time. We are still friends.

FEMALE

Finally I decided that I didn't want to be a virgin any longer. I wanted to find out about sex and so my first experience happened out of curiosity. Unfortunately it was not very pleasant. He was older and more experienced; I was nervous and embarrassed, and it hurt. The guy didn't even seem to notice my reaction but just proceeded to satisfy himself.

FEMALE

My mother is very conservative, has high standards, and is rather severe. My father is very easygoing and teases a lot. He occasionally goes up behind my mother and hugs or kisses her, and I always remember her backing off, or at least not reacting. She seemed embarrassed. I think this is where my attitudes began to form. I saw little physical contact between them, yet I knew then as I know now that there was a deep and lasting love between them. Naturally I began to separate the physical aspects of love, sex, and sexuality from what I saw as a supportive, loving relationship between two people. I was ill-prepared for the realities of beginning and sustaining a relationship which called for open honest expression of sexual and other feelings. This is basically why I am still a virgin; not because I dread sex, but because I have been unable to separate my little fantasies of the white stallion and knight in shining armor from real life situations.

FEMALE

At first, sex was very painful, both physically and emotionally—I felt tremendous guilt and fear that my mom would find out. I compensated for these feelings by separating myself from the act. I thought if I enjoyed it or craved sex it would really make me a "bad girl." Often in the middle of sex, I would think of Mom, and if we were at either his or my home I continually listened for someone coming down the stairs. For three years, I separated myself from the sex; because I felt so guilty, I wanted to "get it over" quickly.

FEMALE

During my senior year in high school, I visited the junior college I was to attend and met a boy there. He treated me like a queen and we wrote to each other. He asked me to the college prom, my first formal dance, and came to my graduation. I thought he had "hung the moon" since he took me out and bought me everything his student budget would allow. I dated him exclusively my freshman year in college. One night when we were out in his car the inevitable happened and we "made love"—his words—in the back seat of his car. I felt badly about it but he kept reassuring me by saying we'd get married as soon as we could. From then on we made use of every spare moment together and had sexual relations as often as possible. I didn't really enjoy it but wanted to be held.

After making the decision to have intercourse, one woman reported feeling satisfied with her decision; two others reported that they regretted having lost their virginity.

FEMALE

I lost my virginity at the age of 17. My hymen was "broken" by a guy named Vic, whom I had planned to marry some day when we were both out of college. We went together in high school until he moved to Alabama when we were juniors. During spring break of that year, I went down to stay at his house for a week and of course there was a lot of petting. One night we took the petting a bit too far for him to handle. I must say, I was a little surprised when I felt what was happening. I wasn't about to wrestle with him because his parents were sleeping in their bedroom about 20 feet away and we were on the living room couch which was plastic. I didn't get much satisfaction out of it, but I didn't feel badly that it happened either. I didn't value being a virgin anymore and I did like him more than anyone else at the time. Wow! Did I ever feel like a real woman the next day! I can remember feeling that I must look different to other people. I felt so much older and prettier and sexier.

FEMALE

I stayed a virgin until my freshman year at college. With my steady and me going to the same school, temptation was just too much. I'll never forget how scared I was and how awful it was. I cried for about an hour afterwards and felt so guilty. My mom used to tell me, rather than warn me, that once you screw one guy there's nothing stopping you from doing it with others. How true! Everything I was and thought before, had turned now into something very trashy. Before, I never drank, was very quiet, and liked to go out to a movie or something like that. Now I wanted to swing, go out with other guys and go to the bars. My roommate was a real swinger, so we used to go to the bars almost every night. I thought it was really neat to have guys pick me up. I did go with a few guys whom I really thought I liked, but their main interest was in sex, not me.

FEMALE

My first experience with intercourse was very painful psychologically. I dated very little in high school and arrived at college very naive. I'd always felt ugly and inferior to other girls, so when a really good-looking guy started paying attention to me, I was swept off my feet. We went to bed soon after I met him (a week and a half). I was very inexperienced and he knew this. Afterwards he made a big joke out of the whole affair. This hurt. I could not understand why he would joke about a matter so serious. Afterwards I realized that he had just taken advantage of me and that I had just lost my virginity. I felt guilty and considered myself to be promiscuous and just a regular slut. I punished myself over and over, but gradually I began to look at the situation more objectively. I finally decided that even though I had lost my precious virginity, I was still normal and healthy. I went through a phase then believing that all men were bastards and just out after ass. Gradually I sorted out my feelings and decided that there are a lot of guys who are really sincere just as there are a lot of girls who are really sincere. I just happened to run into a bastard my first time and got hurt. Now I can see that this was a major learning experience.

"Early petting and intercourse experiences are now more likely to be shared within the context of an ongoing relationship than they were in Kinsey's time. . . . it appears that contemporary adolescents are most likely to be sexually intimate with someone they love or to whom they feel emotionally attached" (Crooks and Baur, 1993, p. 410). Some students gave examples of this when they mentioned that love, trust, respect and commitment were associated with sexual experience for them.

FEMALE

The only person who could make me tingle was Marv. The first time a guy led my hand to his penis (over his pants) I was repulsed. But when Marv did it, it was all right. I'm still repulsed when a guy I don't really like, respect, and trust tries to have anything to do with me sexually.

FEMALE

We met on a ski trip. I came with my family and he came with his. Since both of our parents knew each other, we were introduced and spent a little time together. It was not really until one night when we were alone and talking that we realized our feelings for each other. Three weeks later I flew to Kansas where he lived and stayed with him a week. In the beginning of the trip I had given no thought at all about sex. I guess I figured it would go just as all of my relationships had gone in the past—light petting only. Having limited sleeping space, we spent the week in the same bed. The first night passed without intercourse. He made advances, as could be expected I guess, but I did not allow things to go past the petting stage. My head was in the same place it had always been—fear of the unknown. The next day we talked. Up until this point, my head always controlled my body and I would not let it be any other way. The next night he again made advances which I reflexively began to stave off, but not all that firmly. He was assuming a very dominant role which I permitted. We ended up having intercourse that night which triggered a lot of feelings and very confusing thoughts. I was very scared. I thought it would be the end of the relationship, that he wouldn't respect me anymore, that he wouldn't have any more to do with a girl proven to be easy. These were the things I had been taught about pre-marital sex and our having intercourse totally violated all of them. I also feared that if the relationship did continue, his only attraction to me would be because of sex. I had always figured that if a man really loved me he would wait for intercourse until marriage. I became very upset and cried so much that we couldn't even talk about what was happening. The next morning we did, however, and I came to realize finally that a man can love a woman, have sex with her before marriage, and still have a continuing relationship.

FEMALE

After having had several sexual relationships, I've undergone a dramatic change: I now believe sex is not the most important part of a relationship. I still feel sex is very important but companionship, friendship, togetherness and love now come first on my list. These are the qualities I treasure most in my current relationship and our sex is very beautiful, too! This feels like a true partnership.

MALE

A sexual experience with a woman always has triggered intense feelings in me. I've never been able to handle a one-night affair. Even if I felt nothing prior to the sexual experience, I always felt like I loved her afterwards. That hardly fits the loose, sexually free male role in our society. Though I always tried to fit that role, I always failed miserably. It's still the same for me, except that I have stopped trying to conform. I know if I have sex with a woman, I will feel very attached to her, very possessive, and very dependent on her. Although that's the way I am, it seems wrong to me; it seems as though one should have the emotional attachment first and that sex should culminate it. I think, deep inside, I still yearn for that male "love 'em and leave 'em" role, but neither I nor anyone I know can do it. I think what I'm saying is that because sex is so pleasurable in and of itself, it's too bad everyone can't just enjoy it without the strings attached. But I know I'm not that way.

A common element reported in first or significant sexual experiences was an emotional reaction. These feelings varied depending on circumstances and preexisting beliefs; however, there was little doubt that there had been some impact on the person(s) involved. Rarely was it a neutral experience for people.

FEELINGS OF CONFUSION, DISAPPOINTMENT, OR LONELINESS

MALE

When I was 19, I was extremely lonely and finally asked a girl I hardly knew for a date. After a few drinks, we went back to her place and I ended up participating in my only one-night stand. It was awful. Though willing, her participation was awkward and nonexpressive and I felt even more alone and ashamed as I left her that evening.

FEMALE

When I first started dating one guy steadily, everything was pretty casual—just a kiss and a hug and that was about it. As we continued to date, I found that I disliked his "touching" me on my body. Sometimes I pushed him away and other times I gave up and let it happen. I felt confused and when I gave in, I always felt if things were going too far that it would lead to too much involvement on both our parts. I always felt that his touching me was wrong or more involved than I wanted to get. I guess I wasn't mature enough to handle the situation.

FEMALE

Just after I turned 18 we made elaborate plans to finally do it. Bill was terrified I would get pregnant so he used *three* rubbers. Neither of us felt anything wonderful. After so many years of passionate anticipation, making love with him was terribly anticlimactic.

FEELINGS OF GUILT

FEMALE

When I turned 16, I lost my virginity in the back seat of a car. I remember coming home and thinking that my mother knew for sure. I was feeling some pain, went into the bathroom and discovered blood. That started my tears. I went to my room and cried, feeling frightened and terribly guilty. These feelings continued during the whole time I went out with this guy and still haunt me. I was lucky to have gotten involved with a sensitive male (mostly). It helped that he was very caring and concerned about the relationship. He tried to approach the matter of "us" and convince me we were still okay even with sex as part of the relationship. We continued to date on and off for two years and I still hold him in my heart as a friend and the first young man I loved.

FEMALE

According to my mother and the church, touching anywhere below the neck was a sin. When my first boyfriend and I started petting, I was very confused and guilt-ridden. I would come home from a date and immediately take a shower because touching him was dirty. I tried to talk about it with my church friends and they called me a "slut." Eventually, I ended the relationship because I couldn't handle all the guilt.

FEELINGS OF PLEASURE MIXED WITH FEELINGS OF GUILT

FEMALE

Even though we did some fairly heavy petting, it was many months before I would let Jim fondle my breasts. He thought I was being kind of backwards. I'd felt my breasts were very private parts of me. I really looked forward to going out with him after studying all evening and we almost always ended up in a heavy petting session. I really liked the bodily sensations. I think I was having orgasms but didn't realize it. I also had a nagging feeling that we were doing something wrong or bad. That part of it I didn't like.

FEELINGS OF FEAR

FEMALE

When I was 13, I had my first sexual experience. It sounds like it's right out of a weird novel, but it's all true. I was camping with my family near a dead town in Indiana while my father attended a convention. There was absolutely nothing to do except swim. So I swam until I developed the worst sunburn of my life. There were a few kids around, but for the most part they were ugly, stupid, or swam constantly. There was only one who looked interesting enough to save me from complete boredom. His name was Hot Rod Lenny. He was 16, had bright red hair, and was double-jointed. Late one night, Hot Rod and I took a walk by the lake. After a while, we lay down on a soft, grassy hill and talked. I kept wondering if he would kiss me. He did, but he soon moved to touching my breasts and made motions for the bottom half too. My lips felt blistered—I think it was because of the sunburn. I got scared and left. I felt terrible and thought I was going to throw up. I didn't, and after a long time I went to sleep. The next day I felt better but I stayed in bed till past noon. I pretended to be asleep in the trailer when Hot Rod came around to say goodbye. I was glad he was leaving and I was glad I didn't have to see him. Hearing his voice outside the trailer was bad enough.

FEELINGS OF INSECURITY, SELF-DOUBT, AND GRATITUDE TO AN UNDERSTANDING PARTNER

MALE

Being a virgin at marriage can present some difficulties for either partner—at least my virginity led to some difficulties at the beginning of my marriage. Feeling loving and wanting to give sexual satisfaction and receive sexual satisfaction is one thing. Being able to perform—no, I think the more definite word is function—is quite another. Fortunately, I seldom felt much self-doubt, for my wife was and still is (has to be sometimes) able to help me understand the clumsiness, poor functioning, and mistakes that we faced as sexual partners. Also, she has helped me to enjoy, appreciate, wonder at, and be amazed by sex. She has helped me to understand the nonphysical part of our relationship: the concern, worry, love, pride, and delight that are a part of our total life.

FEELINGS OF RESENTMENT

MALE

It wasn't until high school that sex assumed any real importance in my life. Friends of mine had sex and I felt the pressure to do likewise. When I was 15, I somehow found myself in bed with a girl, but it wasn't very nice. Even getting into bed with her wasn't easy. She was lying in bed looking at me as I undressed, expectantly waiting. I was scared but it was nice in some ways. The lovemaking wasn't coming from a genuine feeling of passion; rather, it was a performance. I was doing what I thought was expected of me, and I was very scared. The overall effect was that I felt unsure of myself sexually for a couple of years. Since then I have very much resented the fact that as a male I am supposed to be the aggressor, the initiator of sexual activity.

FEELINGS OF FRUSTRATION

MALE

The movement from hand to oral petting to intercourse was a long and frustrating process for Jean and me. I was unable to penetrate and enter her, because of her fear and accompanying vaginal contractions, and my own inexperience. This led to two problems which frustrated our sexual relationship: a feeling of inadequacy and incompetency on my part, and in response to my feeling, Jean could not communicate to me what pleased her sexually because she feared that any feedback would reinforce my feelings of inadequacy. The result was my satisfactory sexual pleasure and guilt because I doubted that I could satisfy Jean. I discovered later that she had taken care of that by secretly achieving sexual gratification through masturbation, completely removed from the relationship.

FEELINGS OF BEING INEXPERIENCED

FEMALE

I liked this one guy and used to park with him once in a while. He thought I was very experienced. I was ashamed to tell him that he was the first guy who had ever had his hand in my pants. I never felt ill at ease with sex unless a guy I didn't like tried it; when someone like that tried to kiss me, I'd almost die. I even told one guy that I had mono. When he said it was worth it, I pushed the gas pedal and that was that.

MALE

When I first came to college, there was much more peer pressure to have intercourse than there was in high school. My first experience of intercourse was with a girl a couple of years older than I. She came to the dorm one night looking for her friend. We were having a party and invited her in. We talked for a while and then she went home. She came back a week later and this time we went out to the bar. After a few drinks, we came back and started making out in my room. I began taking her clothes off and I was surprised when she consented so readily. I had a little trouble in the process of balling her, but she was older, more experienced and helped me out. I had fun and we repeated the act several times that night. When not having intercourse, we talked and laughed. On the whole, however, it was somewhat disappointing. It wasn't all I had expected it to be from past discussions with my friends; I remember thinking that masturbation was almost better. [Note: The often reported disappointing experiences during early intercourse are validated by both laboratory research and anecdotal research: Physiologically, experiences of masturbation are often more intense than intercourse. For one reason, the person has discovered specific ways of self-pleasuring which the partner—especially an inexperienced partner—would not know. (*The Hite Report*, 1976; Masters and Johnson, 1966)]

MALE

My first sexual relationship of any kind was with Lora, a sexually experienced 15-year-old; she had been pregnant once, had had an abortion, and was on the pill. All her experience caused me stress because of my lack of experience. When we finally tried to have relations, I couldn't attain an erection. I'd had it up for quite a while because of very long foreplay but I couldn't keep it up long enough to satisfy her. I think this had a real impact on me. Right after this incident of impotence with Lora I lost interest in her and we broke up shortly after. I wonder if I'm subconsciously worried about trying again. I functioned properly in oral sex (mutual) at a later time with another woman but before I could convince her to have coitus I mysteriously lost interest. I have been finding it harder and harder to get a close enough relationship where my partner and I might eventually consider having intercourse.

MALE

As a junior in high school, I couldn't imagine engaging in sexual intercourse with anyone. That was something "grown-ups" did when they were married. But after several nights of messing with Sue, she finally said that that was what we had to do—we had to have sex. I felt just a horrible fear at the thought of it. As we had no place to go, we went out into the woods with several blankets and made love. It was like something out of a Woody Allen movie. I couldn't get my pants off because I was shaking from nerves and from the cold. The nerves and cold made it all but impossible for me to get an erection and then after I had one and we made love I couldn't find the car keys. It seemed that everything that could possibly have gone wrong had done so. I found the keys at last in my pocket and we drove home in silence.

FEELINGS OF PAIN AND/OR DISCOMFORT

FEMALE

The summer before my senior year of high school I had sexual intercourse with my boyfriend who I had been going with for several months. My mother's words passed through my mind just before coitus: "Good girls wait until after they marry to have intercourse because it is so special and men prefer virgins." My only thought after coitus was—bullshit! I was bleeding moderately and making love for the first time was unexpectedly painful! If I had waited years with great expectations for this, wow—what a terrible disappointment that would have been.

FEMALE

My first sexual experience occurred after my high school Junior Prom in a car at the drive-in. We were both virgins, very uncertain, but very much in love. We had been going together since eighth grade. The experience was somewhat painful. I remember wondering if I would look different to my mother the next day. I guess I didn't because nothing was said.

FEELINGS OF COMFORT

FEMALE

In the fall of my junior year in college (a year ago now), I began to date a guy steadily. This relationship proved to be a kind of turning point in my way of dealing with my own sexuality. He was a very open, free-thinking individual. We became very close very quickly. In fact, I worried about how fast I responded to him physically. I was afraid that I wasn't being cautious enough. But my fears were soon dispelled. I have never felt so comfortable and so able to be open as I was with him. He made me feel good about myself, my feelings, and my body. I didn't feel self-conscious around him; I felt like I was loved and appreciated for who I was without demands for changes. He didn't pressure me to have intercourse although he really wanted me to. He accepted and respected my feelings about it.

FEELINGS OF SATISFACTION (AFTER SOME INITIAL FRUSTRATION)

FEMALE

The first time I made love, I didn't know whether to laugh or cry. It changed me and the ways I viewed life and love. I think I cried because I realized I'd always thought about what I should or shouldn't do or be, rather than acting on my deepest feelings and beliefs. Making love helped me get in touch with myself; I no longer had to be lonely to be good.

FEMALE

I became very attracted to a close friend. Until this time we had always just been buddies but I had loved Fred as a person for a long time; now I began to be "in love" with him also. Our sexual life was slow in starting as Fred, being a virgin, went through the same qualms that I had had about losing one's virginity. I recall a great deal of frustration after sleeping with him for three months and being able to play sexually, but not have intercourse. He finally decided that intercourse was a logical step in a love relationship. We spent three very happy years together, sexually and otherwise. Our sex life was very satisfying and it is only now since we have left each other that I am aware that sex was a greater part of our relationship than I had realized.

Some women learned to fake orgasm because their partners were focused on their own pleasure only.

FEMALE

Warren was a very athletic lover. I realize now that even at the beginning there wasn't a lot of feeling with it. Kissing, caressing, and oral sex were all merely a build up to the important part, him thrusting inside me for an extended period of time. He also asked that inevitable question toward the end, "Are you ready yet?" I was never even close but it didn't take an Einstein to figure out what he wanted to hear. He'd pout when I said no and seemed in seventh heaven when I said yes. Being a real pleaser and regularly using a vibrator for orgasms when I was alone, it seemed harmless enough to say yes and go through the motions. He didn't appear to know I was faking, which troubled me, but not enough to say something about it. He liked things to go smoothly.

One woman mentioned a rather disturbing first experience which seemed to have a long-term impact on her. Being uncomfortable in openly discussing her fears and concerns with others made the disastrous experience seem especially painful.

FEMALE

I had many boyfriends but I never experienced any sexual activity (besides kissing) until I was going into my senior year in high school. Then I experienced a very shocking relationship. I started dating an Italian boy who was two years older than I. He never communicated verbally what he wanted from our sexual relationship; he only tested me as to what I liked. The first time he put his hands down my pants I thought I would die, but once he began stimulating my clitoris it felt so good that I said nothing. The relationship continued and I began to visit him on weekends at U of M. I always dreaded night time because I knew I would feel guilty after we had intercourse (especially if I enjoyed it), and most of all I always feared that I wouldn't know what to do. I could never communicate my fears to him because I was too embarrassed; I couldn't talk to my mother because she would have thought it was sinful and I had no older sisters. I told no one and crammed all my fears inside of me. Finally my boyfriend showed me how to have oral sex. He told me he loved fellatio. He proceeded to ejaculate in my mouth and I wanted to throw up. At that point in my development, I had never heard of fellatio. I thought he was just exploiting me. It really frightened me and I broke up with him. I closed myself off from sexual relationships for almost a year after that. I still have a scar from the relationship.

SUGGESTED ISSUES FOR PERSONAL REFLECTION, GROUP DISCUSSION AND INTERACTION, PERSONAL JOURNAL

1. What memories do you have of your first significant sexual experience?
   a. What feelings did you have about the experience?
   b. What about the experience made it enjoyable or unenjoyable?
2. Which of the following were important aspects of your first significant sexual experience?

   _____ Love   _____ Learning
   _____ Trust   _____ Commitment
   _____ Respect   _____ Noninvolvement
   _____ Curiosity   _____ Self-testing
   _____ Other_____

3. Indicate the appropriateness of each activity for each age (a = acceptable, u = unacceptable).

	10	12	14	16	18	Marriage
Holding hands						
Kissing						
French kissing						
Necking (waist up)						
Petting (waist down)						
Petting to orgasm						
Oral sex						
Intercourse						

Talk about reservations or conditions that might affect your answers above.

Chapter 9

Self-Image and Sexuality

INTRODUCTION

Self-image depends on the feedback each person receives from family, peers, community. "Each of us is born with a full circle of human qualities, and also with a unique version of them" (Steinem, 1992, p. 257). Steinem goes on to suggest that males and females with low self-esteem may reject the full circle of human qualities and "seek refuge in approval and exaggerated versions of their gender roles," thus becoming even less complete as they grow up. Male dominance means that admired qualities are called "masculine" and are more plentiful, while "feminine" ones are not only fewer but also less valued. Thus boys as a group have higher self-esteem because they are literally allowed more of a self and because the qualities they must suppress are less desirable, while girls as a group have lower self-esteem because they are expected to suppress more of themselves and because society denigrates what is left. Once adolescence and hormones hit, this lack of a true self in both sexes, this feeling of being incomplete and perhaps also ashamed of parts of oneself that "belong" to the opposite sex, combines with society's intensified gender expectations to make many of us construct a false social persona—in a big way (Steinem, 1992, p. 257).

An individual enters adolescence armed with the sense of himself or herself that has been acquired, basically from the family, during childhood. "Genuine respect for oneself is a prerequisite for the development of intimacy in relationship. This self respect derives from the experience of consistent, loving care given by caretakers during childhood" (Crooks and Baur, 1993, p. 203). During adolescence, a major shift from dependence on parents to independence must occur and this is usually accompanied by inner turmoil and some form of movement away from accepted family values and behaviors.

MALE

I've always felt uncomfortable about sexuality in general and my own sexuality specifically. The line my mom always used about anything genital when I was little was "dirty, dirty." I feel comfortable with my gender (male), but I am still somewhat uneasy about my body. My dad would remind me that I was his son and that boys will some day be men. But since he never discussed any personal things with me (sexuality included) it just made me feel somewhat unsure of myself.

MALE

As a youngster my grandparents and parents had a lot to do with how I saw myself. One grandmother and great-grandmother always made me feel special any time they saw me. My great-grandmother always had a new Chevy that she loved to take us kids for a ride in. She always had her fishing pole in the trunk, so she would stop at the river and let us all fish and look at things in the water. She and my grandmother (her daughter) and my mother had the easiest smiles. They always smiled and laughed. They also made that special effort to see if you were happy. Their sensitive and gentle loving ways really impacted me. They made me feel good to be a boy, even if I was small and bony. It didn't matter to them. They showed how they felt. They could kid me about girls before I was old enough to date. I was always so happy to see my grandmother and give her a kiss. As I became older, I realized how much it meant to her.

The teen years often are an emotional time for adolescents and their families. This is the time physical and emotional changes, increased importance of peers, career decisions, and many other changes exert strong and often conflicting pressures on the maturing individual.

FEMALE

In general, what I learned from my parents was the difference between right and wrong (morally and legally), to respect others, to be honest and to work hard. These qualities did help me to make good decisions regarding my relationship with boys, but it certainly didn't help me to sort out my feelings of confusion, concerns, and doubts about myself on a personal basis. I grew up feeling very unsure about my identity during my teenage years. Just knowing that I wasn't the only one who felt ignorant, lonely, self-conscious, nervous and shy at times would have helped tremendously to normalize those feelings, and in effect, would have helped me to feel better about myself.

MALE

As a teenager, I didn't talk about feelings at home, sharing very little with my parents. However, when I came home from a date angry and frustrated, I would slam doors or kick things, but felt my folks were intruding or prying when they asked what was wrong.

Low self-esteem is perhaps the single greatest barrier to intimacy. Women with low self-esteem are afraid of letting men get too close because their real selves will be seen and may be rejected. Gloria Steinem says that men experience a comparable fear, and that for men there is "often an added fear that dependence on a woman or the discovery of 'feminine' feelings within themselves will undermine their carefully constructed facade of manliness" (Steinem, 1992, p. 259).

FEMALE

I absolutely loved to go fishing and play outside. Did that make me a "tomboy?" It's funny, I knew a few other girls who liked to do the same things. I always wanted to wear pants—never dresses! I wanted my hair to be cut in the current style—short and shaved up close in the back. My mother wouldn't let me have it cut that way. I guess she was sick of the waitresses and cashiers calling me a boy. Actually, I was probably more bothered by it than my mother was. I remember in Big Boy's restaurant one time the waitress said, "And what would HE like?" directing the question in my direction. I lost it! The tears ran down my cheeks uncontrollably. I wouldn't order a thing to eat. I just wanted to leave. I must have only been about seven or eight.

MALE

I have trouble meeting girls. My older sister set up all my dates back home. I am still dating one of those girls. How close have we come to intercourse? She gave me a peck on the cheek on New Year's Eve. I am terrified about dating a college girl because I am afraid she would find me socially retarded and make fun of me.

Some risk only when it is safe.

MALE

I never really chased girls in high school as so many of the guys did. Most of the girls with whom I developed close relationships chased me. It wasn't that I didn't want to "chase" them or that there were none worthy of the chase, but I think it had something to do with my great fear of rejection. Before I asked any girl out, I made quite certain (through the grapevine) that she wanted to be asked by me. Maybe this is common, but I sure worked hard finding the reassurance necessary to make my move.

It is often difficult to understand the changes going on in bodies and in relationships. It may seem as though one is absolutely unique and alone.

MALE

By age 15 I liked and desired female company. My lack of confidence, due to not really knowing how to behave, caused me to become sort of shy about having a relationship of a steady nature. When I discovered that this was also the way my friends felt, I lost my worries and figured what was going on was only natural. My rapport with the women soon improved and I began to frame the positive mental attitude about sex that I feel I now possess.

MALE

Three years ago I had a disastrous sexual experience which I don't even want to write about. I can write, however, about all the feelings that came from it. Up until that time I believe my fears and anxieties were normal. After that frustrating and bewildering evening I became not only scared of the sexual part of a relationship but of any part of a relationship that could possibly lead to any sex. I became very defensive in most of my interactions to avoid being caught in another embarrassing situation. I couldn't possibly talk to anyone about what went on that evening for it would be too embarrassing. I felt alone and trapped. I could obtain factual information about sex with a low degree of embarrassment, but I could not put together any of the psychological pieces of sexual relations. The hardest part was not being able to talk to anyone about it. My buddies were always making jokes and kidding each other, and I didn't talk to any of them for I was afraid of becoming the center of the needling. My parents never brought up the subject of sex around home.

My fear and general confusion continued to increase until this year when I decided I simply had to talk about it. Surprisingly enough I did not start talking with my buddies but rather with a girl. I told her I was a virgin when the subject came up; her reaction was not as bad as I thought it would be. Slowly I started expressing my feelings and she handled it really well. I found out my feelings were not so strange. A good example is that I believed I was supposed to want to jump into bed with every girl, but I really didn't want to unless I liked the girl and understood her feelings. I found out that was okay. I started to open up with my friends on some of the things involved with sex and found out talking wasn't so painful there either.

Because of society's stereotypes, a tall girl has a harder time feeling feminine and desirable, and a short boy has a harder time feeling masculine. It takes years to fully accept one's own body image, and some people never do. Women indicated how much their self-concepts depended on being part of the dating scene.

MALE

One thing I really like about myself is that I'm small. I'm just under average height but on the thin side (that's a polite way for me to say I'm skinny). It used to bother me that I was too small to play football and always the last to be picked for most any team effort, just because of my size. But being small has taught me many things. I had to learn to out-think and out-maneuver my opponents instead of bulldozing them. I feel that I have earned people's friendship and respect because of my personality, not because I'm 6'4" and play football. Though I'm not Joe Popular on campus, I'm happy as I am.

FEMALE

I never dated during high school and this was a horrible thing . . . giving me a terrific inferiority complex that lasted until just last year. I went to an-all girls high school and kept excusing my "social failures" on the basis that I just didn't know any guys. I told myself if they only knew me, they would *love* me. I went to all of the sock hops and when I wasn't hiding in the john, spent my time trying to look inviting and unconcerned that I was the only girl in the room up against the wall. I was tall, heavy, and felt ugly unto death. My parents and teachers kept telling me that I was a lovely girl and that my time would come. They assured me that purely social situations were very difficult and that you did better to get to know young men on a casual basis—as people first. To compensate for this aspect of my life, I threw myself into academic pursuits and became one of the intelligent, upstanding, big wheels in the school. This resulted in a good grade-point, a college scholarship, and the respect of many people, but it didn't scratch where it itched and as a result didn't do all that much for my self-image. For the longest time, I connected my worth as a person and as a woman with my failure to ever have a guy look at me twice. That was one real disadvantage of a female school. They always made a big deal about dances and things like that and if you didn't go, there was obviously something radically wrong with you.

FEMALE

I don't remember having any early feelings about my gender. I realized I was a girl but often played with boys. There was no difference to me between male and female. My mother reminded me frequently to act like a "young lady." She would emphasize the fact that I should look nice and be clean and wear pretty dresses to school. As I got older, there was a difference for me and it was awkward. I never cared much about looking pretty, though, because I was bigger and taller than most boys in school until I was in tenth grade. Because of this I always felt awkward about boys. I never had any brothers so they were really something very different to me. I chose not to have any relationships with boys. As a result, I studied a lot and had one good girlfriend to do things with on weekends. My girlfriend dated a lot and used to try to get me to go out with boys. She always tried to set me up with a date. I began to feel the pressure from my friend and my mother about going out with boys. I felt obligated to because normal high school girls date. I forced myself a few times and had a bad time. The summer I graduated from high school I suddenly started becoming aware of my body and comparing myself to other girls at school. I realized I was attractive and most of the boys were, at last, bigger than I. I began to think of myself more as a woman and enjoyed it.

The agony of feeling fat is widespread for girls.

FEMALE

By the time I was in junior high, I had become very fat and shy. Ever since I was a little kid my dad had asked me why I didn't have a boyfriend. Finally I started to lie, telling him that I did. Even though I desperately wanted a boyfriend I knew that it was pretty impossible, and I resigned myself to being excited about my girlfriends' boyfriends. This made me feel horrible.

FEMALE

I used to hate my body. Most of my life I've felt fat and ugly and I really didn't want anyone to see my naked body. For many years I had chafe marks on my inner thighs. In high school someone asked me about them, wondering if they were bruises. I was so ashamed and embarrassed I said that they were bruises. Soon after high school the marks went away—maybe because I lost weight and stopped wearing girdles. Now I don't mind "gang showers."

FEMALE

I do not like my body. My weight has fluctuated on and off my whole life and no matter what, I feel fat and ugly when I am naked. This lack of a good self-image causes me embarrassment and discomfort when making love or I should say before I make love. I am presently working on loving myself as I am, but I will be honest and say I am not very hopeful. Maybe the right partner will do the trick some day. I hope so.

"Jealousy springs from feelings of inadequacy and incompleteness, and as self-esteem decreases, feelings of jealousy increase" (Steinem, 1992, p. 259).

FEMALE

Throughout my school days I was overweight. However, because of my high academic standing, my involvement in school activities, and my outside participation in clubs and youth groups, I never really tried to lose weight. I was invited to many of the parties. However, my social life, as far as dating was concerned, was absolutely zero. I did not have a single date until the end of my senior year. Instead of dating, I did things with a group of kids. I talked myself into thinking that everything was fine. However, I was lonely and jealous of other girls in my class who went out.

"In a survey of 400 U.S. psychiatrists . . . the majority reported that both women and men with low self-esteem were more likely to be promiscuous, to have difficulty finding fulfillment in sexual relationships, and to be less likely to fall deeply in love" (Steinem, 1992, p. 258).

FEMALE

Many years were filled with self-doubts and so much insecurity. It hurts to remember them. Weight has always been a problem, and if I had to list a single factor as being most influential in my sexuality that would be it. I have not studied much psychological theory but I believe that shaped my life more than anything else. My body image was and still is very bad. I have been obese in my mind's eye from second grade on. There have been years in that time span that I have been physically thin but I have never felt that way. I think these feelings were paramount in affecting my sexual behavior. If I didn't say yes and participate, "he" wouldn't belong to me or I to him. It was a desperate attempt to be needed, useful, and loved.

Big breasts were a status symbol.

FEMALE

I remember Tammy in Ms. Sheathelm's English class. She was passing her paper up to be turned in and ran her finger down the middle of my back, promptly announcing to the class that I was wearing an undershirt instead of a bra. Needless to say, this was the beginning of my body-hating days. Especially my breasts. Between my sister making fun of my breasts at home and kids making fun of them at school, I began to get quite obsessed with growing up and maturing. From seventh grade on, I routinely checked my underwear for my period to start. I looked at a lot of clean panties—didn't get my period till I was seventeen. Today, I am grateful for this fact, back then, devastated. By the time ninth grade rolled around, my friends all had me convinced that something was wrong with me and my mother should have taken me to the gynecologist by now, whatever that was.

FEMALE

I'm thin and a lot of people comment about how good I look in clothes and how skinny I am, and how they wish they could be like me. Without clothes I feel like a flat-chested bean pole with a potbelly. I've been told that I am sexy looking; I have waist-length hair and have a cute face, but I wish I had a chest—just so I could have a little cleavage.

FEMALE

As I started developing a few small curves, I didn't wear many close-fitting clothes. For a while I was very self-conscious about my body, even though I was very slight. It used to bother me that I was relatively small-chested. It seems all boys were attracted by large breasts. That might have been one reason I never felt I was good looking. I always wanted to be beautiful. Men have told me I am very good looking, even beautiful, but I've always felt it was just a line. I find it very hard to accept that I might be beautiful.

FEMALE

In junior high I was flat-chested, skinny, and had pimples on my face. This made me painfully shy with the "opposite sex." Every now and then I'd have a crush on a boy, but rarely would he like me back. Finally around the age of 15 or 16 things started to shape up. My face cleared up and my figure got somewhat better. I was still lanky and very self-conscious about not having much as far as breasts go. Boys started noticing me, though. My girlfriends and I started hanging around with my (one year) older brother and his friends. It was fun but I still didn't have a boyfriend. It seemed like all the girls with the big chests got the guys, even if they were ugly and had no personalities. Even after I started dating, if a guy tried to touch my breasts, I'd push his hands away out of embarrassment.

Early breast development can be a problem.

FEMALE

Grade school was hard. I did not fit in well. I went to a small school and was one of seven girls. I was the lucky early developer of the seven. My parents gave me a beautiful suitcase for Christmas with new clothes in it when I was in third grade. There was a bra. Nothing was said. I did not want it. I wanted to be little. I had the only hair pulling, kicking fight I ever participated in that spring with one of the other girls who made fun of me. The pain was excruciating and I wanted to hurt her back. I slapped a boy that I really had a crush on in fourth grade when he did the same thing to me. My self-esteem was the pits. I was five feet, eight inches tall the spring of fifth grade and my breasts were about fully developed. I had my first male teacher in sixth grade and he was two inches shorter than I was. I towered above everyone. I hated school. I hated everyone. I wanted to be cute and little. I knew I couldn't so I settled for smart.

FEMALE

I developed breasts prematurely and even got my period before most of my friends. Of course these were more embarrassing than beautiful experiences because I was comparing myself to my other friends. I felt different. Therefore, I was uncomfortable and shied away from sleeping over at my friends' houses; even at camp I would turn my back when changing. I also hid what I had by the clothing I wore. I was very sensitive about my figure and was disgusted whenever I looked at myself.

A number of other concerns about physical characteristics can also cause discomfort.

FEMALE

I never thought of myself as pretty or particularly attractive. I have very dark hair and very light skin. My body hair is dark also, and that made me very self-conscious. All the other girls in my class had much lighter hair and very little body hair was apparent. I thought they were much more feminine looking, much more girlfriend-looking to the boys than I was.

MALE

I joined the YMCA to take swimming lessons. We swam in the nude in this class and at first I found it hard to adjust to. I had had an operation for a hernia at six months of age which had left me with no navel; I was very self-conscious about this and it bothered me all through junior high.

FEMALE

When I was very young (four to five years old) I remember pulling at my nipples. My mother caught me doing this one day and told me not to because I would hurt myself. For a very long time (until high school) I thought I had hurt myself and that my nipples were disfigured. I thought nipples were supposed to be pointed and that I had pulled off the points on mine. I felt horrible. After several years of "gang showers" in junior and senior high school, I realized my nipples were normal.

MALE

During adolescence I had a strong attraction to girls, as I know all boys my age did. I saw myself as a gangly, unattractive, acne-infested creature without much drawing power for the girls. While my male peers would verbally fantasize about their sexual prowess and knowledge, I remained silent and rather passive toward them and their conversation. This type of conversation lasted from junior high school through high school. Though I dated and maintained relationships with girls, I didn't have a great deal of confidence in myself as a person, and as a sexual being.

The time comes, after puberty, when each person must reconcile the dreams of becoming a "Prince Charming" or "Cinderella" with the reality of his or her body as it has finally turned out.

FEMALE

I've come to accept my body. Oh, I still wish I weighed 13 pounds less. But my body is me—a part of me—and I like it. When I was growing up, Mother reinforced my "fat, ugly" self-concept. Her idea of my looking attractive was for me to wear dark-colored clothes. And she never realized how much my crooked teeth and skin blemishes bothered me. Well, I got my teeth straightened when I was in college and mostly time has helped clear up my skin problems. Those things have helped me like my body more, though I still occasionally daydream of having the "ideal" body—skinny!

FEMALE

It took me a long time to accept my body. Much to my chagrin I didn't need a bra 'til tenth grade. Heck, I still don't really need one! I'm a "late-bloomer"—small breasts, late periods (16 years old), and very little hair under my arms. My small breasts were always a source of tears (Why *me?*) in my early teens. Now I say, "The hell with it, ya gotta live with yourself and big boobs aren't gonna make you any more of a woman!" But sometimes I still feel kind of sensitive about it.

FEMALE

I used to be very modest and no one ever saw me naked. I guess I never really saw myself in the nude either until one day I took a good look at myself in the mirror. And you know what? I'm not bad. I'm not any beauty from a model's magazine but I'm not repulsive either. I remember hiding behind towels in gym class after showers but now when I go swimming, who cares? No more hiding behind towels. I feel proud that I can finally do this without blushing and cringing with embarrassment. For me, it's been an accomplishment.

FEMALE

I like me. I like my body. The more I learn about my body the better I feel, the happier I am, and the more I love myself and others.

MALE

If there was ever a rite of passage to male adulthood for me, it was shaving. Large biceps, muscular shoulders and a broad chest were things I hoped to see in the mirror but did not. Gradually I accepted bumps and pimples, knobs, and moles as myself—it was a slow, painful process.

Peer acceptance is very important.

FEMALE

Looking back I feel that I was very lucky that teen boys didn't seem to find me very attractive. I was so desperate for male approval at that point in my life that I could have been very easily pressured into some very difficult situations. In my senior year I began dating and became more certain of myself. Luckily, I dated some boys who were very conscientious about doing what was "right" or "moral."

FEMALE

During my high school days, I remember feeling flattered by "wolf whistles" and guys' comments regarding their attraction to my body; in those days I wasn't part of the popular group, and anything that made me feel accepted or liked was desirable to me.

Some adolescents try to win esteem by developing special talents or playing special roles in their peer group.

MALE

When I was in fifth or sixth grade, I acquired an inferiority complex not only because I then started wearing eyeglasses (what a traumatic experience at such an important time in personality building!), but also because I felt that I was a skinny kid, which was exactly the case. I would never wear short sleeve shirts to school, even through high school, because I thought my arms were so skinny. I would wear my long underwear well into spring so that my legs would look bigger! I was in sad shape! Because I wore glasses and was so skinny, I needed to depend on some other quality in order to socialize and make friends; I became sort of a "class clown." I seemed to have a knack of getting people to laugh at dull and boring times. This quality helped me get by in high school.

MALE

I always felt pressure to exaggerate my sexual experience. I learned to be a good liar, which now makes me angry. Usually I just told one of my fantasies as if it were real, but my fantasies have always been so incredibly detailed, so finely honed, that they were believable. Sometimes I got to believing them. It made sex an incredible competitive game and the prize was acceptance in the "in crowd." The "in crowd" went to dances and so on, and then would sneak away for a little "kissy face, huggy bod." That was all I wanted, but I never had the nerve to ask anyone out. I couldn't see that I had anything to offer; I wasn't athletic and though I was smart, the smart women who might have admired me were never into dating.

MALE

I went out for three sports in high school because I needed to stabilize myself and to possibly raise my self-esteem. I eventually gained some stability but was on the whole unsuccessful in all three sports, though I felt I had the determination and the desire to be great. My low self-concept did not help me out at all in sports, which demanded quite the opposite.

Relationships often raised self-esteem; when they ended, self-doubt set in.

FEMALE

My big leap forward in comfortableness about my sexuality was in my junior year, as a result of my relationship with Edgar. We got along together great and after knowing each other for six months we had sex for the first time. We went together for almost two years. When I started college, we started to have problems which led to breaking up. I also had some feelings of despair because Edgar was the first guy I had had sexual relations with, and I sort of felt that we were "meant for each other" and I'd probably never find another lover.

Fears about homosexuality were disturbing to some.

MALE

Lately I have become more scared of my (latent, thank God) homosexual tendencies. The main thing that made me worry about myself was a dream I had in which a (male) friend of mine was sucking my fingers, and giving me pleasure (pretty obvious symbolism). Intellectually I realize that this is OK, but it still frightens me a little. Emotionally I still feel that homosexuality is perverse.

"Am I OK?" is a haunting question. Those who understand and affirm their own sexuality and are reflective about their sexual behavior have taken a giant step toward self-esteem.

SUGGESTED ISSUES FOR PERSONAL REFLECTION, GROUP DISCUSSION AND INTERACTION, PERSONAL JOURNAL

1. Draw two pictures of yourself: one between the age of five and ten, the second between 13 and 17. Respond to the following for each picture:
   a. What did you like and/or dislike about your body?
   b. List words or phrases that describe you at that age—popular, tomboy, athletic, sexy, shy, left-out, etc.
   c. Rate yourself on the following continuum in relation to your peers:

   Loner _____ Most popular
          1   2   3   4   5

   d. How did your parents and siblings feel about you?
   e. How did your view of yourself compare with how you thought others saw you?
2. Whose impressions of you have made the most impact on how you feel about yourself? Why?
3. Draw a line, dividing a sheet of paper in half. On the left side write, Who I Am; on the right side write, What I Do. List five positive descriptive phrases or words under each heading. Then respond to the following:
   a. Looking at the ten items as one list, prioritize them from one to ten in terms of what you can offer in a relationship.
   b. Do you especially value any of these characteristics in others? Which ones? Why?
   c. Are there any you would choose to change? If yes, in what ways?

Chapter 10

Sexually Active: STD'S and Pregnancy

"Students must be provided the infomation needed for good decision-making regarding premature sexual activity and lesening the high risk of sexually transmitted diseases, including AIDS" (Hechinger, 1993, p.68).

INTRODUCTION

Adolescent coital activities have increased dramatically in the last four decades with some leveling-off in the '80's. This leveling-off, however, does not apply to those age 15 and under; their numbers continue to increase quickly (Crooks & Baur, 1993). In Kinsey's survey reported in 1953, the data showed that 20 percent of female respondents and 45 percent of male respondents reported engaging in sexual intercourse by age 19. In a survey reported in 1988 by Mott & Haurin, percentages had shifted dramatically upward to 68 percent of females and 78 percent of males who answered "yes" to the same question. Also reported is a sharp increase in births among adolescent females, particularly in the age range of 15–17 years.(National Center for Health Statistics, 1991). Melchert's (1990) research finding confirmed that the younger the first intercourse occurs, the higher the rate of pregnancies and Thornton (1990) looking at age at first intercourse found that those who were relatively young at the time of first intercourse had more partners and engaged in more frequent intercourse at age 18 than their counterparts whose first intercourse occurred later.

Despite the availability of birth control today, consistent and effective contraceptive use is not widespread among sexually active American adolescents (DeClemente et al., 1992; Orr et al., 1992; Soskolne et al., 1991; Strassberg and Mahoney, 1988; Woods, 1991). This presents problems both in unwanted pregnancy and transmission of STD's, the most threatening of which is HIV/AIDS. Most adolescents in the United States are familiar with the basic facts about high-risk activities that may lead to transmission of HIV but it does not seem to affect their behaviors. Teens are probably particularly vulnerable to STD's because of "... an illusionary belief pattern in which they view themselves as somehow invulnerable and immune to the consequences of dangerous and risky behavior" (Crooks and Baur, 1993, p.413). For instance, often, even when an adolescent chooses to take birth control pills, she does not require her partner to use condoms to protect herself from possible transmission of HIV/AIDS (Crooks and Baur, 1993).

Effective birth control measures are also neglected because of the many inaccurate myths believed by both males and females. For instance: if intercourse is episodic or infrequent, pregnancy won't occur; there is a safe time of the month (without individual record keeping of the cycle); withdrawal is a safe form of birth control.

High value placed on sexual spontaneity and euphoria contribute to nonuse of contraception, especially when combined with drinking (Hacker, 1976). "We got carried away"; "We just couldn't help ourselves"; "There was that sudden feeling and it was bigger than both of us."

Our society persists in some irrationalities about sexuality: for instance, the exploitation of the erotic in public media and advertising, combined with intergenerational silence and/or judgemental attitudes about sexuality, especially nonmarital sexual activity. Confusion and ambivalence abound and are reflected in the ambivalence about contraceptive use.

Many people have internalized such strong negative messages about premarital sexual activity that they seem to prefer the risk of unprotected intercourse to the safety of intercourse with contraception. A curious "moral" thinking process becomes: "I know that when people consciously make a decision, they are morally responsible for the consequences. So, I feel more 'moral' if sexual intercourse happens spontaneously or unexpectedly. If I plan for it by using contraception, I would then have to face the fact that I am sexually active."

FEMALE

We had intercourse regularly for over a year before deciding I should go on the pill. We had talked about contraception many times before, but I was always afraid to go to the doctor because then other people (at least the doctor) would know what I was doing. I was concerned what they would think of me. . . . Finally, a friend's abortion scared me so that I decided to go. The whole experience at the doctor's office wasn't at all as bad as I had thought it would be. I have been taking the pill for two years now. I still feel uncomfortable if other people find out.

MALE

After two months of sharing an apartment, we slept together for the first time. . . . When we talked about it afterwards, we discovered each of us feared the other might want to break off the relationship. With the discovery that we still cared about each other, we continued to sleep with each other, but without any type of contraception. I kept telling him I would take care of it and I never did. I guess my guilt about sleeping with him immobilized me. I didn't want anyone to know; I even stopped going to church.

MALE

I look back now on some of the last months of high school, and I can't believe what I did. I got in with a fast moving set of the popular kids. We made out a lot—usually at somebody's house when the parents were away—but we never did anything about birth control. We figured "It can't happen to us!" And it never did. It was OK to screw, but it was better to screw when you were drunk or really horny than to plan it out and wear a condom. If I had had one with me, then **I** knew and **she** knew that we were actually **planning** on having sex. We were really lucky nothing happened—like parents coming home, STD's or pregnancy.

Some people depended on withdrawal for contraception.

FEMALE

Bill and I developed an intimate relationship over a two-year period. He used a condom for a while, but I didn't like the way it felt. Then he used withdrawal which I found very unsatisfying.

MALE

I had been reading *Penthouse* magazine for a few years, so far as I knew, that was what sex was supposed to be like. Due to my Catholic upbringing, I thought I would be a virgin until marriage. I rationalized that anything except intercourse was harmless and therefore not sinful. Things progressed in the summer; I resisted the temptation to go all the way. But finally passion won over conscience. Once I had made love and experienced what I had only been reading about, I could not get enough. I was seventeen and in my sexual prime. My girlfriend and I got into a routine of making love every time we went out on a date. On weekends we would go out drinking and make love as many as four times a night. We never used protection. I would just pull out before I reached orgasm. During her period I wouldn't pull out at all. If I had known then what I know now about teenage pregnancy, I would have used a condom. We were so lucky she didn't get pregnant.

Some people decided to seek birth control information, even though they experienced internal conflict about doing so.

FEMALE

When I came to college, I attended a couple of birth control seminars that were held in the dorms, and I realized it would be relatively easy to obtain birth control pills. I had already been "lucky" for two years and I **knew** this was a step I must take. After one of the seminars I approached the speaker about how to go about it. That was the first time I had ever admitted to anyone that I was having regular sexual intercourse; it was so difficult for me to talk that I began to cry. But the speaker was so nonchalant about it that I felt reassured. I guess because of my guilt, she referred me to a minister who after talking with me, referred me to a local doctor. When talking to them, I let go of all my feelings about being a slut, and for the first time was able to discuss sex as a normal biological function. I was relieved to take full responsibility for my body. That was a step toward freedom that I will never regret.

FEMALE

I guess I lost my virginity on a beach one night before my freshman year in college. I had dated this fellow some in high school, even though he was three years older. I say, "I guess" I did because we were necking and rolling around on the beach and I had no idea what was going on. I had expected very different things to happen when I had intercourse. A couple of months later I agreed to go to bed with him. I then spent a great deal of time my freshman year making love. I was not proud of myself, but at least had enough sense to use birth control after the first few times. I never admitted to my roommate that I was screwing. In fact I lied to her, even though I talked more about sex with her than I had with any other girl.

MALE

I remember my first few times out buying condoms. I'd have to "psych" myself up just to stay relatively calm. I relived a few of those moments when I saw the movie *Summer of '42* a few years back. I really identified with the kid who told the druggist the condoms were for balloons!

Sometimes fear of suspected pregnancy was the motivation for seeking contraceptive protection.

FEMALE

I felt I really loved Pete and wanted to show my love in other ways than just kissing him. I wanted to make love. He came over one night when my parents were out of town. He spent the night and one thing led to another. Well, it was a beautiful an experience but it gave me the scare of my life. My period didn't come and didn't come. I was scared to death. Finally I went to see my doctor. After a test, he came back into the room where this little seventeen-year-old girl sat scared to death and told me I was not pregnant. I started crying, drove straight to Pete's house and told him the good news. We both decided right then and there that if our relationship was going to continue to include intercourse, I was going to go on the pill.

FEMALE

Terry and I did a lot of petting, and he often "came." (At that point in my life, I didn't know that women really "came" too.) Whenever we could find a private place, we would touch and fondle each other's bodies, always careful that he didn't get too close to me at the end. One time my period didn't come, and I waited until time for the next one. When it still hadn't come, I went to see a gynecologist. He examined me and then said gravely, "Young lady, why did you come here?" I told him I was afraid I was pregnant. He then asked, "What made you think you think you might be?" I told him how Terry and I had been playing around, and that he always "came." He said, "Well, I don't know how you think you could become pregnant with an unbroken hymen." I felt mortified and fled from his office, sure he and all his nurses were convulsed with laughter. I decided I would not go through that again, so Terry got some condoms, and I got some foam, and we continued heavy petting all that summer.

For some, the worst fear was confirmed.

FEMALE

I was debating whether to go on the pill because my boyfriend and I were making love. Before I made my decision, I discovered I was pregnant. I underwent an abortion experience that was so hard for me to get through I cannot talk about it even in this paper. We stayed together, and were even closer than ever. I learned my lesson, and from then on, had no more unprotected sex.

For others, fear led to abstinence from sexual intercourse.

FEMALE

I've been going with a guy now for two years and we've never had intercourse. The main reason is that I would be afraid to admit being sexually active, and using means to prevent pregnancy. I feel like I have no business going to Planned Parenthood or getting an IUD or going on the pill. I'm basically stumped over the whole matter, and my boyfriend is not pressing me. I value how my parents feel and that they trust me. I've tried so hard to be a "good" girl. However, through heart-to-heart talks with girlfriends, I've found they don't worry at all.

FEMALE

A close friend in high school had an abortion. It scared me and confirmed my decision not to have intercourse until marriage. I didn't know about any birth control methods.

After deciding to use some form of birth control, some women encoutered tremendous disapproval from their parents.

FEMALE

My mother and I were very close until she found out I was having sex with my boyfriend. When she found the pills in my purse, she told my Dad and both of them immediately rejected me. I couldn't understand because we had been so close. I started sleeping around. When I look back, I guess it must have been an unconscious way for me to get the love I lost from them. What I wanted was love, and I got sex. It was very hard for me to understand my parents, and to this day I still don't. I know that I hate them in some ways for causing me such confusion and rejection.

MALE

I was sixteen, a sophomore in high school, when I bought my first condoms at the drug store where I had gone on errands for my parents for years. The pharmacist and owner was a close friend of my parents, so I went in and hung around the birthday card rack until he went out of the store for lunch. Then I hurriedly asked for some Trojans from an older woman clerk that didn't know me, stuffed them in my pocket and went home. Now that I think about it, I wonder why I didn't take a bus across town to a different store! As if that weren't enough, my mother found the box on my bed. I was going out to a big dance with Sarah, the girl I had been going with since seventh grade; we had decided it was too scary waiting every month to see if she was pregnant. In changing clothes, I carefully put the Trojans where I would be sure to remember to take them, and my mother brought the laundry in my room. She didn't say anything, but in a few minutes my father came soberly up to my room, and I knew I was in for it. I lied and said a friend had asked me to keep them for him, but I got a long lecture anyway. The main point of it seemed to be that it was immoral for me to have the condoms. It was confusing, and made me feel even more separated from my father than I already did. I just ignored what he said, and Sarah and I never had intercourse without using them.

FEMALE

My mother found my pills while snooping through my purse. She admits she was looking for something of that nature. When my boyfriend and I returned from our date, my mother was freaking out about how guilty I should feel and what a terrible slut she had for a daughter. My father was concerned about me having affairs after I got married and also about venereal disease. I was totally shocked to hear their reactions. My mother dragged me off to the nearest psychologist because she thought I must be sick since I had had sex. Well, I talked to the doctor, he told me there was nothing abnormal about me, and he didn't recommend treatment. Since then, my mother and I have been total strangers to one another.

In an effort to help their children avoid unprotected intercourse, some parents offered contraceptive advice or device. The young persons were offended.

FEMALE

Two days before I was going away to college, my mother told me she would be glad to get me a prescription for the pill. I had skipped a couple of grades in school, and was pretty young, and she told me she thought I couldn't get my own prescription. I felt she was telling me that I ought to be sexually active now that I was going away to college. I had dated a few guys in high school, but was not what you would call popular by any means. My mother had always tried to push me to go to more parties, even to invite a guy. And this felt like more of the same. I have since talked to her about it, and she told me she was just wanting me to know it was all right with her if I got access to birth control—more all right than if I didn't. It didn't come across to me that way at the time.

FEMALE

When my brother was in high school, he dated a girl quite frequently, and my father gave him a condom. My brother was shocked and hurt that Dad thought he would be doing "that" with a girl, but to this day he has never told Dad that.

FEMALE

When I was a senior in high school, my parents came into my room one night to ask me if I wanted a prescription for the pill. I was shocked. I thought they thought I was "fooling around." Evidently, they had discussed it for several months and felt they could probably help me by removing any potential sources of guilt. After I thought about it, I decided they must have been wanting to tell me I wouldn't be "letting them down" by having sex, but they wanted to be sure I didn't have a child. Now when I look back, they were pretty courageous!

Some people tried the "safe" period. Such reliance may be particularly undependable for adolescents. Following menarche, some girls may experience irregular menstrual cycles for several years before ovulation occurs relatively regularly. Therefore, a "safe" period may not be identifiable (Crooks and Baur, 1993).

MALE

After taking a class in freshman biology, I realized I had better watch what I do because a measly drop of sperm was dynamite. After going with a girl for eight months, we began to have external genital contact, but only during her menstrual period. I had read that that was the safest time, and I was worried about pregnancy. After a year and three months of dating, I purchased three condoms from a friend who gave me a hundred percent guaranteed to keep his mouth closed. My biggest actual goal was to keep what we were doing a secret. The relationship developed as we increased our sexual practices. The intercourse occurred, me with two condoms on. I thought it was great, but wondered if it was worth all the worry about pregnancy.

FEMALE

Last weekend I went to visit a boy friend and ended up staying the night, doing some experimenting. We had intercourse. He had an orgasm but I didn't. It was the day after my period stopped and we used no contraceptive. Then I went to classes and found out you can get pregnant during the so-called safe period. I hope to hell I am not pregnant. I don't know what to do or who to talk to about it. I was curious, but not cautious.

Others discovered reliable information in a community agency.

FEMALE

I went to a Planned Parenthood which was specifically designed for teenagers. In order to receive any contraceptive device, I had to attend two co-ed group sessions which discussed various methods, the reproductive systems, and personal relationships. The people were extremely helpful in answering the multitude of questions I had. While writing this now, I realize I did all this on my own. I am proud that I took on the responsibility of sex without the encouragement of friends or parents.

FEMALE

My Mom would answer all of our questions concerning sex—but I didn't feel I could go to her or Dad when I thought I should get on the pill. Though I was a freshman in college, it seemed like that might be straining their liberalism. So, when I made the decision to explore birth control, I asked my best friend about it. She said it wasn't fool proof; she had gotten pregnant while on the pill but said she must have screwed up (no pun intended here!). She had decided to get married because she got pregnant. Anyway, she took me to a clinic she had gone to.

FEMALE

I have a twin sister, Suzi, and she and I have been very close. When we began going out with boys, we talked a lot to each other about what the guys wanted us to do, what we wanted to do, etc. We also talked quite openly with our mom who is easy to talk to. A friend of hers was a counselor at Planned Parenthood, and she asked Suzi and me one day if she could make an appointment for us to talk with her friend about birth control. I felt sort of embarrassed and a little hurt, but Suzi jumped at the chance, so we went. Mom waited in the car (which I was glad for), and when we came out, all she said was, "I just feel better that as you go out with boys, you know what you can do to avoid pregnancy." We both got fitted for a diaphragm because neither of us wanted the side effects of the pill, and we didn't see any point in having to do something all the time (taking a pill every day) when we weren't even doing anything yet. The counselor had been very clear that a diaphragm would do no good in the dresser drawer when we were in a car, so we decided to carry them in our purses.

The possibility of negative side effects for the woman was a consideration for some in choosing a particular method.

FEMALE

I keep wishing there were some way to have sex without having to use anything. I know that sounds silly, but after I had a lump removed from my breast, I decided I wouldn't use the pill any more—which is the only contraceptive that doesn't interfere with the freedom of sex. The doctor said my lump wasn't caused by the pill, but I get scared easily. Now I am using a diaphragm, but I don't like taking the time to prepare it and put it in.

MALE

Before this class, I was quite ignorant about the types of contraceptives, their use and possible side effects. At that time, I had no qualms about a woman using birth control pills but now I am very skeptical about it. I'm not certain I would want my wife to run the possible risk of messing up her body. I have changed my whole outlook on birth control.

". . . studies have revealed that many teenagers do not use any contraception at all the first few times they have sexual intercourse and only a minority of teenagers consistently use a reliable method of birth control even after they have been sexually active for some time" (Crooks and Baur, 1993).

FEMALE

I am one of those people who should not take the pill because I have asthma. During my senior year in high school, I got into a very close relationship with a guy which lasted for three years. I learned to understand a man's feelings, as well as his sexual being. It was two-way as he also learned from me. It was with him that I learned my own sexual feelings, needs, and responses. However, as I look back, I don't remember why he didn't use some form of contraception.

The question of **who** *should be responsible for contraception often seemed to be settled without conversation. It was assumed that it was the woman's responsibility.*

FEMALE

At times I would question myself and say, "Wow! I'm hung-up because I won't just 'do it' when a guy wants it." Then I feel a bit of resentment and say, "Why should I satisfy someone who doesn't know or care about me?" Last year, an old friend came to see me. We had never had any real physical contact before, but he stayed overnight and things just happened without our talking about it. I had finally broken the reservation I had always had, and yet I didn't feel good about the fact that we never really made a decision. He really forced himself on me. I found out that he had taken for granted that I was on the pill. It aggravated me for him to just assume that!

FEMALE

Until halfway through my senior year in high school, I believed intercourse was really disgusting. I couldn't even imagine taking off all my clothes and climbing into bed with a guy. Then I started dating a guy my senior year, and we had intercourse. We talked about birth control and it led to our break-up. He wanted **me** to use something. I wasn't sure that was fair.

FEMALE

Until my junior year in high school, I held the view that people who engaged in intercourse before marriage were "grubby" people. Meeting an already experienced guy changed my attitude. He explained to me that love wasn't complete unless you loved with your whole body. When I turned him down, he threatened to break up, so I gave in. Since I wasn't old enough to get my hands on any kind of contraceptive, we didn't use any. He hated condoms and wasn't willing to use them.

For some, not using contraception resulted in a negative feeling about sexual intercourse itself.

FEMALE

I was sexually active, but I never had regular periods. So I pretty much climbed the walls most of the time. Not only was I scared, but I came to look at sex pretty negatively.

FEMALE

After breaking up with a guy because we fought about birth control, I have had continuing misgivings about sex. Intercourse never did anything for me; in fact, it was constantly threatening to me because I was using no birth control. And thus I psyched myself right out of the mood every time.

For others, there were various forms of frustration.

MALE

After getting my driver's license, I started playing the field. Without going into detail, I met and "ringed" a very cute farmer's daughter. The relationship lasted for about five years, during which I was exposed to about every sexual experience imaginable, but had no real peace of mind. We would have deep, heavy evenings that most often ended in tears and pledges never to do "it" again. But invariably we would be thrashing around in the back seat the next date. My main problem was fear of impregnating my girl, so I would withdraw my penis before ejaculation. In fact, I can consciously isolate the times I have had intercourse when I have ejaculated in the woman's vagina. Each time I feared the possibility of pregnancy.

FEMALE

Just after I turned eighteen we made elaborate plans to finally do it. Sam was terrified I would get pregnant, so he used *three* rubbers. Neither of us felt anything, to say the least! After so many years of passionate anticipation, making love was terribly anticlimactic.

FEMALE

Jack used a condom for a while, but I didn't like the way it felt. We thought the only other alternative was withdrawal. That is a very frustrating method of birth control and it left me quite unsatisfied. However, back then, I didn't even think about having a climax for myself. I wasn't even aware that I had the potential. At the time, it was more than enough for me just to satisfy Jack.

Fear can impair the excitation response in women (Weinstein and Rosen, 1988). There seems to be some evidence that a "holding back" of sexual responsiveness, especially on the part of a woman, may result from fear of pregnancy. This holding back can inhibit responsiveness sometimes even after the original occasion for inhibition has disappeared.

FEMALE

I never dated very much and I never did anything but kiss. Until my present boyfriend, I had never french kissed or been touched in any way. But with my present boyfriend, it just seemed right and I liked being touched and hugged. I am basically a warmer and friendlier person now. We have intercourse but not regularly. I am not on the pill, so we are very careful. I am very good at exciting him. He comes, but I never have. We are quite concerned about this. We keep trying but aren't getting far. I believe the problem is fear of pregnancy, but I do not want to go on the pill.

Adolescents are at higher risk for sexually transmitted infection than are persons in other age groups.... By their late teens a significant percentage of both black and white adolescents have been infected with herpes virus type 2 (Center For Disease Control, 1991). Fear of STD's or AIDS was not strong enough to motivate consistent use of condoms—the only contraceptive device effective in STD prevention.

MALE

In my old neighborhood, it was no shock to discover that many teens were engaging in sexual activities with three to four different partners per week. Surprisingly, none of the promiscuity expanded into orgies or caused an outbreak of sexually transmitted diseases. We all knew, including parents, that sexual relationships were going on but no one made a big deal about it. I mean, no one was kicked out of their house if they happened to have gotten caught in the act. In fact, a few teenage girls got pregnant, but no one was shocked, surprised or thrown out of the family.

MALE

All of the women I made love to were on the pill, so there was no need to use a condom. I tried one once and didn't like how it felt. I decided then that I wouldn't use one unless it was absolutely necessary. As it turned out I never used one again. I guess that I'm lucky that I never contracted any diseases or got anyone pregnant.

With the development of better contraceptive technology, our society is moving toward the successful separation of the reproductive uses of human sexuality from its other uses. As long as reproduction was assumed to be the natural and primary goal of human sexual activity, all nonreproductive sexual activity was considered illegitimate. Abstinence was believed to be the responsible and appropriate behavior when reproduction was not desired. These attitudes have blurred our ability as individuals and as a society to make ethical distinctions between the various nonreproductive uses of the human sexual function. As contraception is more widely available, and more widely legitimized, the bases for judging the rightness or wrongness of a particular sexual act are shifting to some other norms than reproduction.

New, more inclusive norms have important implications for single adults, divorced and widowed people, homosexual people, and all others who choose sexual activity without the intention of reproduction.

SUGGESTED ISSUES FOR PERSONAL REFLECTION, GROUP DISCUSSION AND INTERACTION, PERSONAL JOURNAL

1. There is some evidence that personal and interpersonal dynamics and feelings have more to do with use of contraception than does good information. (People who have had excellent sex-education training at home and/or in school may still fail to use contraception while saying they do not want pregnancy.) What are your ideas about the possible reasons? List as many as you can.
2. Hacker's research indicates that responsible use of contraception occurs when a problem-solving approach is used by the partners involved in sexual activity, and when they talk together about what each one wants. Give illustrations of situations where such communication might not be present, and the impact on the use of contraception.
3. You are the parent of ten-year-old twins, male and female. One evening at the dinner table, the girl says to you and your partner: "We were talking

today in school about how babies get made. It sounded like sometimes people 'do it' a lot and no baby is made. Why would anyone want to do that if they didn't want a baby? How do you keep from making babies?" What will you say? Why? What do you think is especially important to communicate about sexual activity?

4. "Birth control is the woman's problem and responsibility—after all, she is the one who can get pregnant." What is your reaction to this statement?
5. "Abortion is not a contraceptive method." What is your reaction to this statement?
6. Write down three questions you would like to ask the other gender about sexual activity and contraception. Put all the questions from the group in a pile, and have them drawn out one at a time by a representative of the group addressed (men read questions addressed to men). The person who draws a question answers it and then the rest of the group of that gender may add any comments. The next question is drawn, until they all are read or time is up. The other group then does the same.
7. Some people would say that abstinence is the most appropriate contraceptive. Do you agree—why or why not?
8. Are there changes in your family background, peer attitudes, and cultural attitudes that would allow you to feel unambivalent about acquiring contraceptive protection and using it consistently? How can such changes begin to happen?

Chapter 11

Abuse: Painful and Confusing Experiences with Sexuality

INTRODUCTION

Sexual abuse can be defined as the use of power to manipulate, hurt, and control a person sexually. "In the spectrum commonly understood as sexual abuse—from sexual innuendo and leering to ritualistic or Satanic sexual abuse—there is verbal abuse. This can include denigration of the child's genitals, sexual ability, or sexual orientation (Cassese, 1993). The specific act(s) is not as important as the emotional impact on the victim: shattered trust, a sense that the world is not safe and feeling terrified, hurt, shamed, and/or confused (Bass and Davis, 1993). "If adult society can learn to believe in the reality of child sexual abuse, there is opportunity for unprecedented advances in the prevention and treatment of emotional pain and dysfunction. If adults cannot face the reality of incestuous abuse, then women and children will continue to be stigmatized by the terrors of their own helpless silence" (Summit, 1987, p. 172). "At present, it is estimated that nearly 500,000 children each year are sexually abused (Fuller, 1989). However, it is notable that previous reports indicate that perhaps less than 6 percent of child molestations are ever reported (Desenclos, 1992). Some studies suggest that between 20 percent and 60 percent of women have experienced incestuous and/or extrafamilial sexual abuse. Some studies indicate that as many as 16 percent of men have experienced incestuous or extrafamilial sexual abuse. A study conducted by the Canadian government found that one-third of male subjects had experienced some form of sexual abuse" (Cassese, 1993). The long-term consequences are destructive to individuals and pervasive in society. The full impact of abuse on the life and well-being of survivors and their families and communities is only now being fully recognized. Wylie (1993) suggests that if child abuse and neglect could be stopped immediately, in two generations individuals would suffer only from organic, biochemically based mental illnesses such as schizophrenia, bipolar affective disorder, and reactions to accidental traumas.

Children usually experience strong short-term reactions to being sexually abused but are often too confused or frightened to tell. They feel upset, helpless, frightened, guilty and, if physically injured, the pain experienced makes them particularly fearful of future contacts. The child's experience of abuse can be minimized or exacerbated by a nonabusing significant adult's management of the event. Parents (nonabusers) who handle the event as an unfortunate but not devastating experience and who can reassure the child that he or she is in no way to blame, reduce the impact on the child significantly. On the other hand, the impact of the event may be very much intensified by the parents' negating, angry, and hostile responses. Parents often react so strongly and negatively out of their own feelings of anger, powerlessness, and (too often) denial, that they cannot focus constructively on the child, thus isolating the child and providing inadequate help to prevent long-term consequences.

Long-term consequences of child sexual abuse have been identified in many recent studies. Findings: The longer the abuse lasted, the greater the impact; the use of force or the threat of force is associated with greater psychic injury (Beitchman et al., 1992); and early childhood abuse was found to be a significant etiological factor of transvestism (Goodwin and Peterson, 1990). Studies have been done, the results of which indicate differing consequences for female and male victims of sexual abuse: Beitchman et al. (1992) in a review of current literature reported the following data for females. In comparison with nonabused women there was greater evidence of sexual dysfunction, homosexual experiences in adolescence or adulthood, and depression; and abused women are also more likely to be revictimized. Anxiety, fear, and suicidal ideas and behavior have also been associated with a history of CSA.

Several of the outcomes for male victims of child sexual abuse include low self-esteem, depression, learned helplessness, guilt, alienation, distrust, and sexual orientation confusion (Genuis and Thomlison, 1991). Problem areas are described as disturbed adult sexual functioning; repression, denial or normalization of the trauma; self-blame and shame; post-traumatic stress disorder; male gender identity fragility, sexual orientation ambiguity and internalized homophobia; mistrustfulness of adult men; and disturbances of self-esteem and body image (Beitchman et al., 1992; Myers, 1989).

Cassese (1993) brings together significant data from various studies looking at the impact of child sexual abuse and HIV infection. Interview data from a recent study indicated that a disturbing 65 percent of those infected reported physical or sexual abuse in childhood and pointed out a connection between abuse-survivor characteristics and behaviors such as low self-esteem, which predisposes to lack of self protection, lack of firm boundaries, and confusion about how to assess another's trustworthiness, all of which increase the risk for HIV infection.

The public is becoming more and more aware of sexual harassment. Harassment includes behaviors that fall on a continuum from subtle to blatant and was first addressed in the workplace because women's complaints began to be heard.

As a guideline, Cooper (1985) described six increasingly obvious kinds of unacceptable behaviors in the work place:

1. *Aesthetic "appreciation":* These are pseudo compliments that aim at demeaning the target.
2. *Active mental groping:* This makes the targets feel as though a person has undressed them with their eyes.
3. *Social touching:* The offender stays within norms for social touching, though the person being touched finds it offensive.
4. *Foreplay harassment:* The Foreplay Harasser pushes the boundaries of acceptable nonintimate touching.
5. *Sexual abuse:* This includes verbal abuse and propositions, direct touching, including hugging, grabbing, and kissing.
6. *Ultimate threat:* The clear message is to give in or take the consequences.

One woman wrote about her experience as a teenager in the workplace.

FEMALE

When I was in eleventh grade, I got my first job. It was at a theater and I soon found out that the manager was a big flirt. He used to tease me by pinching me and telling me that I was cute. Since I was still really shy and had no other boyfriends, I started to like him. I knew that he could tell that because the teasing turned into petting in the back room. I kept telling him to stop and I'd push him away but deep down inside I guess I really liked it. One afternoon he asked me to come in early to help him take inventory. Instead of taking inventory, it turned into a heavy petting session. He was using his finger and all of a sudden he switched to using his penis. I got really mad and scared and started to fight him off, but he made me do it. When it was all over I was completely numb. I didn't have any feeling about it at all and I never even thought about it until years later. I guess it was too painful. I never told anyone and I didn't quit my job, but he never tried anything again.

It is now being acknowledged that sexual harassment is very much a part of the experience of many children and adolescents, both as victims and perpetrators. In earlier chapters of this book are excerpts written by women who reported experiences of boys making comments and snapping the straps of their newly acquired bras and then laughing. The women reported embarrassment and anger. In a study done with 1,632 students, grades 8 through 11, in 79 schools, the following results were reported:

- *More than 75 percent of girls and 56 percent of boys report having been the target of unwanted sexual comments, jokes, gestures, or looks.*
- *66.6 percent of girls and 42 percent of boys have been touched, grabbed, or pinched.*
- *About 80 percent of unwelcome sexual behavior is done by students and directed at other students; the remainder comes from teachers, custodians, coaches, and other adults.*

- 70 percent of girls reported that they were upset as a result of harassment, whereas only 24 percent of boys said they were upset.
- Nearly 33.3 percent of the girls who reported having been the targets of harassing comments said it made them want to avoid school and that it reduced their willingness to talk in class.
- Nearly 25 percent of the girls have been forced to kiss someone, and one in ten students—both boys and girls—reported being forced against their will to do something sexual other than kissing.
- 66.6 percent of the boys surveyed and 52 percent of the girls said they had been harassed by other students. Of those, 41 percent of the boys and 31 percent of the girls said they believe this was "just a part of school life: and that it was no big deal." (Clark, 1993).

The following excerpts describe young children's experiences of abuse (level 5 and level 6 harassment.)

FEMALE

When I was 12, I had a bad experience with some of the neighborhood boys. I think they were mostly curious and wanted to scare me so they tried taking off my clothes. I told them they'd regret it, and they were being foolish, and finally they left. I never told anyone—I knew my folks would be upset.

FEMALE

Back in sixth grade, while I was out riding bikes with John, Howard and Alfred, we were a ways from home and ran into two older boys. It was time to start for home and one of the older boys, whom I didn't know, wanted me to show him the shortcut. "Sure," I said, "no problem," and we started home. It seemed O.K. until we got to a small ravine. He grabbed me between my legs and scared the shit right out of me! He was carrying a machete, and threatened to cut me with it if I didn't do what he wanted. It made me furious and I said, "No! Go ahead and swing!" He swung the knife, stopped at my neck, and said, "Get out of here!" I ran home and never told anyone what happened.

FEMALE

I recall an older boy of perhaps 15 or 16 taking advantage of me when I was only about nine or ten years old. It happened one afternoon as I was on my way to the store. Actually, I believe it was about five o'clock because it was beginning to get dark. The grocery store was a block away from my house, so it was easy and even enjoyable to walk there.

I had to pass his house on the way. I was wearing pants. As I walked past his house I noticed that he wasn't out on the front porch as usual, but I really didn't give it another thought. There was an alley in back of the store, and a long bench close to the building. As I crossed the street and approached the side of the store, I heard a voice softly call out my name. It was a high-pitched voice, but I knew that it was male. I turned to see a tall, lean teenager peeking from behind the back of the store, and beckoning to me to come to him. My first reaction was to run as fast as I could. But then he said, "Come here, I want to tell you something. Don't be afraid, I won't hurt you."

Curiosity got the better of my fear, and after all, I reasoned, I did know who he was. "Come here, quick. It'll only take a minute," he said. So I went. He walked closer to me and put his arms around me. Then he hugged me. He touched my face, said I was pretty, and asked if I would like to be his girlfriend. I said no, and he began telling me of all the things that he would buy me if I would be his girlfriend. I thought of the things my mother had told me, one of which was that I was too young for boyfriends, and I told him this. He said that I should be his girlfriend for just five minutes, and began kissing me. I was too stunned to say anything. I tried to pull away slightly. Then he asked me if I'd ever been kissed before on the mouth. I said no. He began kissing me harder and more and more. His hand reached toward my pants. All of a sudden a group of kids, my age and younger, came up the alley. He let me go, and I ran into the store, terrified, not only of him, but of everything that happened in the alley. This was one of the most disturbing sexual incidents of my life. I've never forgotten it, nor will I. This happened two more times before I could say no to his beckoning, and I dreaded going to the grocery store until I learned to say no. For a long time, I didn't like boys.

A young man chose not to follow his father's abusive modeling.

MALE

When any of us worked with my father, he yelled. I admired his strength and mechanical abilities, but I never wanted to see my mother yelled at and I never wanted to be like that. When I was out of high school I felt obligated, to help on the farm. One day he started yelling at my mother, since she always did things wrong in his eyes. I yelled back at him to stop. He didn't and I told him if he treated her that way I was not coming back; I was leaving. He was silent. I stayed. Mom cried. To this day I cannot tolerate someone purposefully hurting someone else.

When considering children's sexual behaviors, the question arises as to the difference between childhood sex play and abuse. A useful guideline is: An invasion which overpowers another's ability to understand and/or resist falls into the category of abuse. Abusive activity involves an element of power: through age, size, or experience. Sex play or other sexual activities are entered into by mutual consent.

MALE

When I was about eight, my older brothers began involving me in sex play. At first it was just with my oldest brother. I thought it was neat. I could become excited by his excitement, and I had no idea of right and wrong, so it seemed OK—until my mother caught us. She didn't say anything to me, but my brother got a very big lecture. I knew then that "sex play" was wrong. So, when my next oldest brother started asking me to mess around, I couldn't understand it. If it was wrong, why was he insisting? After a while, I got tired of it and told Mom about it. She lectured him, but it didn't do any good. He kept right on pestering me, and it took my own personal refusal to make it stop.

FEMALE

I remember the summer after second grade. The neighborhood kids would play army and I was a nurse. There was a boy who lived across the street who was three years older and kind of a tough, troublemaker type kid. My first encounter with him was in a pup-tent as the nurse, and the second one was in my basement. Both times I had my pants down and he was doing all the exploring. I carried around a lot of guilt through my adolescence and young adult life for not being able to say no to him, as my mom and all those teen books and magazines said to do.

Sometimes, an age difference creates a different experience for the two people. The experiences in these excerpts were not seen as abusive by those reporting (all males).

MALE

When my sister and I used to play doctor, we would examine and touch each other's organs. Later, as I began to acquire some sexual "knowledge" from the boys behind the barn, things between my sister and me went a little farther. I would con her into performing fellatio (I didn't know what it was called then), and it was very pleasurable to me. I, in turn, would perform cunnilingus (another word I didn't know then). On occasion I would persuade her to allow me to rub my penis between her vaginal lips, although penetration never happened. This went on until she was about 10 or 11, and I 15 or 16. We stopped then because I was afraid I might possibly make her pregnant.

MALE

I used to go to my sister's room after everyone in the house was asleep. However, I would not return to my bed. In the morning, mom would ask why I was there, and I would say I had a bad dream and I didn't want to bother her and Dad. Actually, the meetings were by mutual agreement, but the actions weren't. My sister is eight years older, and was just into puberty. She would fondle me and become excited, but her breasts were too sensitive for much stimulation and everything else was off-limits to me. However, I did enjoy the one-way activity, and I believe the first time I ejaculated was in my sister's hand long before any of the other beginnings of puberty.

MALE

An early incident that happened before I knew the penis had any other purpose than urinating woke me up to my parents' sex taboos. My older brother knew I liked canned peaches. One day he showed me some peaches he had hidden under his bed. He offered me the peaches if I would place my mouth over his penis. "No big thing!" I thought, and those peaches looked good. So I did it. My mother came into the room and yelled at my brother, and I never got the peaches!

Experiencing an incident of exhibitionism had different impacts depending on the circumstances.

FEMALE

Once when I was in seventh grade, my girlfriend and I were walking down the street at dusk. A man drove up and exposed himself. My friend realized this and walked on, but I stood there for a few seconds longer. Because of my inexperience I didn't know what I was looking at and it interested me. He had his hand down there. Also it was dusk, and I didn't have my glasses on.

FEMALE

I was 11 years old. I was walking and he stopped his car beside me. He asked me for directions. . . . Being young and innocent I approached the car to respond. When I got to the car and looked in I discovered that this man had his male organ fully exposed. I ran away from the car stunned. I went home and told my parents. They called the police, and the policewoman came to our house to ask me all sorts of questions. I still think that that incident has an effect on me today.

Until the parents became aware of the situation, the children responded positively to a neighbor's requests and rewards.

FEMALE

When I was almost five years old, my neighborhood friends and I frequently visited a friend of ours who let us play on the wide variety of playground equipment in his backyard. While we were there he regularly exposed himself and asked us to lick his lollipop (penis). If we were compliant we received a donut as a reward. (However, I recall that we all received a donut each time before we went home anyway.) Our friend was a man who looked about as old as my grandfather and he lived alone. Our parents eventually found out what went on when we were there. My playmates and I realized that something was "wrong" because of our parents' reaction and his immediate departure. We really did not know that what he was doing with us was wrong. I guess our parents watched us more carefully after that.

Immaturity combined with peer pressure may lead to situations in which abuse may occur.

FEMALE

My best friend had her first sexual experience at age 13. This bothered me. I knew I wasn't ready yet, but my best friend was having sex. I felt pressure to hurry up and get ready. I was confused. Later that year, my friend was still having sex with the older guy. I was still a virgin. The guy's younger brother started to pay attention to me. We would go on bike rides together and sometimes walks. He was a few years older than I. One day we were walking and he started to kiss me and touch me all over. It made me really uncomfortable. I didn't know how to make him stop. He pushed me on to the ground and tried to convince me to have sex with him. I started crying and finally he stopped trying. He said his brother was right—I was a baby.

If a woman's self-image is low, then it may be easier to exploit her.

FEMALE

I came to think of myself as someone who was not sexually attractive and did all I could to maintain this image—dressing sloppy, staying fat, and always falling in love with the wrong person. I was like a puppet: doing anything people wanted, being all things to all people—when they said "Jump," I only asked, "How high?" I let myself be used by people for a long time and but one day I woke up and finally blew my stack, "Damn it, I have needs and feelings and I hurt." It took me a while to really believe it myself, but life was better after that.

FEMALE

When I was 11, I was already developing breasts. This made the boys notice me. I enjoyed being noticed, but it was also a hassle. I was very shy and had low self-esteem. I was also easily manipulated. Boys were always trying to take advantage of me and make me do things that I didn't want to do. When I was 11, a group of older boys trapped my friend and me, and tried to talk us into doing sexual things with them. It was very frightening, but my friend got away and got help. When I was 13, I had three high school boys chase me with handcuffs and threaten to do all kinds of sexual things to me if they caught me. They never caught me. When I was 14, I had a boyfriend make me do things I didn't want to do. He put his hands on my breasts and my vagina, and he made me touch his penis. I tried to stop him, but I couldn't. By this time I learned that boys were going to take what they wanted from me. It was not my right to decide. Therefore, I had my first experience with intercourse at the age of 16. I figured I might as well "give it up" because it would be taken from me anyway. It was horrible because my boyfriend was rough with me. He just kind of threw me on the bed and did it. I gave him permission, but he did not try to make it any easier for me. This same boyfriend forced me to have sexual intercourse with him, later on in the relationship, another time against my will. I went with this boyfriend for almost four years, and he was physically and emotionally abusive. By the time I got out of this relationship I was a real mess. After this I dated many guys and slept with a good share of them. If I was given any kind of pressure at all, I would have sex with them. Well, I finally got myself some counseling, the counseling I should have gotten when I tried to commit suicide at age 16. At that time my family refused the recommendation that I go into counseling. The counseling I'm getting now has really started to help me.

Being fondled by a "friendly neighbor" can be a confusing and frightening experience.

FEMALE

There was a neighbor who used to take me places, the best being out on his motorboat. He was married to a very nice lady but they had no children. Once while we were alone in the boat, he held me very close and put his hand in my swimsuit, and began fondling and rubbing my breast and genital area. I was so afraid! I tried to get away from him. I remember trying to keep it from my parents and having frequent nightmares about it. To keep anyone from knowing, I still went with him when he asked my parents, but began making up excuses to avoid him. Since he was just a "regular friendly neighbor" I'm sure no one suspected it or would have believed it anyway. I felt horribly guilty about it.

FEMALE

I was the youngest of four children, with two older brothers and an older sister. I felt wanted and loved as I grew up. The first time I can remember thinking about my body as an interest for somebody else was when I was about four. I remember being at a girlfriend's house, being all bundled up to go outside and play. Just before going out the back door my friend's father stopped me and I looked up at him expecting a question. Instead he put his hand between my legs and rubbed. I ran out the door. He did not stop me. I didn't like him doing that but I never told anyone. Sometime later he did the same thing, but I don't remember how much time was between the events. This time I cried when I was in bed that night (although I don't think I did when he was touching me). My mother discovered me crying and stayed with me until I finally told her what happened. I didn't understand how to explain to her, but I do remember it took a long, long time for me to get the words out. This man never undressed me, I do remember that. My mom told me not to worry and he would not be touching me again. I wasn't allowed to go over to that house again for many years, although my friend was always allowed to visit at our house and often did until about fifth grade. Years later my mother told me she called the wife the next day, explained what had happened and that if it ever occurred again she would call the police. She never questioned me or the truth of my statements.

FEMALE

A very unpleasant thing happened to me in eighth grade. I babysat for my basketball coach and his wife who was our cheerleading coach. My birthday is in January and one day I asked my coach what he was going to give me for my birthday. He said, "A great big kiss." I laughed and said "No thanks." In February he asked me what I was going to give him for Valentine's Day. I said "Nothing" and he said, "How about a big kiss?" I said "No." A few weeks later when I was babysitting for them, my coach said he'd take me home. On the way, he asked if he could have his kiss now. I didn't really know how to respond so I said "Yes," thinking I'd give him a little peck on the cheek when I got out of the car. Well, he decided to pull off the road and started to french kiss me. I didn't know what to do. I just sat there. I didn't kiss back, I didn't pull away—I just sat in shock. Finally, after what seemed like forever he pulled away. To this day (seven years later) I won't look at, talk to, or associate with that man. I still can't believe he took advantage of me like that. I also can't believe I was so vulnerable. I told my best friend what happened about six months later. No one else knows.

FEMALE

I was sexually fondled by an old man when I was ten years old. He said he wanted to teach me what I should not allow little boys to do to me. I loved and respected this old man. He was like another grandfather in our neighborhood. He hurt me and I was afraid to tell anyone. My mom scolded me for not wanting to go see him anymore when he invited me over. She asked me how I could be so unkind and ungrateful to an old man who had been so good to me in the past. She still doesn't know the truth.

One woman was particularly vulnerable to authority figures.

FEMALE

I was always a very good student and I really worked at it. I became an excellent pianist. I started teaching the day after my thirteenth birthday and had 23 students when I was a junior in high school. I got straight A's. I was a leader in school. I gave up my childhood and became an adult. Sexually I was becoming an adult too. My hormones were racing at 14. I was ready for an intimate relationship. Society said I was too young, but I felt I was living the responsible life of an adult without any of the rewards. My choir director in ninth grade became attracted to me. His relationship with his wife wasn't very good. I helped him teach because I was so musically accomplished. He held me and kissed me after a performance in the spring of my tenth grade year and then he transferred to another school system. During eleventh grade my chemistry teacher spent long hours tutoring me with his arm around my shoulder. I was so attracted to him. He really led me on and I was very vulnerable. The repeated physical arousal was driving me crazy. I started messing around with boys my own age even though I was not attracted to them; they were legal—so to speak. At least they were not married men. We did everything except intercourse because I was afraid of getting pregnant. Still not very satisfying. During my senior year I received a full scholarship to Ohio University to study optometry. My mentor, my optometrist, a married man with three children, started making sexual advances. He arranged to meet me in his office one Saturday morning to talk about optometry and college, but he ended up suggesting we make love on the floor. I refused, but it was exciting to have another man interested in me.

Children often kept the experiences of sexual abuse secret and hidden, while experiencing feelings of disgust and shame. If a child senses that a parent will react with shock, disbelief, or disapproval, it does not seem worth it to break the silence.

FEMALE

The message I got from my mother as I was growing up was that talking about sex was bad. Nudity was not allowed and sex was a "dirty duty" that a wife had to endure. When I was about eight, I decided that was pretty confusing because of what my dad was doing with me. For some reason mother began to suspect there might be something inappropriate occurring between my father and me. She asked only enough questions to find out that her suspicions were correct. Then she took my little sister and me to stay at an aunt's home. The next day she took me to the doctor and either she or the doctor must have contacted the police, because they talked to me a number of times trying to get me to tell. At first I wouldn't talk to them because I'd learned that I shouldn't talk about sex, and because I was embarrassed. I also overheard one of my sisters saying that dad might go to jail. Then I wouldn't tell the police or the psychologist anything. I learned about hiding anything sexual very well!

In many but not all cases of sexual abuse, the offender is a family member. In some cases the victim was too fearful to tell; in others, it was possible to tell a parent. Kissing and hugging in a sexual way and exhibitionism were the behaviors children most often reported. Adolescents most often reported kissing and hugging in a sexual way and fondling by an unrelated male (Stewart and Lykes, 1985). Long-term negative outcomes of abuse generally increased in severity where victims were closely related to the perpetrators, the abuse was more severe, and the victims' immediate negative responses were not to tell and self-blame (Wyatt and Newcomb, 1990).

SIBLINGS

Survivors of sexual abuse by siblings may often resist telling because of guilt and shame. They also may choose not to tell because of the problems it probably would cause in the family (Canavan and Meyer, 1992).

FEMALE

When I was 11 and my brother was 13, we went through a difficult time. I had many friends besides my best friend. My brother was very fat, and his personality reflected how he felt about himself. He didn't have any good friends and so had no one to share his fears, questions, and thoughts with. I suppose he was curious about sex just as my best friend and I were, but we didn't like him and certainly didn't want to spend time with him. Several times he forced me to let him see me in the nude. I didn't tell my folks because he threatened to beat me up. He said he was just looking and it didn't matter if I didn't like it. Then, of course, he was no longer just satisfied to look; he wanted to touch. Although he was fat we were the same height so I had been able to fight him off. One day my mother walked in while we were fighting at a doorway—me trying to close it and him trying to open it. By then I didn't care what he threatened and I told my mom what had been happening. It was quite a rude awakening for her. My folks talked to him and he promised it would never happen again. A lock was put on my bedroom door that I could use to guarantee my privacy and safety. Of course it was not the last time it happened. During the next year, no matter how careful I was to plan it so I was not home with him by myself, something would go awry and he'd make another attempt (I am still uncomfortable writing about it). After the third time my parents realized there was a more serious problem than they could deal with. They set up an appointment for my brother to go in for counseling. Resorting to that was quite unusual at that time. At least we all thought so. It started out with just him going, and then my parents went with him and then I was told that I had to go too. I couldn't believe it. There was nothing wrong with me. It was his problem. I was furious. I did go—twice, I recall. My brother went for about a year. He never approached me again and we never talked about it again. By the time we were 16 and 18 we were double dating quite a bit and he directed his sexual curiosities to other girls. At least, I guess so because it was never an issue between us again.

FEMALE

I've been carrying a difficult sexual memory around with me since I was 11 years old. It's something that has bothered me a lot since then, mainly because I don't know if this really happened or if it was a dream. It was a winter evening and I was home alone with my oldest brother. I remember we were watching a movie on the television and it was about two lovers. My brother told me to unbutton my shirt and lie on the floor. He started kissing me and I remember asking him if my shirt was unbuttoned enough. When he heard my parents drive up, he yelled at me to hurry and "straighten up." It's been eating me up inside because I don't think I'll ever find out if it was a dream or if it really happened. It really frightens me and I have never told anyone before. In fact, this is the first time I've *ever* released this, and it's been over ten years now.

FEMALE

The earliest experience I can remember involved my oldest brother, John. I was somewhere between eight and ten years old. I don't remember how long it went on, or when it started. What I vaguely remember is that he'd "touch" me. And eventually it got more involved. I remember one night fairly clearly. My whole family was in the living room watching TV. John and I were on the couch covered up with a blanket. My pants were half off and he was fondling my crotch. Another time we were in the kitchen and he tried to pull up my shirt to suck my nipples. I pushed him away and said "No." I'm not sure if that ended it or not, but anyway it eventually stopped. Now I cannot stand it if he so much as comes near me. I practically get hysterical if he touches me. As far as I know, we are the only two people in the world that know about it. I don't know if he remembers what happened or not. Not a word has been said about it since it stopped.

FEMALE

When I was in ninth grade a situation happened with my brother who is a year-and-a-half younger than I. I woke up in the middle of the night to find him standing next to my bed with his hands on my breasts. I was only half awake and he ran out of the room. I felt weird. I got up and shut and locked my bedroom door. Then I hugged my teddy bear and eventually fell asleep. The next day I told my dad what happened. That was awkward. I felt weird telling my dad, but I had to tell someone so that it would stop. If I told my mom, I think she would have gotten furious and made a big scene by yelling at my brother and the whole family would have found out. My dad simply said he'd take care of it. The next day he told me that he had had a talk with my brother and that it wouldn't happen again. But to this day I dislike my brother for doing that.

FEMALE

I was sexually abused as a child beginning about the age of three-and-a-half to four, by my brother and it lasted till I was 15. He told me if I told anyone I would be in big trouble. I told my mother about my brother fondling me and making me touch him. My mother confronted my brother who said I was lying. I was then punished for lying. I began to act out and, eventually, some of the neighborhood children and I were caught with our pants down. I was banned from playing with the neighborhood children and wasn't allowed to even go near their house. I didn't really understand why, only that what I was doing was bad, and I was bad. When we moved, I lived up to my "badness" in the new neighborhood. I lifted up my skirt in the cafeteria for anyone who wanted to see. I was taken out of class by the teacher and sent to the principal. He called my parents who punished me severely. I think it caused me to start stuttering and develop learning problems in school. We moved again out into the country. There wasn't anyone around to play with, so I spent hours playing with my dolls. My dolls were the only control I had over my environment. Once I got in trouble for having Barbie naked on top of G.I. Joe. I was still being molested by my brother. When my brother went off to college, he finally stopped bothering me.

There are differing circumstances under which women sexually abuse children. These circumstances may vary from those reported that cause men to abuse. Many of the studies depict female abusers as socially isolated, loners, alienated, having abusive backgrounds and emotional problems (Wakefield and Underwager, 1991).

MOTHERS

FEMALE

Sometimes my mother was nice. If I woke her up in the night because I didn't feel well, she was there in a minute, soothing and attentive. She'd make peppermint tea, sit with me until I felt better, and tuck me into bed. However, for as far back as I can remember, she gave us enemas for anything and everything—a cold, a stomachache, a fever, the flu, measles—any symptoms that persisted. When it came to enemas, she was different—harsh, belittling, and unsympathetic. She got the most bizarre look in her eyes, and also made a production out of giving one—almost a ritual. Not until last year did I remember that my father was also present. He held me down. I don't remember struggling.

FEMALE

For most of my adult life, I've mourned not having a connection with my mother. Going back in my mind and emotionally reexperiencing the abuse that took place with her, I realized just how connected we were at those times. I also remember the pleasure and sexual sensations I felt. I was surprised that instead of hating her for what she did, I felt very sad for her, and us, because that was the only way she knew how to connect with me. All the shame that bogged me down for so long seemed to lift when I was able to accept that I had no choice back then about what to do in those situations with Mother. I coped as best I could, and as an adult, I realize that the sensations I felt were natural for what was being done.

FEMALE

For the Record

My brother is a mother-fucking son of a bitch.
He told me on my 50th birthday.

Mornings in her bed
Wondering now if he penetrated her.

Her peculiar over-attentions
    peeling his grapes
    sterilizing his toys to take to nursery school
    fastidiously cleaning and oiling his baby boy penis.

His memories triggered by mine
    hours of baby girl neglect
    while he was my mother's preferred partner

I couldn't have been half as exciting
Except for her peculiar nightly ritual with my body.

Brother in the morning
Sister in the evening.

I want to throw up.

It went on and on and on.
No voices anywhere.

At brother's adolescence, father said, "No."
One night in my adolescence, I said, "No."
    She turned stonily
    voice heavy with blame
  "Well, if you don't want *that* anymore."
Mind-fucked too.

Now I lie on a massage table with no feeling.
Once after a session I felt my chest and arms for 3 days.

He ain't so bad, that
mother-fucking son of a bitch
brother of mine.

Greater long-term harm is associated with abuse involving a father or stepfather and abuse involving penetration (Beitchman et al., 1992).

FATHERS

FEMALE

Some of my siblings treated me differently after I told about the incest. They acted as though I had done something wrong—was tainted or bad. Until a few years ago I thought I was the only one of us that my father had molested. I now know that at least two of my other sisters were also victims. Ironically, these two are the ones who treated me the worst. One of them made it clear that she didn't trust me to be alone with my nephews. The other didn't trust me around her boyfriends—even though there was a nine year difference in our ages.

FEMALE

When I was six or seven, I often had bad dreams and would call for my mom. One night she didn't answer so I went into my parents' bedroom, woke my dad and asked where Mom was. He told me she had gone to my older sister's house after I'd gone to bed. I asked if I could sleep with him because I was scared. He said I could. That was the beginning of the most confusing and scary part of my life. My dad started doing what I now know was oral sex. This was my dad, and he wasn't hurting me physically, although I sometimes felt like I was choking or suffocating (perhaps that's why I suffer from claustrophobia). I liked the attention, yet I felt that I was doing something bad or naughty. I was afraid my mom would find out and afraid she wouldn't. I didn't know what I should do. My dad told me that if I told, no one would like me anymore. Judging by the way some of my family treated me after I told, that wasn't far from the truth.

FEMALE

Dear Father,

In some ways I wish I could hurt you the way you've hurt me. I happen to know for a fact, though, that there is absolutely nothing I could do to you that would hurt you in the same way and impact on your entire life the way what you did to me has on mine. And I guess I wouldn't really want that for you when I really think about it. I wouldn't wish that on anyone.

What I would wish on you though is that you could have some appreciation for the impact of your acts. I wish that you'd educate yourself on the subject. I wish you'd look at the patterns that incest victims have in their lives and see what you've done to me. Because it isn't just a matter of what you did to me—both physically and sexually—but what having experienced that abuse did to my life, the things I have to go through as a direct result of what you did to me.

One of the things—the little things—that comes to mind is how you've never been proud of me . . . that I've never done anything you were proud of. Just remember that the person I am and what I've "accomplished" reflects directly on you. So if you're disappointed in me, look first to yourself and how you impacted me.

Well, I'm not your victim anymore. And I'm not protecting you anymore. And I'm seeing you as the person you really are. And I'm taking responsibility for my life now.

I am grateful that I somehow came out of a dysfunctional family with some inner strength. I had the strength not to believe everything you ever said to me. I didn't have the strength to not believe *most* of the things you said about me. I still struggle with that. Somehow, though, deep inside me I knew there had to be another way to live and love than what I was taught at home by example. I realized that I needed to get the support and love I needed from people who were not crippled themselves. That led to me reaching out to others and that's what saved my life. I was able to find some healthy adults to help me and guide me on my way.

The thing that I think you should be most proud of me for is facing reality and doing things to help myself heal. Between my individual therapy and group therapy I'm going to survive in spite of you.

I guess you'll have to live with that.

FEMALE

I had a bad habit of getting into my parents' bed and I got more than I bargained for one morning. Mom got up to fix breakfast and I stayed on their bed snuggling with my dad. He was hugging me and then he started to touch me inappropriately. I froze. I did not say a word. I just wished he would stop. I never climbed into his bed again. I never sat on his lap again. I never got close again. I set up boundaries to protect myself and I lost all physical closeness with my father at the same time. I still grieve this loss because I still can't get close. When I started school, I fell in love with one of the big boys. I wanted him to put his arms around me and hold me. I didn't know it then, but I missed my dad. I got into trouble in second grade because I told another girl that I did not think that the boys in our class should sit around looking at pictures of naked native women in *National Geographic* magazines. My teacher was an old woman and she overheard our conversation. She scolded me for talking about looking at naked women, but she did not do anything to the boys. This was very troubling to me because I knew that my father kept "girly" magazines in the bathroom cupboard. I did not think that was right either. Why did he want to look at women? Soon after that I overheard my dad and an uncle talking about women and their big breasts. It was very negative. I was angry. They did not have the right to talk about women like that. I was female. I was going to grow up to look like that. I felt sick inside. Not long after that my family went to a fair and much was said about the female strippers. I started to hate men and the way they talked about women. Yet for some reason I was still very drawn to boys. I fantasized that my particular boyfriend would never act that way—never make fun of a woman's body. I believed that he would think a woman's body was beautiful, like I did. There was always a particular boy or man in my life. This seemed to be necessary. It filled a vacancy, satisfied a need. I missed being close to my dad. He was a part of my life and was there for me, but he did not touch me and I did not touch him. He was very supportive and he made me believe that I could do, be, and accomplish anything I wanted in life. But, he awakened my sexuality too early and so contributed to my shame. I believed that somehow something was wrong with me. I felt frigid on the outside, yet burning with desire on the inside.

When relatives make children feel uncomfortable through unwelcome touch, parents need to help their children by stopping the unwelcome behavior and setting appropriate boundaries. Unfortunately, adults too often choose to ignore children's discomfort, considering it disrespectful of other adults.

GRANDFATHERS

FEMALE

One experience I had as a youngster I have yet to tell anyone because it is surrounded by so much guilt and shame. My grandfather used to french kiss me when the family would all say good-bye on a Sunday afternoon. Now, I didn't know a french kiss from a Hershey's kiss, but I did know that I hated the taste of the tip of Grampa's tobacco-stained tongue moving along my lips, and sometimes inside my mouth. I used to wrinkle my nose, wiping my mouth with the back of my hand, saying, "Ewwh! He put his tongue in my mouth!" Gramma, Mom, and Dad would just laugh—probably thinking I was joking. Then there were the times Grampa would feel me "down there," and I would feel guilty. I think that having this experience with my grandfather affected me more than I was aware. Now I recognize points in my current relationships where the old fear of exploitation returns.

Two women described experiences with uncles and neither knew how to cope. For one woman the long-term pain centers in part on the attention given to the uncle, rather than the victim. And there is a double-bind. Sex is taboo; to be disloyal to a family member is also taboo. Even the victim may not focus on his or her own trauma but rather on the adult aggressor. The child is fearful of what the adult may do to him or her, and also of what will happen to the adult if he or she tells.

UNCLES

FEMALE

When I was ten years old an uncle took me up to a bedroom in his home while my family was visiting. There he fondled my genitals. I have no recollection of masturbating as a child, so this was the first time I had experienced these sensations. It has taken me about 18 years to be able to admit to myself that it really did feel good, and that is why I let the incident with my uncle be repeated two or three times. Then one day I was feeling confused, to say the least, and I said something about it. Later my mother told me that my uncle was getting psychiatric help. We continued to go visit them and the subject was never mentioned again. I carried hate, guilt, and mixed-up feelings with me until I finally worked through that situation with a counselor at age 28. I'm sure much transpired between my parents and my uncle, and I will never understand why my parents never mentioned it again or tried to find out how I was feeling about it.

FEMALE

As a child, I had little awareness of my sexuality; in fact I was naive, and I had little desire to learn. When I was about 13, I was molested by my uncle. I must use the term "molested" loosely because I didn't scream or anything, but it was against my will. Being the playboy he seemed to think he was, this 35-year-old man took me and made me feel things I had never experienced before. In doing so he made me feel deviant because I didn't understand my own sensations. After this experience, I was fearful of all members of the opposite sex.

FEMALE

My dad's first cousin's husband tried to fondle me at a party when I was 15. He had been drinking and he cornered me when I was alone. I told no one. It would only hurt the innocent and he was well liked in the family. It would have destroyed his wife and it was simply easier to keep my mouth shut. I do not think refraining from telling is that unusual.

IN-LAWS

FEMALE

An ex-brother-in-law regularly exposed himself and made lewd suggestions to me and two of my nieces about my age. He tried to force his hands down my pants. I managed to get away from him by telling him I'd scream if he didn't let me go. Ironically, my sister never trusted me around her boyfriends; he had been one of those boyfriends! Much later, when I was 15, and pregnant for my son, he raped me. I never told anyone about this. I was afraid of the consequences of telling. Another of my brothers-in-law made suggestive comments many times, but never followed through on any of them.

It is now being recognized that some children sexually abuse other children. Researchers are trying to discover the causes and settings of this phenomenon. In all incidents studied by Johnson (1988), coercion was involved. Data indicated that prior to their own sexually abusive behaviors, 49 percent of the children had been sexually abused and 19 percent physically abused. The victims all knew the people who victimized them, and all the child perpetrators knew the children they molested. In 47 percent of the cases, it was a sibling who was abused. In the majority of the families of these child perpetrators there was a history of sexual abuse, physical abuse, and substance abuse. In a study done specifically on female child perpetrators, Johnson (1989) found that all the perpetrators had been sexually abused, 31 percent had been physically abused, and 85 percent had been molested by family members.

FEMALE

When I was about seven, we used to play in a lot in a large field across the road from our house. Just before it could be harvested for hay, it made an excellent place to hide so that no one could find you. We would play many games and it seemed that I often ended up with the boy next door. We spent some of our time alone exploring each others' bodies out of curiosity. He was different than I and so I was interested in seeing how, and vice versa. We also played "doctor" quite often, as I think most little kids do. This was also encouraged by my 14-year-old cousin who babysat for us. She was a very self-oriented person and used both my brother and me to gratify her sexually, young as we were. As I said before, she encouraged us to play "doctor" and usually took part in playing it also. After a while it reached a point where she would make us suck her breasts and just play with her whole body in general. I hated that with a great passion but I was afraid to tell my mother about it, so it continued for quite sometime. Finally, I got really fed up with it, and though I don't remember how much I told my mother, I did say enough that my cousin wasn't asked to stay with us any more than absolutely necessary.

"To a woman the definition of rape is fairly simple. A sexual invasion of the body by force, an incursion into the private, personal inner space without consent—in short, an internal assault from one of several avenues and by one of several methods—constitutes a deliberate violation of emotional, physical and rational integrity and is a hostile, degrading act of violence that deserves the name of rape" (Brownmiller, 1975, p. 376). Researchers have identified several conditions under which rape occurs. Jaffee and Straus (1987) report that sex magazine readership, urbanization, poverty, and a high percentage of divorced men were each significantly associated with the incidence of reported rape. They report that their findings also suggest that rape is a function of social disorganization and hypermasculine gender roles and sexuality. Muehlenhard and Falcon (1990) affirmed this, reporting that the research subjects who accepted traditional gender roles or male sexual dominance were more likely than other subjects to have engaged in both verbal sexual coercion and forceful rape.

Drugs and alcohol create vulnerability to violation, including rape.

FEMALE

I lost my virginity in a not so positive way. At age 17 on Friday, the nineteenth of December, 1983, I cheered at a high school basketball game and afterwards had my first and only date with my best friend's 23-year-old brother. We went out and after drinking some beers I felt exhausted and asked him to take me home. Instead of taking me home by turning left toward my house, he turned right to go to "his place." I ended up sleeping in the car on the way home and when we got there, he woke me up and I made it to his couch and collapsed. This man then carried me into his bedroom. I was so "out of it" I only vaguely remember "it" happening, but I still cringe at the thought. The incident had a great influence on what I believed about how sex is supposed to be. From that incident I got the notion that I really had no say in how I felt in a sexual encounter with a man. It seemed that I was supposed to let him initiate and then go along with it whether I liked it or not. I've just recently—in the last few months—come to terms with what really happened to me that night and how inappropriate my conclusions were.

FEMALE

I married young, and my husband was into heavy drugs, and on two occasions slipped acid into my drinks. It was a bad nightmare! I remember vaguely the fright of the high and what followed. During these two times, I was tied and raped by eight males. My mind left my body during and after the events. There were violent arguments in the marriage and he beat me severely on eight different occasions. I was married to him for three years. At the end, my "Love Bubble" broke and I left. I went for counseling for one and one-half years to straighten it all out for myself.

FEMALE

The most difficult experience for me to talk about was when I was raped at age 22. Actually, I was raped twice but the second one was more date rape. I was drunk and in a blackout so I don't remember the actual event. I remember the shame and disgust I felt the next morning, though. The first rape was really traumatic. I was high on drugs and alcohol but I remember it clearly. When something like that happens, it's like you're instantly stone cold sober. It was a motorcycle club and they had set the whole thing up, but due to my intoxication I didn't realize what was happening. Later this became quite an issue because it was hard not to blame myself for it. I thought if I hadn't been so loaded I would have realized the danger and left the situation. Today I know that what they did was wrong regardless of what mental state I was in. As for myself, I think this was one of the experiences that taught me I can't use alcohol or drugs and still protect myself at the same time. It sure was a painful lesson. I don't know if I have healed completely from that rape; I have done recovery work on it and continue to do so when it comes up. The self-loathing I had after it happened gave way to self-pity and eventually anger (at them and myself). Today when I think of it I just feel incredibly sad.

FEMALE

What happened in the year following seventh grade changed me. That summer I went to a Girl Scout camp as a counselor in training. I was with three other girls who were several years older than I. I was allowed to go because I had been a camper there for five years. During that summer, I smoked my first cigarette, took my first real drink of alcohol (as a child I would sneak sips of my dad's beer and everyone thought it was cute, but this was something very different), and I had what I thought at the time was my first experience with sex. My cohorts talked very highly about sex; how wonderful it was, how adult it felt, and how it brought out the "woman" in you. They were all very impressed with the ranger's son, John. They talked about him as being a prize catch and that "any woman would love to screw him." That dreadful night in July, John brought various bottles of alcoholic beverages to the tent. I drank a lot. I wanted to fit in. I wanted to be "grown up." I wanted to be accepted. John ended up carrying me to the latrine to throw up. He also ended up carrying me to my tent where he informed me that he wouldn't hurt me and then raped me. It hurt. It was not wonderful as I was told that it would be. It was degrading and it was violent. I did not share the same views as my compadres after that experience. After I had passed out, the bottles were put in my foot locker and they were discovered the next day. Three of us were sent home. My parents never asked me what happened. They also failed to notice that I isolated myself for the rest of the summer in my room. They didn't notice that I began writing intense stories about "boy meets girl, they fall in love and he is killed in a gruesome accident." They didn't worry when I woke up in the dark screaming from the nightmares. My sister knew. She heard me cry out for help in my sleep. She told me many times at three o'clock in the morning, "Go back to sleep . . . it'll go away . . . you'll get through it . . . he's not here." I never told her but she knew.

FEMALE

I few times I felt pressured to go home with guys we'd met at the bar. One time, the last time, I did go home with what seemed to be a nice guy. (How do you accurately judge this after six or seven beers?) He wouldn't take no for an answer. He penetrated me without permission. The first penetration of my life. What a fucker! He stripped me of more than my virginity.

> *And women recalled situations of being in a relationship which had some previous bounds that were suddenly and forcefully overthrown, and rape occurred. These incidents illustrate some of the confusing aspects of rape. Is the victim consenting or collaborating? "The victims' collaboration comes about because of the inability to consent or not consent due to their stage of personality or cognitive*

development. The primary person involved, the assailant, stands in a relationship of power over the secondary person, the victim, because of being older, being an authority figure, or for some other reason" (Burgess and Holmstrom, 1974, p. 11). The victims in our excerpts remained silent. Being in a relationship and participating to an extent were probably some of the reasons why the women did not label the experience "rape." "The feeling persists that a virtuous woman either cannot get raped or does not get into situations that leave her open to assault" (Brownmiller, 1975, p. 386). Part of the confusion about what constitutes rape "is the underlying cultural assumption that it is the natural masculine role to proceed aggressively toward the stated goal, while the natural feminine role is to resist or submit" (Brownmiller, 1975, p. 386). The complex interplay of participating, enjoying it, being coerced, resisting, and finally forced to submit is confusing to the victim. Feelings of fear, hate, and anger remain within the victim as testimony to the violence.

Sexuality education should be about "learning about how to live together, respectfully, with other human beings; how to understand our thoughts, feelings, and fantasies; and how to make informed choices about which behaviors are appropriate and which are not. The principle around which this question should revolve is that of nonexploitation—what it means and how we must apply it in everyday living. This is the essence of morality" (Hacker, 1990 p. 7).

FEMALE

When my body started to develop, one of my male cousins, who was several years older, started to take notice of the changes and took advantage of my family often being at his home. I don't know how it really started, but soon he began making advances to which I was receptive. Maybe that was because I never got much attention from anyone. At first he wasn't bold. He primarily focused on my budding breasts for satisfaction, but eventually he explored farther. At the same time the son of one of my parents' friends started making advances. I didn't really mind as I didn't know the potential danger in it. At one point he explained to me how a girl gets pregnant in very general terms, such as you put this (penis) down there some place. He said he wouldn't try that but eventually he did try a little. My experiences with him lasted a little longer than with my cousin for that reason. One night my cousin tried to penetrate me. That infuriated me because it was primarily by force and I wasn't exactly sure of what was going on, except that I knew I didn't want to do it. When I said no, he threatened to tell my parents, so I went along with it. I didn't want my parents to know that I had done anything like that. Had I been wiser, I would have said, "Go ahead," because then I think he would have left me alone. Looking back, I am almost positive he wouldn't have told because it would have gotten him in more trouble than me. And even if I had said something about it, I still might have been better off because then perhaps my mother would have been compelled to tell me about sex and the facts of life.

Courtois (1988) describes shame in relation to the victim of incest: "A significant number of incestuously abused children come to believe that something about them, something inherently wrong with them, caused the incest to occur. These beliefs, coupled with guilt and anxiety, result in a shamed sense of self—that the self is unlovable, deserving of abuse, and unworthy of care and good attention" (p. 217). This self-hate is experienced by most victims of sexual abuse.

FEMALE

Eighteen years ago, something happened that I have only just begun to remember. Last fall I attended a five-day conference and began reading a book on shame. About halfway through the book, an old memory came back in the form of an image of being raped the summer after my freshman year of college. I began to recall in detail the events of the rape and the feelings I had surrounding it. I remembered blaming myself because I had not resisted. I had believed it was obvious to my assailant that I had been sexually active (one time only), and this was the consequence for doing wrong. I even remember thinking through the possibility of becoming pregnant and decided that if I did not say anything that my parents would assume that I was having sex with a boyfriend and that I would allow them those assumptions. I had been at a beach party and walked into the woods to urinate. A man followed and raped me. I did exactly as I was told. It was totally dark and I did not recognize the person. I assumed the blame for the entire incident and did not tell anyone. I have kept it locked inside, hidden even from my awareness all these years. Now I wonder if there are other secrets that might unexpectedly reveal themselves to me.

FEMALE

At 14, I was walking down the street and was abducted by three older males in a car. They took me for a ride and they made me perform oral sex and raped me. I didn't know them or what to do. The incident left me ashamed, uncertain, and frightened. I also kind of liked it too, which really worried me.

Rape makes a first-hand impact on the victim's friends.

FEMALE

I just found out that one of my friends was raped recently; the trial still hasn't come up yet. What good can it possibly do to prolong her agony by keeping a trial date off in the future, always keeping her from forgetting, always reminding her. Besides that, they'll try to make her out a whore—some justice! She was raped by three guys, not of her own race. Rationally I know they aren't representative of their race, but emotionally I'm afraid of them even now.

Exploitation: Our culture says it is OK for men to use prostitutes. A first experience with a prostitute proved confusing. Does this cultural norm set up exploitation of both?

MALE

Having four sisters and knowing the "lust of mankind," I decided that I would only do with a female what would be OK for someone to do with my sisters. When I graduated from high school, I got a job. I was ready, young, hungry, and eager. On my eighteenth birthday, I decided to have my first sexual experience—with a prostitute. I went down to the district and approached the young lady with confidence. We went up to the apartment and she had me drop my pants and shorts. First, she washed my penis, then she started sucking for an erection. I did not get a solid erection. Since it appeared the sucking was not working, my hostess decided to mount what there was and jumped up and down, said, "That's it—good-bye." Talk about a confused male! I didn't know what had happened, it seemed so fast and empty.

Exploitation can occur between persons in what appears to be a good relationship. "It is precisely when men and women conform to traditional roles most rigidly that abuse is most likely to occur" (Steinem, 1992, p. 259).

FEMALE

I have only one negative experience during my sexually active past years. Ironically it happened just short of a year ago. My ex-boyfriend and I occasionally saw each other when I visited home and sometimes things went further than they should have. It was obvious (not to me then) he wanted only one thing when we saw one another. I saw it as hope that we might get back together and hope that he still cared. So I played his games. One night his game was going too far. I repeatedly said "no" and asked him to stop, but I used to do that before and it often meant he could keep going and I would eventually give in. He knew that and kept trying. I knew where I wanted to stop that night but could not convince him of that. He began to get physical. He was already intoxicated and upset at my refusals. This went on for about 15 minutes, him fighting me and me fighting him. I finally was able to get up and demand that he leave. I don't believe it was date rape but perhaps sexual harassment. Maybe both. Whatever it was, I knew it hurt, both physically and mentally. I drove around, crying, for hours. I kept asking myself what I could have done differently do prevent what happened. I blamed myself. I thought of how terrible I was to have let that happen to me. Now I know those are typical thoughts for a woman in this situation. I'd always believed I had control over my body and myself and when something got out of control the fault would be mine. I thought the guilt, too, should be mine. I do not view him as a "bad" person. I know I have nothing to fear. I also know it will never happen again with him. He was in the wrong, not I. I neither allowed nor provoked it. I may have accepted his kisses but when I said no to something that pertained to my body he should have respected my wishes. I feel confident believing in this now.

"In the confusion of adolescence, in the chase of young adulthood, the sexes were often set up to persist and to resist. Many young men were taught that 'no' means 'try again.' Many young women were allowed to excuse their sexuality only when they were 'swept away'" (Pellaver, Chester, and Boyajian, 1987).

This is the chase from one man's point of view.

MALE

With the advent of the pill, the miniskirt, and liberated women I decided to try a little experiment. I would try to seduce girls on our first date. It worked so well that if they didn't put out the first time I didn't give them a second chance. Only two fell by the wayside. One was a virgin who wanted to save it for her husband. The other was one of the, "Well you don't expect me to make it with you on the first date, do you?" type of girl.

Research has detailed long-term consequences of experiences of sexual exploitation: a steady, significant and progressive increase in maladjustment from the nonabused through the nonincestuously sexually abused to the incest victims (Parker and Parker, 1991). Results from another study indicate that childhood sexual assault victims could be distinguished from nonvictims by a pattern of elevated anxiety, heightened interpersonal sensitivity, increased anger problems, more paranoid ideation, and increased obsessive-compulsive symptoms. The age at which the sexual assault took place was related to current adult functioning: Victims assaulted in adolescence displayed more elevations in hostility, interpersonal sensitivity, obsessive-compulsivity, anxiety, and paranoid ideation than nonvictims. Victims assaulted in early childhood displayed only elevated anxiety symptoms as adults (Finkelhor et al., 1989). Those who were victims of childhood sexual abuse involving penetration were more likely than others to report a disrupted marriage, dissatisfaction in their sexual relationship, and a tendency to be a religious nonpractitioner (Murphy and Kilpatrick, 1988).

Reports of the above were reported in the "Who Am I Sexually?" papers. Women recalled feelings recurring long after the event. Women writing about their early childhood sexual memories recalled both isolated and repeated episodes of abuse.

FEMALE

In October of my freshman year I lost my virginity. I was not drunk. I had spent Thursday night in the dorm, studying for a chemistry exam. My roommates had gone to the bar. They brought home three guys. One for each of them, and one for me. Shit. It was simple. He and I were left alone. He approached me. Smelled like alcohol and smoke. Began feeling my shoulders, and kissing my mouth, moving down my neck. I was getting sick. I asked him repeatedly to stop. He did not stop. He became more aggressive. I said no a thousand times. He didn't listen. He won. Twice. I felt dirty, ashamed, and guilty. He slept (passed out) in my bed. I took a long shower. Then I spent the rest of the night on the couch, with my chem book open, and a box of kleenex. I was hurt, and I hated myself. I never told my roommates. How could I tell them? They had brought this guy home for me, though I never asked. The great charade began the day after. I gained weight, drank more (every day—if not more), and felt like shit. Maybe I had experienced all sex had to offer but I decided that maybe I was just inexperienced and needed to look for good, fun, enjoyable sex. I prepared for the next bar date and the next, etc. I became promiscuous and had sex with different guys, in different situations, at my and his request. The chase and challenge was more fun than sex. I hated the sex. My promiscuous behavior lasted for two years. Then I found a boyfriend and he liked my dirty talk and my chasing. We had fun. One night, he had drank a fifth of Tequila and mixed a couple different drugs. We planned on having a great weekend. My roommates were not home. He became violent, physically attacking me, and demanding me to have sex with him. I refused. He did not accept. He won. And I lost. I lost my courage, the temptation of the challenge, the desire to chase, and the need to understand sex. A possible pregnancy, a couple of STDs and a confused sexuality sent me into a dungeon. I went through a severe depression. I vowed to myself, I would never have sex again because I was not going to go through the torment, the pain, or the shame again. I was tired. For months I denied my sexuality completely. I was depressed, and did not care about anything or anyone.

FEMALE

I got into a serious relationship that ended two months ago. It lasted one year and four months. I honestly thought we would get married even though it was not all that wonderful for the last five months. He was never pushy, rude, or anything else. He was very caring. But things got rough last fall. I was raped by a guy I didn't know. My boyfriend stood by me but it was not that easy on him. I was angry, afraid, paranoid, and generally emotionally screwed up. One minute I laughed, the next I cried. I felt dirty and had no self-esteem. I hated men—literally. At first I would not even let him touch me. It was awful. He was my main support. He reassured me that it wasn't my fault. He comforted me when I had nightmares. He told me I wasn't dirty. I was moody and withdrawn and I hated me. It was really hard on him. I was insecure and accused him even more than before that he was cheating on me. He was tired of the distrust and we broke up. Later I found out that all my suspicions were true even before the attack. He was unfaithful. Talk about a distrust for the male species. Counseling helped me with that a lot and still is. He was a jerk but at least he helped me through one of the hardest times of my life. Now I'm dating a few guys but allowing nothing to go on. Smart finally! AIDS is scary, I still am distrustful a little, and my life is too important. What does all of this say about me? A lot! I've grown up a tremendous amount over the past few years. Gullible no longer, and realistic about life. My childhood beliefs were too idealistic. Life is not that way.

Victims of sexual exploitation suffer. It is most helpful for victims to talk through their experiences soon after the event(s) with someone who understands and is supportive. If the initial sharing is experienced as nonsupportive and/or judgmental or if the victim is unable to talk about the experience at all, there may be a decidedly negative impact. Then, talking with someone competent can help them to shed the often reported long-term consequences of such experience: the heavy feelings of guilt, fear, confusion, and/or helplessness. Many victims of child sexual abuse find help through therapy.

FEMALE

I remember enduring lots of enemas when I was little. When Mother and Dad forced their way into me, yelling at me not to be such a baby and to hold the water longer, I went somewhere else. Several weeks ago in therapy, I revisited that place and reexperienced the feeling of getting out of my body. There was a little girl where I went, she was around five, holding a doll and a blanket, with her thumb in her mouth, calmly telling me it was okay and not to be afraid. The feeling of being taken care of was overwhelming; it just washed over me. That little girl also frightens me. She's only there when I'm at my limit of pain and desperation. So when I connect with her it means I'm in major trouble. Something else I've discovered through what I've written is a pattern of entanglement with pain, pleasure, and intimacy. When I reexperienced the abuse, I also connected with some pleasurable, sexual feelings I had. What a mixed message for a little girl. Invading my body, inflicting pain, and telling me it was for my own good. And from these otherwise distant, cold parents came attention and intimate touching. I finally got attention but I had to hurt in order to get it.

FEMALE

My attack brought a whole new reality into my life. It was definitely the most terrifying night of my life. I can think of nothing worse. Even the emergency procedures were humiliating, making me feel like a criminal not a victim. It has affected all aspects of my life. School has been hit the worst. I'm scared to be here at the university. My grades have fallen, and I miss a lot of classes because I go home on a whim because of my breakdowns. Counseling is helping a lot. It is a necessity.

FEMALE

At 19 I went away to college. That first year at school I was raped by an acquaintance I'd just met. I went to the hospital to make sure I didn't catch anything and that I wasn't pregnant. I was lucky that I was okay. After that day I didn't think about the experience until a few years later. I didn't even think of myself as being raped. Two years later I was raped again. This time it was by a stranger by the roadside after having a flat tire. He told me he was going to kill me. This experience had a great impact on my life. I moved back home to be close to my family but I didn't tell them what happened. We *don't talk* about those things. I experienced a lot of anger toward my family because I couldn't tell them. The next semester I went back to school. However, I denied my feelings to myself and everyone. I was afraid of men and afraid of sex but I didn't want to admit it. I slept around a lot because I didn't care about myself and I wanted to prove to myself that I wasn't scared. Then one day I was sitting in a health education class listening to my professor talking about date rape. To me he seemed to be talking to the women in class. He was telling us that it was okay to say no. It seemed patronizing to me. He did not put as strong of an emphasis on the males' part in it. After all, the men are the ones that should curb their behavior and not force their dates against their will. It really made me angry. I didn't know what to do about it. I decided that maybe I should go to counseling. I got counseling at the counseling center and joined a support group for sexual assault survivors. I've graduated from the group and have started to get into relationships with men again. I still get counseling and I still have trouble beginning relationships with men but it's getting better . . .

In conclusion, although abuse injures a victim, that victim can become a survivor. The sooner the survivor can tell her story, the sooner the healing will begin. The pain and degradation of the trauma can be resolved. "As you heal, you see yourself more realistically. You accept that you are a person with strengths and weaknesses. You make the changes you can in your life and let go of things that aren't in your power to change. You learn that all of your thoughts and feelings are important, even when they're painful or difficult" (Bass and Davis, 1993, p. 68).

SUGGESTED ISSUES FOR PERSONAL REFLECTION, GROUP DISCUSSION AND INTERACTION, PERSONAL JOURNAL

1. Do you have any memories of being sexually exploited as a child?
   a. What feelings did you have *then* about the experience?
   b. What feelings do you have now about the experience?
   c. What kinds of changes in your behavior did you notice at the time of your experience?
   d. Were you able to discuss the experience with anyone? If not, what made that difficult for you? What would have made it easier?

Note: The questions in 1 are for your personal use. You will not be expected to share them.

2. What are your own personal guidelines for determining if a child has been sexually exploited, or has been involved in a "normal" experience which is part of growing up?
3. What roles should be played by family, schools, community, concerned adults, and lawmakers to decrease the likelihood of any individual experiencing sexual exploitation?
4. What are some helpful responses from parents?
   a. How can parents be sensitive to the child's feelings about the experience and not make the incident worst for the child?
   b. Where and how do parents deal with their own feelings of rage, powerlessness, and guilt at not protecting their child?
   c. How can parents open doors for children to talk?
   d. How can parents teach a child what is appropriate affection and what is "sexual?"

Chapter
12

Sexuality and Personal Values: Drifting, Rebelling, Acquiescing, or Deciding

INTRODUCTION

*I*n 1966 Ira Reiss reviewed what he called "the sexual renaissance" of that era, and made some predictions for trends in the future. There was not then much research evidence that sexual *behaviors* had changed appreciably over the previous 25 to 50 years. What had changed were *attitudes,* especially toward premarital coitus. He suggested that behaviors usually precede attitudinal acceptance, rather than the other way around. The pluralistic ignorance (privacy and secrecy) which has surrounded human sexuality kept people unaware of the changes in behaviors until the advent of the sex research movement, which made public the fact that many proscribed sexual behaviors were more widespread than previously believed. Attitudes then began to change in the direction of acceptance.

Reiss suggested that in the late 1960s the attitudes in this culture had approximately caught up with behavior, and so we might expect another upward cycle of increasing sexual behavior and sexual acceptance. Assessing future trends, Reiss predicted:

> We are headed in an increasingly permissive direction, but one in which sexual permissiveness is strongly linked with affection. . . . There are many key structural features of American society that will continue to provide pressure toward premarital permissiveness. Our emphasis on love is certainly one such feature. If love is stressed as crucial to marriage and as an essential ingredient in a happy life, then it is likely that people in love feel justified in taking sexual liberties; when love is so valuable, it justifies many things. Our free, participant-run courtship system . . . also encourages permissiveness, by allowing young people access to each other in a myriad of ways. The

respectability of choice, and stress on diversity and tolerance, also encourage permissiveness. . . .

Persons who say they like the emphasis on love, the free dating system and the allowance of choice in sexual standards are at times the same people who decry the increased permissiveness which the factors they favor promote! . . . I doubt if such people would be moved to change these causal factors, for they are valued highly. The choice then would be to maintain the inconsistency, or to become more acceptant of the increased permissiveness. . . . (Reiss, 1966).

Students writing in this chapter about their struggles with moral and value issues and with sexual decision making demonstrate many of the predicted trends: There is a continuing struggle about virginity, which is frequently resolved in favor of coital activity if affection or commitment is present; a strong emphasis is placed on the quality of relationship and the expectation of love, rather than on the norm of virginity.

Research that was carried out in the two decades following Reiss's predictions also seems to corroborate his thesis. The pattern of coitus with commitment emerged in research. Researchers found that women's reports of frequency of intercourse approached the frequency reported by men. This research finding was confirmed for high school as well as college students.

In a review of the research on the relationship of sexuality education and contraceptive availability to teen pregnancy prevention, the data showed that these factors have helped limit or reduce teen pregnancy rates (Scales, 1987). However, the focus in our society with regard to teenagers continues to be on stopping their sexual activity, rather than focusing on what is now clearly known about making sexual activity relatively safe (with regard to pregnancy and sexually transmitted diseases). Scales concludes that the current societal debate is about teen sexual activity rather than teen pregnancy.

Traditionally, the sexual behavior of older adolescents has been the target for concern and education. However, the focus needs to shift to younger adolescents (10 to 15 years of age) so they have a chance to make informed decisions. This is especially important since there are currently no generally accepted societal norms that guide adolescents' sexual behaviors. The availability of alcohol and drugs makes the increased sexual behaviors at younger ages of special concern.

Education must include not only the biological facts about sexuality, but also important information about interpersonal communication and health concerns as well as the emotions surrounding sexual activity, and the emotions during it. Other factors important to teaching wise decision making include the availability of knowledgeable and trustworthy adults for the teens to consult with and, where possible, a health care setting where adolescents could easily seek information and treatment. Adolescents need a basis for making informed, deliberate decisions rather than ignorant, impulsive ones about matters that have large, lifelong consequences (Hamburg, 1993). In a study done in Baltimore, a clinic was established close to the junior high schools involved, and was staffed by social workers and nurse practitioners who were available through both school and clinic. "Education, counseling, and medical services, including the dispensing of contraceptives, were available to all students on a confidential basis. The program resulted in increased contraceptive use for all who used the clinic compared with those who did not. Knowledge of contraceptives and of the risks for pregnancy went up 13 percent; . . . Rates of pregnancy and childbirth were reduced; . . . In less than three years of the program's operation, the proportion of sexually active ninth- to twelfth-grade girls who had babies was down 25 percent. In addition, girls became sexually active at a later age after being exposed to the program" (Price et al., 1993, p. 48).

Sylvia Hacker (1990) has offered a proposal for new sexual norms:

> With our former restrictive, strictly procreative, sexual norms eroded, controls on sexual intercourse are currently severely weakened. Not yet having consistent guidelines on how to handle sexuality responsibly, we remain tenaciously tied to the old morality or norm that "sex" equals sexual intercourse only . . . We should broaden our views and focus on pleasuring with or without intercourse as a path to caring, respectful behavior between genders. . . . Teenagers . . . do not accept themselves as sexual beings and so do not plan for intercourse—this would be akin to "planning for sin." In addition, our lingering (albeit largely subconscious) sex-for-procreation attitudes continue to devalue other forms of sexual behaviors. Pleasuring is still suspect! Therefore, engaging in alternatives to sexual intercourse, simply for pleasuring per se, is still thought of only as preliminary foreplay to the "real thing."
>
> . . . The new norm that I suggest may be conceptualized as follows: *SEXUALITY IS GOOD. UNWANTED PARENTHOOD IS BAD.* (pp. 1–4)

Our sexuality is an inextricable part of our identity. If we learn to celebrate it as something beautiful, pleasurable, and treasured, rather than as something dirty and shameful, we will not allow it to be harmed or used; rather, we will be positively disposed and motivated toward protecting such a wonderful gift. The second half of the norm, which states that unwanted parenthood is bad, does not say unwanted pregnancy is bad; often an unintended pregnancy can be resolved positively. However, the psychological damage wrought to both parents and children from unwanted parenthood is profound (David, 1986). There are three major premises encompassed by the proposed new norm:

1. Sexuality is far more than sexual intercourse.
2. Children and older people are sexual.
3. Thoughts, feelings, and fantasies normally occur. Our focus should be on the behaviors that must be monitored, disciplined, or changed.

Deciding for oneself who one is sexually, how one will relate to the same and other gender, what specific sexual activities are on limits and off limits, when one expresses oneself sexually and why, is a lifelong process. But decision making and choices about personal values and lifestyle are especially crucial in late adolescence and early maturity (Gagnon, 1977). The feelings, experiences and influences related to sexuality during childhood converge with maturing physiology, increasing privacy, independence, and opportunity for new and diverse relationships. Conflict results—internally and externally. Intentional decisions about values and attitudes become urgent, and confusion increases. Old guidelines are challenged.

MALE

In college I underwent a change in my views. During my freshman year I started petting on dates and developed a new view of sexual intercourse. I decided sex was a good, natural, and beautiful drive in people, and that there was no need to suppress this urge or wait till marriage. But, to my surprise, I found that my new ideas did not make me able to act in a new way. Even though I believed this genuinely, I simply could not allow myself to have sexual intercourse. I felt hypocritical and confused, and ended up staying safe by snubbing any girl I was attracted to, thereby putting some distance between us. Or—maybe this was my way of making sure I didn't get hurt by a girl.

FEMALE

My third high school relationship began in the final months of my senior year and lasted two years. Things started slowly, but intercourse soon became a part of our relationship. I was in love with him so that helped me see it as something closer to right than wrong. Guilt feelings were still there determining where we had sex, how often, and in what manner. My mind worked very traditionally, yet I allowed my body to go along with his desires. I decided that if I thought having sex was not okay—if I thought it wrong while I was involved in it, then it was not so bad or wrong. If I were to have thought sex was good then I would be a bad person. Therefore, I could never say yes or initiate sex because that would have meant I wanted sex. So, though I always said no, my partner could always persuade me.

I became more aware and afraid of the long-term consequences that could come with having sex, so we almost always used condoms. Half way into our relationship, when I turned 18, I decided to go on birth control pills. I did this on my own. My parents never knew nor did my sisters. I think I would have shattered an illusion they all had of me as an upright Catholic young lady. I did not even tell my boyfriend till some time later, for fear that sex would then be abused.

I tried very hard to come to terms with myself sexually during this relationship. We were very close and it was a nice feeling to believe in the love I was giving and receiving. I think in my relationships it was important to me that I felt love for the person in order to feel there was a reason why we were having sex.

FEMALE

I spent eight years in a religious school, and I was thoroughly indoctrinated with the church's values on sex and sexuality. All the way through high school, I took virginity and not touching another human being as a cardinal rule without really thinking it through or considering myself, my happiness, and especially my needs. I learned to repress my physical feelings as if they weren't there. I also got so I repressed my emotions too.

FEMALE

My first high school boyfriend was like a dream come true. He was a year older yet I was his first girlfriend. My parents seemed to like or at least accept him and our relationship. We learned about our sexuality together; we were deeply involved and our feelings for each other also ran deep. However, I still felt guilty and had trouble dealing with my religious beliefs.

FEMALE

My parents, like most parents, I suppose, have certain prejudices against sexual attitudes and practices different from their own. We were taught that homosexuals are sick and bad for society, and that any kind of oral sex is perverted. I believed these things for quite a while during my teens. After I learned that my parents weren't perfect, but were human like everyone else, I started to think that these attitudes toward sex weren't so perfect either. Except for these, however, my values now are quite a lot like those of my parents.

Experience often changes perceptions.

FEMALE

After going together for about a year and a half, I decided I couldn't receive all the pleasure while poor Dan was dying for some touching too. Until that time, guys' bodies had always grossed me out. But I learned with Dan to touch him—and that was partly because he never pushed me into doing anything I didn't want to do. We really got to love one another's bodies and used to delight in lying naked on a bed and just holding each other.

FEMALE

I remember learning about french kissing. A girlfriend's older sister told her what it was, and she told the rest of us. I thought the idea of sticking my tongue in a guy's mouth and his doing the same in return was the most repulsive way of kissing there could possibly be. Somehow, once I got older and began to date it wasn't so repulsive after all. Funny, isn't it, how our ideas change from one extreme to another within a few years!

Students wrote about the influence of parenting (functional and dysfunctional) on their values.

FEMALE

I had only one date in high school and it was a disaster. I am not really even sure how he did it, but my father made me feel cheap and dirty because he saw the boy put his arm around me. I still feel bad about the boy. He never understood what happened and since I really could not verbalize it either, I'm sure we both lost a lot of confidence. After that it was easier not to date and wait until I got away from home and in college. I remember one weekend when my father was taking me back to school. He informed me that if I got pregnant he would protect me, but kill the guy. Now that was really not a comforting thought since all I had done was kiss up to that point.

FEMALE

I think what amazes me the most is that my values have really remained unchanged since childhood. The most important things to me are honesty, loyalty, caring and accepting people on an individual basis. My feelings about sexuality are probably the healthiest thing about me right now and that is because my parents stayed out of that aspect of my life. Almost everything about me is a contradiction to the way I was raised. I only know that although I've experience a lot of pain in my life, I am glad I am who I am. It has taken a long time to be able to say that and mean it.

FEMALE

My mom said that a boy would keep his hands to himself if he really loved and respected me. She also said good girls say no. Good girls weren't even supposed to like sex. I kept remembering Dad's girly magazines I had seen years before. I wanted to be sexual. I did not want to be a good girl any more. I wanted men to be attracted to me.

Rethinking old guidelines for behavior does not resolve sexual decision making. Parental or religious pressures are often replaced by peer and partner pressure.

FEMALE

Coming to college I began to question my values. I learned a lot through my experiences and I began to doubt the importance of my virginity. But the other side in me was saying "Wait until you find a relationship that includes love before you have intercourse" (this value coming from one of my sisters). I think every time I felt myself getting deeply involved, I would break off our relationship because I just wasn't ready emotionally to handle intercourse. Winter term both my roommates had the same intention—to rid me of my virginity. I'll admit it was a close call but they didn't win the war! They did confuse my head, though.

FEMALE

My father instilled his sexual attitudes in my sisters and me at a very early age. They were that any woman who had sex before marriage was a whore. But it was acceptable for men to have sex before marriage. I never had to question that double standard until I came to college. I met a guy during my freshman year who I cared for a lot. He started pressing me to have sex and I started to talk to him about it and how I felt. He laughed and told me not many people believed like my father did anymore. After three months and much coaxing, I finally agreed to have intercourse in order to please him. I did not want it for any other reasons. As a result of giving in before I was ready, I felt guilty about our relationship for about a year, and never enjoyed sex.

Peer pressure does not always push toward a "liberal" value position.

FEMALE

After we had been going out for about a year and I felt that I really loved him, I decided it would be okay to sleep together because of my love and because we would probably be getting married. We had sex. It was the first time for both of us. I felt really happy about our decision. We were both scared. We were so scared that he used two condoms! The next day I was so happy. He and I were talking about it. He asked me if I went to confession. I was so hurt. He felt that we had sinned. I said, "No, I didn't." I thought it was right. Our relationship wasn't too stable after that. It was hard for me to understand how he could think just like my mother. I did not believe that sex was something evil.

FEMALE

I was in a small discussion group in a class where we talked quite openly about many things. I felt that because I was "liberal" in one respect (living with a guy), the people in the group took too many things for granted. They generalized that I was liberal in every other sphere of values, almost to the point of not having any. I remember coming home once thinking, "Wow! Am I really that much more lacking in strong values than the rest of them?" My reaction was foolish, but the encounter helped me realize I do know where I am and what I value.

Males sometimes act out "macho" attitudes.

FEMALE

Steve continually pressured me for sex and I would often cry and feel worthless about myself. A few months of that and I got out. After that experience, I decided to just "date" different guys without getting serious. This is almost impossible to do on a college campus. Guys, at least the ones I dated, always wanted more. When they pressured me for sex, I would get out and go onto something new.

MALE

My adolescent years were filled with peer pressure to conform to the then popular motto, "Enjoy sex now and until you die." With no direct prohibitions and willing partners, I began at age 15 to have intercourse on a regular basis. Of course, these activities were very pleasant and they gave me a sense of authority, manhood, and self-respect. I could care less if the female was enjoying the act; all I cared about was my pleasure. Soon I was having upwards of seven sexual encounters a week with various girls. Boy, I thought I had it made! But then emotional pain, abortions, and the such began to happen during my freshman year at college. Along with that, I began to realize that I wasn't enjoying it as I once did. I began to feel worthless, manipulative and selfish, but continued the behavior. I guess I was somewhat addicted to sexual pleasure. I couldn't resist my sexual urges. I had to have sex even though I knew of the pain I was causing women who trusted me.

Sometimes pressure comes from a partner in the form of emotional blackmail or a threat regarding the relationship.

FEMALE

As time went on, I began to feel pressured into having sexual intercourse. Jerald would push me by saying things like, "You must not really love me if you don't want to be close to me." I (like a fool) would give in because it was easier than fighting about it—which would always happen when I refused. Sex for me was "okay" but not fantastic. When I was pushed into it, however, I felt like crying.

FEMALE

My second high school boyfriend still makes me cringe. Though a year younger than I, he was quite "experienced." I never had any sexual feelings for him but I liked him because he was fun, funny, and spontaneous. But, he always used sex for power or control. It was always, "You would if you loved me" or he would threaten to break up. He never really gained my parents' approval because he was afraid of them and never took time to try and get to know them. We always went to his house and spent time with his family. This upset me, but it didn't change anything. He didn't seem to consider my feelings at all. He would cheat on me but not allow me to even talk with my male friends. During all of this, I didn't feel I had anyone to turn to. The last years of high school should have been great but for me they were full of frustration and tension. Sex was all he wanted and all I wanted was someone to do things with, a buddy. I began cheating on him and doubting my worth. I didn't think I'd ever be capable of having a good, strong relationship. Because our school was so small, there weren't a whole lot of guys to choose from. Plus, I figured that if the girls he cheated with thought he was OK, it must just be me. Sex was just something that prevented arguments and it only took him five minutes. I always pictured myself someplace else and so my feelings were never involved. My good friends would tell me to break up, but then I would have been alone and at that point I didn't have any self-confidence and thought I couldn't manage that.

FEMALE

I had a number of boyfriends, but Darryl was direct and right to the point about sex. Right from the start he told me that the only way our relationship could last was if we had intercourse. At the same time, though, he said that even if we did, our relationship would not last long. Under these circumstances, I didn't see how he could expect me to live up to what he wanted me to do. . . . but he had a knack for making me do things which I wasn't really sure I wanted to do. He used to come and visit me at school, and he would tell me that when he went back, he slept with someone else every other night. If he had someone else every other night, I figured he really didn't need me. Maybe that was a "copout," but he meant more to me than I did to him, and I really couldn't handle that. However, there were still many times when I felt that I really wanted to give in to him.

Some males, more interested in intercourse than the relationship, carry through on the threats.

FEMALE

About a week ago I met a real nice guy at a meeting. We talked some, then went our own ways. A few days later I saw him again and he asked me out. We went out, had a great time, and later went back to his room. We necked, but he was quite upset with me. He couldn't understand why I was still a virgin, and also he couldn't understand my not wanting him to touch my breasts that night. "Why?" he asked. He said there aren't too many girls like me left, and someday I'd be really sorry because of all the good times I had missed. (I believe a psychological relationship must grow and then a physical one will also grow in time.) During the course of the evening, he asked me out for the next night—to go dancing. I stayed a little while longer, then left anxious to see him the next day. I waited the next day and night, and he stood me up. He never called or came over. What was I to think? Because I refused to let him touch me, he decided not to see me again. I wanted him to call, but because we had only kissed passionately and nothing more, he wouldn't.

Sometimes students reported being influenced by what they thought was expected of them; "everybody is (nobody is) doing it."

FEMALE

I had a great time in high school. I was always popular, more so with the boys than the girls. I was involved in most of the activities and most of the positions that were filled by females: class president, student council representative, student librarian, in-class plays, on the homecoming court, and on the cheerleader squad. I began to feel I was quite attractive, having dates with many different guys. I loved every minute of it, but after a while I got so tired of fighting these guys off sexually! In those days, it wasn't as common as it is today to be having sexual relations, or so I thought. I was still quite young and naive. I would wait until the second date before having sexual relations with someone. That way I felt I could tell if a guy was dating me because of my personality or because of sex.

FEMALE

It has been a hard transition for me, going from marriage to the life of a single person again. Especially because I feel things are very different now than when I got married. I stepped into the dating game thinking all dates ended up in bed. I've been able to swing back a little now. I've decided there still is a place for me to be a little old-fashioned, and there may still be guys around who feel the same way.

A few women felt pressure because life was passing them by.

FEMALE

In college I met a man that I eventually married. He and I started having sex about three months after we began dating. I felt guilty about having sex with him because we were not married and yet I really wanted to see what sex was all about. It was not very pleasurable and as I look back I recognize that I was having sex for all of the wrong reasons. It was not because I was extremely attracted to this man but because I felt that life was passing me by. He was the sexual aggressor and I the participant. I married him because I wanted to get away from my parents' home and because I was feeling very old at the age of 22. I felt that I needed to be out creating a life of my own. It is sad that I felt I needed to be married to do that.

Needless to say our love life was never very good. Sex with him was boring and afterwards I would lie there feeling dirty and used, wondering what the big deal was. I think I also felt guilty because we had had sex before we were married and I began to resent that fact. I felt he had forced me to have sex.

The depth of one's convictions and feelings may be tested by a painful experience; the attempt to take on new values may prove to be difficult.

FEMALE

I went through a stage where I could accept premarital sex for others, but not for myself. I felt that intercourse was a total giving of mind, body, and soul. That's a big risk—to give all and then have somebody take off the next day. But I began to question my belief; I talked to others, and finally decided that there was no reason why I couldn't involve myself in a temporary sexual relationship and come out unscathed. Then it happened. I had known the man for some time as a friend; then our relationship became sexual. It was a good thing as long as it lasted, but when he left my life, I was in shreds. All of my intellectual coping went to hell and I was an emotional wreck. I decided then that I'd wait until I was sure it would last before I gave up such a large part of my heart.

Deciding rather than drifting or being pushed (from internal values or external pressure) is also accompanied by many conflicts. One of the major conflicts mentioned was between the physical urgency experienced, and the values one has chosen or inherited.

FEMALE

College has been a time when I have gotten in touch with my body. I am no longer afraid to experience the various parts of my body and find pleasure in being "in touch" with myself. I have played around with men, but always without intercourse. I feel very strongly about not having intercourse, but on occasion, find it very tempting. I don't enjoy oral sex, and I want to satisfy my partner. These two values have collided with my no-intercourse stand. I have become very confused, and sometimes temptation seems greater than self-control. It's like I am playing a game: Can I hold out?

FEMALE

My parents were very strict about dating in high school, and had a million religious reasons and Bible quotes to support all their warnings. When I was a sophomore, I started dating Jock, the "king" of the senior class. Keeping in mind my parents' warnings, I really tried to suppress any sexual activity. But slowly things began to get out of hand, and within a year we had made a commitment and were having intercourse. It was a time of tension because my parents caught me in several lies. But my desires won over my guilt and I felt my sexual relationship with Jock was just about the most important thing in the world. I justified my sexual activity because "I was in love." After he went to college, I began casually dating a guy who was still in high school. Because I was still committed to Jock, I would not allow my relationship with the other guy to be more than casual. Not once in two years did he ever give me a hard time. I really respected him for that. Now I wonder if perhaps he loved or respected me more than Jock did because he held back his desires at my asking. I suppose that kind of respect is outdated and that kind of guy is in a fast-fading minority. Too bad!

MALE

I didn't go out with girls until the summer following my high school graduation. Then it was with only one. We went together for a little over two years, and our relationship developed to the point where we were having intercourse. We used rhythm for birth control, and she never got pregnant. I guess we were awful lucky! It was the sexual relationship which eventually broke us up. We wanted to stop, but were unable to, so we split up. That was two years ago this February, and since then I have not even kissed more than a couple of girls. I am afraid to make any kind of sexual move because I don't want to frighten them away, and I don't know whether my experience with my old girlfriend will be repeated.

MALE

My attitude toward sex now is somewhat confused. On one hand, I recognize that girls are persons and not just things. I don't want to have intercourse with a girl if she is going to be hurt by the experience, or if she feels that I am misleading her. I always try to be as honest as I can, and I don't really put lines on girls just to get them to go to bed. On the other hand, I have a strong sex drive and struggle with the dilemma of wanting to use girls to satisfy it. But not wanting to use them as sexual objects only. I also want to avoid getting into a relationship which I can't get out of, or one that leads to the girl getting pregnant.

Another conflict, both with others and with oneself, has to do with the question of when sexual intercourse is appropriate.

MALE

At one time I saw intercourse as a way to prove myself sexually. Now, I feel comfortable with my ability to perform sexually. So my remaining struggle is to establish criteria for helping me decide when sexual expression is harmful to the persons involved, even though it may be pleasurable.

FEMALE

I started dating at the end of my junior year in high school. By my senior year I was "in love" for the first time. We went together for about ten months. But there was a certain point in petting that I wouldn't (couldn't?) go beyond, and at the end of my senior year we broke up. The next major person lasted one and one-half years with still a resistance on my part to engage in complete sexual intercourse. All during this time (senior year in high school and my first one and one-half years of college) I felt that my resistance was due to my personal beliefs that sex went with marriage. Of course now I'm not sure what the reason was. I would guess it was a combination of my past experiences and my values.

MALE

I have not had intercourse yet. I believe in physical expression of feelings. I often touch and embrace my friends because I just feel like it and no explanation is necessary. I feel close to them or glad to be with them and I express it physically. But, for me, the question of intercourse is different. It needs to depend on whether the relationship is right. I was taught that this could only be in marriage. Now I do not believe a line can be drawn that clearly. On the other hand, marriage is a commitment and involves the bond and declaration of the church. Right now, I'm leaning toward believing that marriage is not always necessary.

MALE

I have had so few good sexual experiences that I have no reason to feel good about myself sexually. That is why I feel so strongly about the need for the proper setting for sex to be experienced. I need the security of knowing the person with whom I'm sharing myself. She must respect me and want what I have to offer—a very deep and very special part of me.

*Several people, in deciding **when** were open to intercourse when they were in a long-term, loving and committed relationship—some only in marriage while others did not require that.*

FEMALE

A fleeting relationship, it seems to me, does not give the security and caring concern which is necessary for long-term sexual interchange. I need the security of marriage to live with the ebb and flow of sexual desire—to know that if it is not good today, it will be tomorrow, and that he will still be there the next day. I should say that I am an older student, returning to university life after 25 years of marriage. I have been married to the same man all that time, and he has been my only sexual partner, and I his.

FEMALE

I met my present steady, friend, lover, and companion three years ago. I guess that is when many of my ideas started changing. Possibly because the others were "fast," or he was just skillfully tactful, or I was ready for a combination of these things. Anyway, I had to stop and define to myself where I stood sexually for the first time—not in theory but in actuality. I once thought premarital sex was sinful. I have, however, developed a wonderful sexual relationship along with a wonderful emotional relationship with my partner. I am very much against promiscuity, but where once I stood fast on virginity till marriage, I now am wondering about living together first.

FEMALE

Sex should be experienced only when true love is present, and I feel it should be experienced after the wedding vows. To me, sex is the final giving of true and everlasting love and should be experienced only with your husband.

> The act of sexual intercourse is only one small part of a smorgasbord of sexual activities, and, in fact, has the potential of becoming a health hazard. Also, the act itself is highly overrated in terms of sustained pleasure ... Of the hundreds of written questions collected by the author from teenagers over the years, the overwhelming majority revolve around sexual urges and relationships, and what to do about them ... When the author reveals that it is possibly not intercourse that brings the greatest pleasure, that many females do not have orgasms, and that males often have their biggest orgasms when talking about them in the locker room with their buddies, the audience always expresses recognition with great roars of laughter ... Yet, despite the fact that the act of sexual intercourse may be an overrated focal point, and that it can be hazardous to one's health, the reality is that the expectation in a dating relationship is not whether to have sexual intercourse, but when.... It may be far better to teach about a wide range of pleasuring activities than to incur the higher risks that are involved in just sexual intercourse. (Hacker, 1990, p. 5)

For some, the process of exploring, touching, and pleasuring each other is very meaningful, and need not lead to intercourse.

FEMALE

My current romance does not carry as much electricity as my high school romance did. I am sure there are many reasons for this but I think it was partially due to choosing not to have sex in high school. We were always on the edge. We went out every weekend and we went parking just about every weekend but we never removed our clothing. It was great to hold each other and kiss for hours. The petting got more and more serious as time went on, and we had to talk about what was happening and what we wanted to happen. We both agreed that we loved each other but that we were not ready for marriage. We also agreed that we did not want a pregnancy. Basically, we were scared to have sex, even if we used birth control so we decided we were not ready to have sex. Most of our friends were sleeping together and I am sure our friends thought we were doing the same. We planned our children's names and we planned to build a house. When I was offered an athletic scholarship by a college and accepted it, he was very angry. He did not want me to go away. We went out one evening and got drunk while we were parking. He was being rough and kept trying to take my clothes off. I realized that he wanted to have sex and maybe even make me pregnant so that I would not go away to college and I started to cry. He stopped and started the car to take me home. We did not talk all the way home and when we got there he would not walk me to the door. That was the end for us. I called him from basketball camp that summer and he told me that he never wanted to see me again. A short time later he started dating a girl that he worked with and she got pregnant. I feel we have unfinished business. I would at least like to tell him that I am sorry about all the heavy petting and no sex. I think that it must have been more painful for him not to have sex than it was for me. I will always remember that special man, my first love.

FEMALE

My first relationship developed when I was in high school; it lasted for almost two and one-half years. All our friends thought any couple going out as long as we, must be having sex. Whenever I told them we weren't, they laughed. But we really never did. He had high expectations for our relationship and so did I. We both wanted to wait until marriage. That is a surprising idea for a male. There are times when we came so close and had to stop ourselves. I look back sometimes and wish that we had made love. He is still a very dear person in my heart. I feel as if I'll always love him. He attends college here also, so I see him a lot. I sometimes wish we could get back together, but he has his girlfriend and I have my boyfriend. We've had some very good long talks about ourselves and our memories. In our family living class in high school the two of us were married and had twin eggs that we had to carry around. It was a great experience for us to go through together. Maybe it had some influence on our resolve about intercourse.

FEMALE

Ken and I enjoyed a very pleasant sexual relationship—the only one I have had yet. He was very understanding and not pushy. We probably did everything up to intercourse (heavy petting in the upper and lower regions), but we both felt intercourse was very special and we should save it for when we got married. I had a very hard time letting him see my body naked. At first, I felt a lot of guilt when we would sleep together nude.

FEMALE

I have slept around quite a bit—especially after my first few efforts at having a "steady" relationship failed. Now I realize that what I mainly want is the closeness, the warmth (emotional and physical) of another human being, and the response to me as a special person. This does not have to be expressed with intercourse. In fact, my experience has been that intercourse confuses everything. So, I like to sleep nude with a guy about whom I care, and with whom I share other things than our sexual activity. I know this would blow my mother and father's minds. They seem to think that any time a man and woman get within 20 yards of each other, sexual intercourse is the next step!

Intercourse was a disappointment to some.

FEMALE

I came to college. Since I was now out in the world and on my own, I was an adult ready to assume adult responsibilities and take on the world. I just knew I would find the right man who really loved me and we would settle down and marry. Things did not work out that way. I remained a virgin until my sophomore year. Then I met a young man whom I thought I really liked. At first I was reluctant, but then I started sleeping with him. He could make me feel so good, and our petting sessions were so stimulating. I liked his arms around me, or so I thought. I knew we had the perfect union and our love and sex had been made in heaven. But to my amazement, intercourse was not as exciting as I had dreamed of. I did not always reach some glorious plateau and then sink into oblivion. Also, I did not know how to stimulate him. I was nervous and timid, and my partner became impatient with me. Sometimes he would force me or demand that I have sex with him. I dreaded the thought of his body on top of mine and him driving into me. And sex lost all its glamour after I discovered the truth about my "lover." I was not his only love—there had been and were then numerous other women in his life. I felt used, degraded, low, and common. There was no tenderness, no compassion—just demanding and submission.

Differences in sexual lifestyle often cause conflict between parents and children. Parents usually hope their sexual values will be adopted by their children. The results of one study indicated that the greatest similarity in values between children and parents occurred in those families having good parent-child communication about sexuality (Fisher, 1986).

FEMALE

The older generation keeps repeating the comment that the climate on college campuses is "amoral." Then they go on to say: "It was so much better when the dating game was played—waiting for the phone call, teasing, chasing, deceiving; more exciting than today's straightforward sex." They seem to think the college dorm today is one big fornicatorium! That type of thinking also says it's best for the man to search out, date, and eventually marry the "nice girl," but at the same time date the town girls for the real kicks. It seems to me that most people who have those values about game-playing carry them into adult life; it's all right to have a downtown "wife" or "wives" while the good wife at home presents a facade of monogamous contentment. It bugs me to see these sexist patterns so deeply ingrained in both men and women—by religion, society, and the family.

FEMALE

I am a college junior. I slept with "him" a year ago. I had never slept with anyone before. I had never had sexual intercourse before. We have been living together seven months now and we're happy while both of us are still adjusting. When we discuss our feelings, we often get around to my feelings of regret that Mom doesn't know that we live together. At times these thoughts haunt me. But what we've done has come about very naturally and I will not give it up. The proper time will come, I'm sure, when Mom will find out.

The younger generation can have an impact on their parents and help them understand that their fears and anxieties may not always be justified.

FEMALE

I have grown children, and am completing my college work that I stopped when I got married. One of the greatest milestones in my sexual learning was provoked by my oldest daughter. She was in college on the East Coast, and she set up housekeeping with her boyfriend and made no bones about it to us. It was a bitter pill for me to take. I was worried that my friends might find out and that it would reflect on me and embarrass me. I think deep down I really envied her for having the courage to consummate her sexual feelings without the fear of pregnancy or of the scorn of society which I had been confronted with at her age. So long as her sexual activities took place far away, and she did not indulge in them at home, I was able to live with it. So, it seems my convictions about premarital sex are based more on fear than on morality. We went out to visit her on one occasion, and I went with fear, trembling, and knowing she wouldn't pretend something that wasn't. What we found, rather than something nasty and shady, was a beautiful relationship. They were living as much "married" as any married couple we know—going through the same adjustments to each other, and with the same consideration for each other as any young married couple. They entertained us royally in the apartment, just as though they were married (though we stayed in a motel). Out of that experience, I feel I have a deeper understanding for and respect for the young people who choose such a commitment.

Evidence from a longitudinal study involving 1,184 girls (initially surveyed at age 14–15 and again at age 19) shows that higher self-esteem, positive attitudes about school with higher educational expectations, nontraditional views on family and gender roles, and strong internal locus of control indicate a lower probability of nonmarital childbearing (Plotnick and Butler, 1991). Choices, carefully made, about contraception show responsibility.

FEMALE

My first sexual experiences took place when I was a sophomore in high school. I started dating a guy my age. We went out for a long time before any petting or making-out happened. I think we both just felt too young and scared to do anything else. A year later when I was almost 17, we had sexual intercourse for the first time. We were both nervous and scared and we took every precaution against pregnancy. Neither one of us would ever disgrace our families so we took great pains to protect me from getting pregnant.

Choices about parenthood require thoughtful decisions that fit into an individual's preferences and chosen life styles.

FEMALE

I'm really quite old-fashioned when you come right down to it. I would eventually like to marry and have children. And one relationship is all I want. I often become worried about what kind of guide I can be for my children. What will I teach them?

FEMALE

When I told a group in the dorm that I had chosen to most likely not bear children of my own, the response I first got was a laugh and "But you're a child development major!" I was floored! I had come to realize that by the time I graduate and finally get some money together, Lanny and I (I hope) will finally be able to spend our free time visiting relatives in Europe, canoeing around Canada, and just seeing all this beautiful land. I can honestly say that by the time we'd be ready to settle down, we might be too old to start a family, or not be financially secure. I believe that childbirth may be a strong emotional experience between husband and wife, but not a mandatory one. I don't think I am cut out for childbearing—and I know we would consider adoption.

MALE

My parents "had to get married" and, as a result of their experience, I chose not to have sexual intercourse until I was 20. This was several years behind my peers. I had decided never to cross that line until I was fully willing to become a parent. This was deeply ingrained in my personality. I've realized I had been sabotaging all my relationships by dating girls I didn't like all that much or who were unavailable for a long-term relationship. I guess this fit into my unconscious agenda. This is something I didn't fully understand, but it became obvious to me as the pattern repeated itself. Finally, I grew to the place where I could take full responsibility for a family in case of any unplanned pregnancies. I'd achieved my personal, nonfamily goals satisfactorily. Two months after this decision I met my wife-to-be. While writing this paper, I came to understand the terrible thing I was attempting to avoid; I did not want any child of mine ever to think their conception may have been the only reason I married their mother.

The importance of communication in a relationship was mentioned by several students as a strong value.

MALE

I sometimes wonder what it feels like for a woman to get turned on. . . . What I would like to do is to have the woman I love receive as much pleasure and joy in sex as she wants and I can provide. . . . I suppose the only way I can do this is to communicate well enough and know as much as possible about what her needs are and how to satisfy them. In the past, however, I have usually had a hard time doing this. Although I am usually open to discussion, many women are not. Unless both of us can be frank and communicate freely, not much can be accomplished.

FEMALE

A month ago I started dating someone whom I'm very fond of. I have gone into this relationship very differently than I would have last year. We have not gone to bed yet; we talked about it but decided our heads really were not ready for that. In the past, if my body was ready, I did it. The longer we go without jumping into bed, the better I feel about myself. I am sure that in the past I have gone to bed with guys just because I didn't feel free enough to talk with them about alternatives. That seems rather self-defeating on my part, because there is no way I am going to feel good about myself if I'm not free enough to talk to my sex partner. I'm very pleased about the open communication we have, and I am going to work very hard to keep it.

Experimentation with nonrelational sex is intriguing for some and frustrating for others.

FEMALE

Frank and I stayed overnight with Gary and his girlfriend, and we had sex with our respective partners. Then something we had often talked about and figured would happen took place. We switched partners. Frank and Gary's girl promptly fell asleep, but Gary and I had sex several times that night. All four of us felt good about it in the morning. We had all wondered if we would have doubtful feelings later on, but none of us did. After Frank and I broke up (for reasons other than sex), I began dating different people, and was faced with many decisions about whether I wanted to have sex and if I wanted to have sex with someone I was not in love with. Right now, I can see the value in having sex without love as long as there is mutual understanding. However, since I have had sex with someone I don't love, I can also appreciate better what an ultimate expression of love sex can be.

MALE

As a ninth grader, one of the most popular subjects of debate for my friends and me (all virgins) was the question of having sex with or without love. At that point I thought sex without love would be a bummer and basically that's where I am now. However, reading Albert Ellis has made me more open to the idea that sex without a deep emotional involvement might be nice, to the point where I might like to experience it myself. Intellectually, it makes a lot of sense, but emotionally I'm not there yet!

MALE

At this point in my life, I find it hard to separate love and sex. I have experienced one without the other, and I came out feeling like one of the lowest persons on earth.

MALE

When two people open themselves up to each other through sexual intercourse, there is great potential either for joy and contentment or for grief and frustration. Even though I can verbalize this, I still find myself allowing my needs to take priority over the woman's, and I enjoy it less because of guilt feelings. Why can't I realize that until I am ready to accept the responsibilities of an intimate relationship, I'll never enjoy sex without regrets?

For some, affection is more important than sex.

FEMALE

I don't really need sex, I need affection; I need to know that I'm loved. Sex just isn't necessary. I often wonder why so many people crave it. Probably because society tells us it is something you have to control, and that makes it a source of curiosity that triggers all sorts of strange ideas. It's a problem for me because I like to know guys and be known by them as an equal, but often it seems like all they want is a sex partner. And I find myself playing games to get out of it. I hope I can find the courage to just tell a guy what my feelings are and why I am feeling uncomfortable.

Although sexual decision making will continue throughout life, there are times of clarity and integration when past and present join, and the confusion and ambivalence are stilled.

FEMALE

I decided that whatever a consenting adult couple chose to do behind closed doors should be strictly up to them. As time went on, I found that I wanted to make some modifications to this basic concept. First, that all prior commitments be respected, otherwise known as fidelity. Window shopping is OK, but look, don't touch. Where this rule came from I'm not sure, it must be something I picked up in early childhood. Another thing that I feel strongly about is the part about "behind closed doors," keep it there. I don't care what others do but I don't want to see it or hear about it. This includes humor of a sexual nature, it amuses me not. Beyond these core beliefs there is only this: every pregnancy should be *PLANNED!* I don't care what anyone thinks about romance or spontaneity, the world can't afford any more accidents. Quality of life, not quantity.

FEMALE

My sexual relationship with my husband deteriorated. I started therapy about a year ago and I began to see why and how I buried feelings, especially anger, with people I saw as authority figures. Since I've begun to speak my mind with others and not always play the pleaser role, I've had more interest in sex ... and have begun to experience orgasms again. I don't think my healing work is done. I still need to grieve the losses of my youth; I still feel a lot of anger toward Duane and myself. I've done much to understand and analyze this and now I'm ready to do the feeling work.

MALE

As a result of difficult experiences, I now highly value the act of intercourse. It is an emotionally binding act that allows individuals to express and give of themselves to one another in a pleasurable way. Because of my convictions and desire not to hurt anyone else, I have for the past five years abstained from sexual intercourse. My mind is at peace, there are no more abortions and I now treasure my own sexuality the more. I'm special and whoever gets this person to agree to be their husband, will be receiving more than a sex partner. If and when I do decide to become sexually active again, it will be within the confinements of marriage. I truly believe that the fullness of intercourse can only be achieved when both parties understand marriage, the purpose of sex, love each other and respect one another's bodies. Knowing now what I know about sexual relationships, I realize I must grow in the area of oneness with my to-be partner. It's not enough to say "I love you so let's jump in the bed and experience an orgasm." I need to explore and define intimacy, pleasure, and bodily reactions in order to ensure that consciously I have made an attempt to reach the point of being mentally ready for on-going sexual activities. When implemented correctly, sex becomes more than an act, it becomes love making which in all essence is the highest form of human-to-human adoration.

FEMALE

In high school, I made love with my boyfriend. Fears and guilt followed. He was the only love I had, and I desperately needed that security. After our break-up, I went through stages from hating men to indulging in "free love." I was mixed up about my sexual beliefs, morals, and identity. Today, things are quite different. I can identify where I am as a sexual being, and what my feelings, values, and beliefs are. My husband has reinforced my values and helped me cope with my previous frustrations. I believe there is sex with love and sex without love. I learned from my previous sexual experiences; they were beneficial in developing my present sexual values in which intimacy and love are primary. Finally, I know who I am sexually. I am aggressive, sensitive, and curious. I love to touch and to be touched, to taste and to be tasted, to feel and to be felt. I love to be warm and to give warmth. I love my body more than I ever have in the past. I have learned that a big part of a sexual relationship is communication. My sexuality is becoming part of my whole being. It's so exciting. I feel that my sexual growth will be a continuing process throughout my life, always needing evaluation and re-evaluation.

CONCLUSION

Sylvia Hacker has developed an important format:

> The principles of being a great lover: *The principles of being a great lover are based on slowing down and getting in touch with one's sensuality, i.e., what "turns you on" and what "turns your partner on."* . . . *Great orgasms can be achieved when partners concentrate just on bringing pleasure to each other, without an "agenda" of sexual intercourse. Most importantly, however, great rewards occur in regard to intimacy when partners learn gradually how to communicate what their sexual preferences are, both nonverbally and verbally, with one another. The willingness to slow down and do this may be characteristic of person who can give to another in a truly loving way beyond just sexual expression.* . . . *Some skepticism and resistance seems to stem from a deep reluctance to deposit or experience semen on the outside of the body. This may come from our culture's persistent reproductive imperative, but in the author's experience it is also strongly associated with an aversion to any of the body's byproducts. Semen is considered by many to be "yucky and sticky" and equivalent to other "dirty" bodily excretions, like urine and feces.* (Hacker, 1990)

The CAR principle: *This has three characteristics:*

1. (C)aring. *Caring people are those who do not take their sexuality lightly but value it enough to take pride in it and avoid harm to themselves and to others.*
2. (A)ttentiveness. *Attentiveness means being interested in and paying close attention to what gives you and your partner pleasure, and discussing who both of you are as unique individuals.*
3. (R)espect. *Having respect for yourself and your partner means not doing anything against your wishes and theirs—and not forcing anyone to do anything. Young people need to be trained in assessing their CAR potential so that they can address the double standard of males who want to "score" and females who feel compelled to submit so as not to "lose him"* (pp. 6,7).

It is important for young females to know, for example, that although there are responsible young men, a great majority of the males who impregnate females will leave them within a few years, married or not (Gordon and Gordon, 1983). It is also crucial that males learn that scoring is "stealing" (Cassell, 1987) unless three conditions are present:

1. *Time is taken to get to know one another so that each can find out if and when both are ready to be sexually intimate.*
2. *They know how to protect themselves against unintended pregnancy and STDs.*
3. *They are knowledgeable enough to ensure enjoyment for both partners.*
   If young people are not willing to consider alternatives to sexual intercourse, then they are morally obligated to use condoms (and to know how to use them correctly).

The fear is sometimes expressed that if we consider sexuality as good, it is equivalent to saying, "if it feels good, do it." This is hardly what is being recommended under the new proposed norm. This norm is based on a view of morality far more encompassing than our former narrowly defined norm. It entails a close examination and an ongoing study of how to develop into healthy, whole human beings, sexually and otherwise, and how to become responsible adults in dealings with others . . . " (Hacker, 1990, pp. 5–8).

SUGGESTED ISSUES FOR PERSONAL REFLECTION, GROUP DISCUSSION AND INTERACTION, PERSONAL JOURNAL

1. Human sexuality is not only a "bedroom matter." There are numerous "public" issues which require citizen decision making. If you were a member of your city council, what guidelines would you use to decide these questions:
   a. Should there be massage parlors on the main street? Any regulations? Laws?
   b. Should pornographic materials and films be available to anyone who wants them regardless of age? How can the rights of those who do not want them be protected?
   c. Should prostitution be legalized?
   d. Should a medical clinic specializing in in-office abortion procedures be licensed in your town? Any regulatory procedures?
   e. Should people engaging in homosexual solicitation in bars be arrested?
   f. Should police be allowed to be "decoys" in "entrapment" procedures?
2. A proposal has been made that all private sexual behaviors—cohabitation, anal and oral intercourse, homosexual lovemaking, prostitution, marital

lifestyle, and others—be considered just that, with no legal connotation of criminal status.
   a. What is your viewpoint?
   b. What are other "public" sexuality issues that should be regulated by laws or ordinances?
3. In personal decision making, people use various guides to come to a decision. Identify one or two of the most difficult sexual decisions that you or your friends are having to make. If you are now in a group, these can be written anonymously on slips of paper and placed in the center of the group. They can then be read out loud without any identification of who wrote them. The group then chooses one for focus, testing whether the following guidelines for decision making are useful, or identifying other guidelines.

   James Nelson (1978, p. 120) says: "We may not be consistent in how we make our decisions . . . but we give some consideration to each of the following, in some cases giving more weight to one element than another:

   • *Motive: Why* would I (or why shouldn't I) do this?
   • *Intention: What* am I aiming at in this act?
   • The nature of the act itself: *How* will I implement my aims? Are certain acts always right or wrong—or does it vary with the situation?
   • The *consequences: In what way* will I be accountable for the results and effects of such acts or relationships?"

   Discuss whether these four items are important considerations for you in making a decision. Are there others?
4. Tear a sheet of paper into eight slips. On each slip, write one thing that is important to you in a sexual relationship. When you have something written on each slip, rank them, with the most important one on top, and the least important one on the bottom. The top one should be something that is virtually nonnegotiable for you—something that is a strong value of yours. When you face a sexual decision, which of the values that you have listed is most influential in your decision? Does its place in the priority list reflect that?
5. Using the matrix of sexual value positions shown here, put an X in each box that represents your present value position. What are two reasons that support that position, and two that you think could be given against it?
6. Sexual decisions are sometimes made by default: "We got carried away"; "Love made me do it"; "Chemistry is more powerful than thinking." What truths and myths about human sexuality are represented by such statements? Give examples of situations where *drift* rather than *decision* was the major influence. What could change that situation?
7. In the past few years, much has been said about "generational gaps," especially with regard to sexuality. List areas where you feel your values and/or decisions about sexuality differ from your parents. Choose one of those and formulate what you would say to your parents to "tutor" them about your viewpoint or lifestyle. Some people say they would never discuss such matters with parents—it would kill their parents. What do you think?

MATRIX OF SEXUAL VALUE POSITIONS

	Relational	Nonrelational
Sexual Intercourse	**Committed**	**Recreational—Fun—Experimental**
	Sexual intercourse appropriate as an expression of love and affection, not appropriate otherwise.	Sexual intercourse does not require an ongoing relationship. May be engaged in for fun and pleasure and/or for purpose of gaining sexual experience and knowledge.
No Sexual Activity	**Companionate Relationship**	**Self-chosen Celibacy (Abstinence)**
	Strong, supportive emotional relationship without heavy petting or intercourse.	Deliberately refraining from sexual activity in order to better experience and define one's own sexuality irrespective of a partner. May or may not have been preceded by sexual intercourse.
Sexual Expression without Intercourse	**Petting Within Relationship**	**Recreational Petting**
	Petting appropriate as an expression of love and affection; sexual intercourse not appropriate, petting to orgasm appropriate.	Petting including orgasm, but not intercourse. Appropriate with partner to whom physically attracted. Does not require ongoing relationship.

Chapter 13

Prices of Silence: Some Concluding Remarks

INTRODUCTION

*H*uman sexuality is defined by Lynn Leight (1988) as "the total of who you are, what you believe, what you feel, and how you respond. . . . It refers to all your relationships and intimate encounters. . . . Sexuality is all this, including the way in which religion, morals, family, friends, age, body concepts, life goals, and your self-esteem shape your sexual self. It is expressed in the way you speak, smile, stand, sit, dress, dance, laugh, and cry . . . our sexuality is a lifelong evolutionary process" (pp. 6–7).

Although sexual attitudes and values are learned in the early years from family modeling, sexual "information" is learned from peers. What the young do not learn in either place is accurate information and the ability to talk about sensitive sexual issues with one's partner (Kelly, 1988; Scales, 1987). In spite of the increase of sexually intimate behaviors by younger and younger adolescents, there seems to be no evidence that these behaviors have reversed the "conspiracy of silence" about serious, personal, direct, and reflective talking about sexuality. The excerpts in this chapter testify to the possibility that such a reversal can indeed occur and illustrate some of the consequences when it does not. Whether the positive learning from a sexuality course is generalizable remains to be tested.

Growing up sexual continues to be for many persons a confusing and not always pleasant process. The tapestry of coming of age is woven of many threads:

1. *Mystery and silence:* Adults' reticence about talking directly about sexual concerns, often combined with negative warnings, communicates to chil-

dren a powerful message that something mysterious and hard to understand is involved.
2. *Am I normal?* The silence and secrecy surrounding sexuality, the inaccessibility of accurate information, and the myths (misinformation) perpetuated in many quarters combine to raise doubts in some children's minds about whether they may be somehow "abnormal" because of thoughts, explorations, and fantasies that they assume to be uniquely their own experiences.
3. *Lack of affirmation of one's own sexuality:* Family and religious teachings are often interpreted or misinterpreted as, "sexuality, and anything associated with it, is dirty and shameful." Since open discussion and talk seldom occur (even between partners), such messages and impressions are not corrected until late adolescence or early adulthood, if then.
4. *Guilt:* Strong negative judgments about certain sexual acts tend to permeate the child's conception of sexuality; without subsequent questions, conversation, and reinterpretation, he or she comes to feel guilty about anything sexual—thoughts, fantasies, feelings, and actions.

The following excerpts illustrate some consequences of guilt.

MALE

I had a "nervous breakdown" some time ago. It was not all related to sex, but lots of sexual concerns were involved. I'd been carrying a lot of guilt about masturbating, petting, and sex play in the nude. All these were "wrong" in my mind, yet I kept doing them. There was so much to feel guilty about! As I think about it now, it doesn't seem right to have had to feel guilty about everything sexual; it didn't make me stop doing anything—it only made me link sexuality and guilt.

FEMALE

I still feel that my sexual upbringing has caused me many problems. Operating as long as I did under so many misconceptions affected the way I thought about sex; sex was only allowed in marriage and for the purpose of having children—not for pleasure or intimacy. I'm feeling less guilt about my premarital sexual behavior and my decision not to have children. I haven't managed to throw out all the guilt, but I have managed to get rid of some of it. I want to continue to work on that, because guilt can really destroy a relationship.

MALE

It seems that I have always felt guilty about whatever it was that I was currently doing sexually. I felt bad about masturbation and mutual masturbation in high school. But the guilt wasn't strong enough to make me stop. I remember that once I was successful in cutting it out for a three-week stretch but I just didn't have the self-discipline necessary to deny myself the pleasure involved. I have had much guilt about my sexual actions with girlfriends. It seems strange to me now at this point in my life, but my guilt was caused mainly by thoughts about whether my parents would find out and what they would think.

FEMALE

I was taught to remain a virgin until marriage; I am presently unmarried and *not* a virgin. I know that sex with a person whom I love dearly has been a very rewarding experience. At times, however, I'm afraid that maybe my mother will turn out to have been right and when I marry I'll suffer the consequences.

Abusers often control their victims by making them feel guilty and convincing them that they are to blame for being abused. If parents have not talked with children openly about sex and boundaries, the child may feel too uncomfortable to ask for help.

FEMALE

When I was in the sixth grade, one of my uncles molested me. The sexual abuse only happened a couple of times that year, and I was too scared to tell anyone. The next year my father was murdered. My uncle, being his younger brother, visited us much more frequently after that. He was good for my mother, giving her much needed support. She needed him and my uncle knew it. Due to the loss of my dad, my mother was going through a great deal of pain. My uncle knew that I would not want to cause the family any more pain or problems, and he took advantage of this by beginning to abuse me regularly.

My father was murdered outside our home, and because I was the only witness to his death, my family did not question the "special" treatment that I was receiving from my uncle. My older brother, sister, and mother assumed that he felt sorry for me and wanted to do everything that he could to "make me feel better." They saw him as a "great guy." He bought me presents, took me places, and came over to our house every day. What is incredibly hard for me to understand is how my family could believe that this so-called sympathy could go on so strongly for three years.

The trial of my father's killer also went on for three years. It was very hard on all of us. Outside the court room, I recall hearing several people say, "Thank God your mother has had your uncle to lean on. He's been so kind." I was the only one to see my uncle as he was. At the time I did not know he was manipulating me. I just knew that he was scaring and confusing me. His visits to my bedroom lasted about twenty minutes. Yet, still no questions from my family. I deeply regret not telling anyone what was going on behind that closed door. My uncle told me over and over again that it would hurt Mother, and she would probably be very angry with me. I was scared of that. Thus, the abuse stayed "our little secret."

In my family, we never "aired dirty laundry." My mother believes that talking frequently about something bad that has happened will only make matters harder to cope with. Therefore, I was under the impression that if I did not think about it during the day it would get better. I learned to be a real pro at blocking things out. It was to the point where I was almost able to numb myself at night when my uncle would visit my room. I was in my own little world. I prayed every night that someone, anyone, would walk in or knock on the door while my uncle was in my room. I no longer cared about being blamed. But no one ever knocked. I began to believe that God was not listening to me because I was doing something so wrong. I should have stopped it. I was not some little child who was helpless. At this point I was almost 14 years old. I should have known better. My only consolation during this time was that since my dad had died, I felt somehow he could see what was going on; somehow he knew. I felt I had finally told someone.

We are a Catholic family and I honestly believe that is why my mother would never even have thought that something immoral, like incest, could be going on in her home. We were never taught about sex, let alone abuse. We never talked about it; therefore it could never happen. I went to a Catholic school for 12 years and learned nothing about sex there that would have helped me. I was too ashamed to even tell this sin to a priest in confession. Due to all the religion classes, and talk about mortal and immortal sins, I was almost convinced that I would be going to hell. The guilt had gotten unbearable; the amount of hatred inside made me feel like I was going to explode. I developed an ulcer. Everyone said it was understandable because of all I had been through concerning my father. Maybe that was part of it, but all that filled my mind was how much I wished they knew that the real cause was my uncle's behavior. But how was I going to tell them? I knew it had to stop. I had to do something before it destroyed me.

The next night when I heard my uncle coming into my room, I began crying and shaking uncontrollably. I was not able to numb myself. I pulled the covers up around my neck real tight. I did not say a word to him. He reached down and felt my face and the tears that were there. To my surprise, he did nothing but turn and walk out of the room. I remember keeping the covers up real tight for a long time that night, afraid he would come back. After all, I thought stopping the abuse could not be that easy. But he didn't come back that night or ever again. I remember getting up to change my pajamas because I had perspired so much that they were almost completely wet. The abuse was over! After three years, it was finally over! But I did not know that for sure. I still lived with the fear of it happening again. I could not believe this was all it took. I was expecting a fight with him. I was convinced that if I tried to stop the sexual abuse it would result in physical harm to me.

I finally told my mother when I was 16 years old, and then only because fear and nightmares still haunted me. Her only regret was that I had not come to her sooner. My uncle was not allowed to see me again. I don't know what my mother said to him because it has never been discussed since. I guess, in a way, I was expecting that to happen. However, I wish she had talked with me about it. Instead, she thought it would be best if we kept it "our little secret." So again, I was sworn to secrecy. I was to be strong, not cry, and not talk about it.

I was not aware of the effect that whole experience had on me until I slept with my boyfriend for the first time. It became clear then that I had some problems to work out. That is why I am now in therapy attempting to deal with flashbacks and certain types of touches and feelings. My biggest concern is that I may never be able to have a "normal" sexual relationship. Hopefully, with the help I am receiving, I will someday be free of the fears and frustrations that haunt me today.

Values are absorbed from significant family members, usually unconsciously, from infancy on. Because of limited exposure, individuals assume these values to be universal—believed by everyone. They are accepted as "The Truth." During adolescence, as these excerpts demonstrate, the old values begin to be challenged; they may be affirmed, amended, or discarded as new information and alternative values challenge old assumptions.

Human sexuality is one of the major areas in which the younger generation might tutor their elders. Some years ago, Margaret Mead indicated that the Vietnam War and civil rights generation was probably the first young generation in history to reverse the instruction/wisdom process. Perhaps for the first time, elders were being drastically influenced by young people. This same phenomenon may now be occurring in the area of sexuality. Younger people, by ferreting out their own sexual values, are causing a gradual shift in the attitudes of older people. Rather than "shift," some would use words such as "erosion," "decay," or "compromise," indicating that such change is not always welcome.

The anecdotes in this chapter are of a different character than those in previous chapters. These were written by students who had been involved for a semester in a university course on human sexuality. The particular format of the course made possible, indeed required, personal participation in a small discussion group of six to eight peers, and comparing, in writing, one's own growing-up process with the research and information currently available about human sexuality. Therefore references in particular excerpts to "my group" or "the group," should be understood within this context.

This concluding chapter explores the following question: What happens when people have access to sexuality information and an opportunity for ongoing discussion and interchange about that information? How does this affect prior conceptions?

Sexuality itself is redefined and seen in a new light.

FEMALE

I no longer automatically associate guilt with everything sexual. I am increasingly able to accept my sexuality as a basic part of who I am. If I step outside of *my* boundaries and give more of myself than I feel the relationship deserves or can handle, then I feel guilty and worried.

FEMALE

During this course, I have come to realize that sex is not a dirty, shameful thing. This has been a big step for me. When I was younger, I was taught that anything beyond holding hands was sinful.

FEMALE

I have realized that sex is not a thing to hide, fear or feel guilty about. It is a function of two people (be they homosexual or heterosexual) exploring, expressing love, and understanding each other better. Previously, I was more or less a frigid and frightened female, because of a lack of knowledge and because of my training that all sexual encounters should be saved for marriage.

Information counteracts old fears and doubts.

FEMALE

I can thank this class for taking a big load off my mind. Previously, I had not understood that the clitoris is involved in having orgasm. I had gone through agonizing times wondering why I could not have an orgasm with vaginal sex. I thought that perhaps something was physically wrong with me, and I should see a gynecologist. Or I figured that perhaps there was a psychological barrier, and I should see a psychologist. If this class had done no more good for me than this, I would consider it worthwhile. I had resented my sexual partners because I rarely had an orgasm. Now I understand that the problem was basically a lack of knowledge on both their part and mine. Thank God I discovered this now and not ten years from now!

FEMALE

After meeting the gay people on the panel in a class session, and doing some reading on homosexuality, I have a new respect for them. The whole idea of homosexuality was previously repulsive to me. I think now I can approach it more on a "head" (rational, thinking) level than simply a "gut" (irrational, nonthinking) one.

FEMALE

My perceptions of homosexuality and masturbation are the two things that have changed most drastically this term. I had a very distorted view of both, because I didn't know much about them. The information I got was new to me and very enlightening. What I previously thought was grossly perverted, I now realize may be natural, and not evil or sinful. I still have a difficult time coping with homosexuality, but I have cast aside many of the stereotypes I once had.

FEMALE

I am still a virgin, but much more knowledgeable about a number of things. I am now aware of what actually happens in intercourse. Of course, I had heard what happens, but everything is beginning to make more sense to me now—past talk, gossip, and even jokes. It is easier to understand. And even though I am no longer uncertain about the process, I don't crave to have intercourse. I had only heard how great it was; I still imagine it might be fun, now and then, but for the present I can live without it. I get my greatest pleasure from simply being near a man—lying next to him or even just holding his hand. I don't think intercourse would be just "the greatest thing" that would "bring us together."

I am also glad I was exposed to more information concerning male genitals. There is still much more I would like to know—such as what circumcision actually does—but I can find that out for myself. I also never knew how a male masturbated, and having never masturbated, I am still not sure how a woman does it.

Self-understanding increases: as one male said, "I have a new awareness of who I am, or at least who I'd like to be. . . ."

MALE

I've learned that there is a great deal of good in me; I am caring and loving, and other people can care about me. It is really hard for me to believe that sometimes. I tend to let my life rest on one thing or one person, and when that doesn't come through, I feel really worthless. I've come to think that a decent self-image for each partner is really important to any solid relationship.

FEMALE

I think I have finally come to grips with my own sexuality. I've come to accept it as a real and good part of me, rather than something to be repressed and ignored. This course let me look at sexuality openly, without embarrassment or secrecy. I finally had the chance to explore an area about which I had many questions, but really nowhere to get straightforward answers. I have been able to look at myself and finally decide what I want and how I feel sexually. I no longer blindly accept other people's standards. I have been able to establish my own.

FEMALE

It was good to saturate myself with readings covering a range of opinions on different aspects of sexuality. It helped me gain perspective on where I am and what I want, at least for now. I've gotten in touch with exactly what is important to me. Being a virgin does not seem to be the main issue for me now. Rather, it is my self-esteem and how my partner and I feel about each other.

MALE

I am beginning to respect my own feelings more instead of relying on how other people feel about me. I am also beginning to understand (not accept, but understand) how my parents feel and act.

FEMALE

For the last seven or eight weeks, I have had really good feelings about myself sexually. I feel I can be very attractive and seductive and, to me, feeling this way is very important. I also know that I am adequate as a woman and that I am capable of being soft and gentle. I am about 25 pounds overweight and very self-conscious about it. In the past, I felt very self-conscious being close to a man, but that has been changing recently. I used to think that if I could just find the right man and get married, all my problems would be solved. But I now know that this is untrue. I've learned that others are more likely to accept me if I accept myself. Also, I've learned from this class that the person I am is unique, and how I am sexually is unique; there is no reason in the world why I should act a particular way just because others do. I must be *me*!

FEMALE

I think I need more time to develop my identity before I will be secure in an intimate relationship. I am just beginning to get myself together after two years at college.

Part of self-understanding is a reassurance that one is not unusual or "weird."

FEMALE

I have discovered in this class that many other people have had similar experiences to mine, and also have many of the same fears and guilt feelings that I do. It has made me feel much less alone and more "normal," which is very comforting.

FEMALE

I haven't really changed any of my ideas since I came into this class. I just feel that a lot of my ideas are not as far-out as I was beginning to think, and I am not as alone as I thought I was in things I do, like petting to orgasm.

FEMALE

I no longer feel that somehow I may be wrong in feeling as I do. I even found some people who agree with my opinions. And I don't feel quite so dumb or shy because of my past inexperience. Now that I know a little more, I am less afraid of saying something that makes no sense or that shows my ignorance. My values have not changed; I have learned, however, to be somewhat more open-minded toward others' values.

FEMALE

Open and objective sharing of opinions, experiences, and problems concerning sexual matters has broadened my acceptance in many areas, but I have not changed my behavior. I am more willing to listen to others, and feel freer to speak about sexual matters. I feel better about myself as a healthy sexual human being.

It is useful to find that one feels quite differently about certain things than do other people.

FEMALE

It has helped me a great deal to talk to different people about their beliefs and values. I was very surprised to hear what many of the other students thought, both those who I assumed thought like I did, and those who seemed different to begin with.

FEMALE

I've done more intentional thinking about sex this term than ever before in my life, and it has benefitted me tremendously. I've been forced to determine the roots of my values and their strengths. I have gained some competency in dealing with differing opinions.

Talking directly and seriously about sexuality with other people in a class may affect the quality of other relationships.

FEMALE

As a result of talking in my group, I have become able to communicate more openly about sexual matters. I have discussed several things with my mother which I could not have done before. After our discussion, we agreed that we'd achieved an openness that was long overdue. I'm also experiencing a new and better kind of communication with my boyfriend. We are working on talking more openly about everything about our sexuality.

FEMALE

As I think about the impact of this course, I realize that the most meaningful learning is my new ability to communicate about sexuality and sexual matters. In one of the first sessions of class, we were talking about sexual physiology, and I laughed through the entire class to cover my embarrassment at the mention of these words. Now, toward the end of the term, I discuss with my roommates a variety of matters relating to sexuality and no longer need to laugh! This new openness has helped me to communicate with guys I date.

MALE

I took this class with my girlfriend. Every week, we would go to the library and do the readings and write our papers. As we read, we discussed the readings with each other. We slowly developed very open and free communication on any topic of sexuality. Our relationship has deepened. We've not only grown sexually closer, but more importantly, we've grown affectionately closer.

Sometimes the new skill in communication facilitates healing.

FEMALE

As a result of the confidence I gained from talking in class, I talked with a retired woman in my home church whom I have known all my life. She knew both me and my first husband, who discovered he was gay after we were married. I dated her son before I got married. I told her how my parents and the church told me that boys would respect my body and keep their hands off if they really loved and cared about me as a person. I told her that I married my first husband because he was the first one that did not "grope." I also told her that her son did. We talked a lot about nonuseful messages about sexuality from the church. She said, "It is not your fault that situation occurred. The important people in your environment did not give either of you the information you needed to make decisions about your life and relationships with others. This church and this community failed you as a teenager. We tried to overprotect our kids and that got them into even worse situations. We acted as though if we ignored your sexuality it would somehow go away. We did not teach you, my son, or any of our youth how to grow up into normal, healthy sexual beings." I can't begin to explain how much our conversation meant to me. She accepted responsibility and did not blame me for the terrible mistakes I had made. I feel so much better about myself.

More direct communication about sexual matters can impact marriages positively.

FEMALE

I have begun to be able to put into words how I feel, using the communication skills I learned in class. My husband and I have become more open with each other, and more understanding of the feelings we both have but didn't know how to express in a constructive way. We now perceive more of each other's frustrations and have found new ways to resolve them.

FEMALE

I am more comfortable speaking about sex—scientific names and all. Previously, my husband and I avoided the subject. And in my being able to speak with more ease, I believe I've put my husband more at ease. And anything that will help us have a better relationship is well worth it. Five years ago, if I ever had even imagined myself lying in bed fully clothed, trying out one of Masters and Johnson's intercourse positions, I would have died of embarrassment. I still feel a little uneasy about my own body, as does my husband about his, but I believe we will soon outgrow that.

Affirming one's own values and convictions about sexuality may enable a clearer and more direct communication with family members.

FEMALE

There was poor communication in my family, and also lots of rules:

    Direct statements were inappropriate.

    Nonverbal messages were to be understood and followed.

Listen to your parents.

No questions asked.

Parents are allowed to say "you're too young" when children do ask about difficult subjects.

Never, never say "I don't know" or "because" when Mom asks you why you did something. Reasons, real or not, are the only acceptable response.

I can see now how there could have been a much better way to grow up. I want to provide that for my children.

FEMALE

My family was rigid, religious and nonaffectionate. Not only did we not talk of lust; we did not talk of love, either. My expectations for family communication have become much more positive, thanks to what I have learned in this class.

FEMALE

My values, attitudes, and beliefs have basically remained the same throughout this course. I am still conservative in my sexual viewpoints, feeling that sexual interaction should be for me a means of expressing emotional attachment and not just a physical attraction. And I have a firm determination to give my children honest information about sexual issues. My parents never did this, and I see how important information is for one's self-confidence, one's ability to make rational choices, and to live in a mature manner. It seems to me that an atmosphere of openness is essential if a child is not to fear his or her sexuality.

CONCLUSION

The focus in this book has been on remembering and understanding personal experiences of growing up sexual, so that persons may find more integration and wholeness in their sexual identity as adults.

The reflections of students about the outcome of their participation in a human sexuality course seem generalizable to other settings, such as the family, the media, religious and educational institutions, and peer groupings. The conclusion is that it is important that we find ways in this society to provide settings where direct and serious conversation can occur between generations and with peers. These conversations should cover a wide range of sexual topics, in such a way that the emotional and feeling aspects of the subject are reflectively and respectfully dealt with. As a result of such interaction, it is clear that people are less vulnerable to pressure or coercion, and more able to identify and express what they feel and believe. They are better equipped to identify and choose what they themselves want, and less swayed by others' viewpoints or values. They are likely to be less fearful, less confused about sexuality, and less lonely than the present and past generations. They are likely to be more accepting—both of themselves and of others—and, therefore, more capable of an interchange of love and caring. According to student self-reports, traditional societal fears that information will lead to more sexual activity are ungrounded. In fact, there seems to be some evidence that increasing acceptance of diverse sexual values and behaviors does not necessarily lead to their adoption.

SUGGESTED ISSUES FOR PERSONAL REFLECTION, GROUP DISCUSSION AND INTERACTION, PERSONAL JOURNAL

1. As a result of your experience in this class, what confirmations/changes have occurred in the following areas:
   a. In your knowledge?
   b. In your values?
   c. In your behaviors?
   d. In your feelings about your own sexuality?
   e. In your relationships?
2. Who or what do you think triggered these confirmations/changes?

References

Acosta, D. (1993). Providing HIV/AIDS education: Recognizing all teens. *Crossroads: Supporting Lesbian, Gay, Bisexual and Transexual Youth, 2*(2), 8.

Allers, C. T., and Benjack, K. J. (1991). Connections between childhood and HIV infection. *Journal of Counseling and Development, 70*(2), 309–313.

American Friends Service Committee: Bridges Project. (1993). *Crossroads: Supporting lesbian, gay, bisexual and transgender youth, 2*(2, fall).

Atwood, J. D., and Gagnon, J. (1987). Masturbatory behavior in college youth. *Journal of Sex Education and Therapy, 13*(2), 35–41.

Barnard, K. E., and Brazelton, T. B. (1990). *Touch: The foundation of experience.* Madison, CT: International Universities Press.

Bass, E., and Davis, L. (1993). *Beginning to heal: A first book for survivors of child sexual abuse.* New York: HarperCollins.

Beal, C. R. (1994). *Boys and girls: The development of gender roles.* New York: McGraw-Hill.

Beitchman, J. H., Zucker, K. J., Hood, J. E., DaCosta, G. A., Akman, D., and Cassavia, E. (1992). A review of the long-term effects of child sexual abuse. *Child Abuse and Neglect, 16*(1), 101–118.

Bell, A. P., and Weinberg, M. S. (1978). *Homosexualities: A study of diversity among men and women.* New York: Simon and Schuster.

Bell, A. P., Weinberg, M. S., and Hammersmith, F. K. (1981). *Sexual preference: Its development in men and women.* Bloomington, IN: Indiana University Press.

Bem, Sandra. "The tight little lives of fluffy women and chesty men." (Sept. 1975) *Psychology Today 9* (4).

Brownmiller, S. (1975). *Against Our Will: Men, Women, and Rape.* New York: Simon and Schuster.

Burgess, A., and Holmstrom, L. (1974). *Rape: Victims of Crisis.* Bowie, MD: Robert J. Brady Cr.

Burns, A. L. (1994, April 28). Collectivism and interpersonal orientations: Is gender culture? *Questioning the Universals of Gender and Social Attitudes Symposium.* Kona, HI: Western Psychological Association.

Calderone, M. S., and Johnson, E. W. (1989). *The family book about sexuality.* New York: Harper and Row.

Caltrider, S. (Ed.). (1992). *Moving forward: Lesbians and gay men at Michigan State University* (Vol. 1). East Lansing, MI: Michigan State University Press.

Canavan, M. M., and Meyer, W. J. (1992). The female experience of sibling incest. *Journal of Marital and Family Therapy, 18*(2), 129–142.

Carnes, P. J. (1991). *Don't call it love: Recovery from sexual addiction.* New York: Bantam Books.

Cassell, C. (1987). *Straight from the heart.* New York: Simon and Schuster.

Cassese, J. (1993). The invisible bridge: Child sexual abuse and the risk of HIV infection in adulthood. *SIECUS Report, 21*(4), 1–7.

Centers for Disease Control. (1991). Premarital sexual experience among adolescent women—United States, 1970-1988. *Morbidity and Mortality Weekly Report, 39*(51–52), 929–930.

Clark, J. K. (1993). Complications in academia: Sexual harassment and the law. *SIECUS Report, 22*(6), 6–9.

Cohen, C. J., and Stein, T. S. (1986). Reconceptualizing psychotherapy with gay men and lesbians. In T. S. Stein and C. J. Cohen (Eds.), *Contemporary perspectives on psychotherapy with lesbians and gay men* (pp. 27–54). New York: Plenum.

Committee on Sexual Offenses Against Children and Youths. (1984). *Sexual offenses against children: Report of the committee on sexual offences against children and youths.* Ottawa, Canada: Canadian Government Publishing Center.

Cooper, K. C. (1985, August). The six levels of sexual harassment. *Management Review,* 55–56.

Courtois, C. A. (1988). *Healing the incest wound: Adult survivors in therapy.* New York: W. W. Norton.

Crooks, R., and Baur, K. (1993). *Our sexuality.* Redwood City, CA: Benjamin/Cummings.

David, H. (1986). Unwanted children: A follow-up from Prague. *Family Planning Perspectives, 18*(3), 143.

Desenclos, J. C. (1992). Pediatric gonococcal infection, Florida 1984–1988. *American Journal of Public Health, 82*(3), 426–428.

Diamond, M., and Diamond, G. H. (1986). Adolescent sexuality: Biosocial aspects and intervention strategies [Special issue]. Adolescent sexualities: Overviews and principles of intervention. *Journal of Social Work and Human Sexuality, 5*(1), 3–13.

DiClemente, R., Durbin, M., Siegel, D., Krasnovsky, F., Lazarus, N., and Comancho, T. (1992). Determinants of condom use among junior high school students in a minority, inner city school district. *Pediatrics, 89,* 197–202.

Etaugh, C., and Liss, M. B. (1992). Home, school, and playroom: Training grounds for adult gender roles. *Sex Roles, 26*(3–4), 129–147.

Fairchild, B., and Hayward, N. (1989). *Now that you know: What every parent should know about homosexuality—updated edition.* San Diego: Harcourt Brace Jovanovich.

Finkelhor, D., Hotaling, G. T., Lewis, I. A., and Smith, C. (1989). Sexual abuse and its relationship to later sexual satisfaction, marital status, religion, and attitudes. *Journal of Interpersonal Violence, 4*(4), 379–399.

Fisher, S. (1989). *Sexual images of the self: The psychology of erotic sensations and illusions.* Hillsdale, NJ: Lawrence Erlbaum.

Fisher, T. D. (1986). Parent-child communication about sex and young adolescents' sexual knowledge and attitudes. *Adolescence, 21*(83), 517–527.

Ford, C. S., and Beach, F. A. (1951). *Patterns of sexual behavior.* New York: Harper and Row.

Friedman, R. C. (1988). *Male homosexuality.* New Haven: Yale University Press.

Fuller, A. K. (1989). Child molestation and pedophilia. *Journal of the American Medical Association, 261,* 602–605.

Gagnon, J. H., and Simon, W. (1973). *Sexual conduct and the social sources of human sexuality.* Chicago: Aldine Publishing Company.

Gagnon, J. (1977). *Human sexualities.* Glenview, IL: Scott, Foresman.

Gagnon, J., and Greenblatt, C. S. (1978). *Life designs: Individuals, marriages and families.* Glenview, IL: Scott, Foresman.

Genuis, M., and Thomlison, B. (1991). Male victims of child sexual abuse: A brief overview of pertinent findings [Special issue]. Child sexual abuse. *Journal of Child and Youth Care,* fall, 1–6.

Giddens, A. (1992). *The transformation of intimacy.* Stanford, CA: Stanford University Press.

Goff, J. L. (1990). Sexual confusion among certain college males. *Adolescence, 25,* 599–614.

Golden, C. (1987). Diversity and variability in women's sexual identities. In Boston Lesbian Psychologies Collective (Ed.), *Lesbian psychologies: Explorations and challenges* (pp. 19–34). Urbana: University of Illinois Press.

Goodwin, L. J., and Peterson, R. G. (1990). Psychological impact of abuse as it relates to transvestism. *Journal of Applied Rehabilitation Counseling, 21*(4), 45–48.

Gordon, S., and Gordon, J. (1983). *Raising a child conservatively in a sexually permissive world.* New York: Simon and Schuster.

Green, R. (1987). *The sissy boy syndrome and the development of homosexuality.* New Haven: Yale University Press.

Greenberg, D. F. (1988). *The construction of homosexuality.* Chicago: University of Chicago Press.

Hacker, S. S. (1976, October 18). The effect of situational and interactional aspects of sexual encounters on premarital contraceptive behavior. Paper presented at APHA Conference.

Hacker, S. S. (1990). The transition from the old norm to the new. *SIECUS Report, 18*(5), 1–8.

Hajcak, F., and Garwood, P. (1988). Quick-fix sex: Pseudosexuality in adolescents. *Adolescence, 23*(92), 755–760.

Hamburg, D. A. (1993). The opportunities of early adolescence. In R. Takanishi (Ed.), *Adolescence in the 1990s: Risk and opportunity* (pp. 8–13). New York: Teachers College Press.

Harry, J. (1990). Conceptualizing anti-gay violence [Special issue]: Violence against lesbians and gay men: Issues for research, practice, and policy. *Journal of Interpersonal Violence, 5*(3), 350–358.

Hechinger, F. M. (1993). Schools for teenagers: A historic dilemma. In R. Takanishi (Ed.), *Adolescence in the 1990s: Risk and opportunity* (pp. 64–81). New York: Teachers College Press.

Hendrix, H. (1992). *Keeping the love you find.* New York: Simon and Schuster.

Herek, G. M. (1984). Beyond "homophobia": A social psychologial perspective on attitudes toward lesbians and gay men. *Journal of Homosexuality, 10,* 1–21.

Hite, Shere. (1976). *The Hite report: A nationwide study of female sexuality.* New York: Dell Books.

Hooker, E. A. (1957). The adjustment of the male overt homosexual. *Journal of Projective Techniques, 21,* 17–31.

Hoyenga, K. B., and Hoyenga, K. T. (1993). *Gender related differences: Origins and outcomes.* Needham Heights, MA: Simon and Schuster.

Humphreys, L. (1973). *Out of the closet.* Engelwood Cliffs, NJ: Prentice-Hall.

Hunt, M. (1974). *Sexual behavior in the 1970s.* Chicago: Playboy Press.

Isay, R. A. (1989). *Being homosexual: Gay men and their development.* New York: Farrar, Straus, and Giroux.

Jackson, L. A. (1988). Gender, gender role, and body image. *Sex Roles, 19*(7–8), 429–433.

Jaffee, D., and Straus, M. A. (1987). Sexual climate and reported rape: A state-level analysis. *Archives of Sexual Behavior, 16*(2), 107–123.

Johnson, T. C. (1988). Child perpetrators—children who molest other children: Preliminary findings. *Child Abuse and Neglect, 12*(2), 219–229.

Johnson, T. C. (1989). Female child perpetrators: Children who molest other children. *Child Abuse and Neglect, 13*(4), 571–585.

Juhasz, A. M., and Sonnenshein-Schneider, M. (1987). Adolescent sexuality: Values, morality and decision making. *Adolescence, 22*(87), 279–590.

Kantor, L. (1994). Who decides? Parents and comprehensive sexuality education. *SIECUS Report, 22*(3), 7–13.

Kaplan, H. S. (1987). *The illustrated manual of sex therapy.* New York: Brunner/Mazel.

Kasl, C. D. (1989). *Women, sex and addiction.* New York: Harper and Row.

Katchadourian, H. (1989). *Fundamentals of human sexuality.* Chicago: Holt, Rinehart and Winston.

Kelly, G. F. (1988). *Sexuality today: The human perspective.* Guildford, CT: Dushkin.

Kinsey, A., Pomeroy, W., and Martin, C. (1948). *Sexual behavior in the human male.* Philadelphia: W. B. Saunders.

Kinsey, A., Pomeroy, W., and Gebhard, P. (1953). *Sexual behavior in the human female.* Philadelphia: W. B. Saunders.

Klein, F. (1990). The need to view sexual orientation as a multi-variable dynamic process: A theoretical perspective. In D. P. McWhirter, S. A. Sanders, and J. M. Reinsch (Eds.), *Homosexuality/heterosexuality* (pp. 277–272). New York: Oxford University Press.

Klein, F., Sepekoff, B., and Wolf, T. J. (1985). Sexual orientation: A multi-variable dynamic process. *Journal of Homosexuality, 11,* 35–49.

Lansdown, R., and Walker, M. (1991). *Your child's development: From birth through adolescence.* New York: Alfred Knopf.

Leight, L. (1988). *Raising sexually healthy children: A loving guide for parents, teachers, and care-givers.* New York: Avon Books.

Lerner, H. G. (1989). *The dance of intimacy.* New York: Harper and Row.

Lewis, J. M. (1989). *The birth of the family: An empirical inquiry.* New York: Brunner/Mazel.

Marmor, J. ed., (1965). *Sexual inversion: The multiple roots of homosexuality.* New York: Basic Books.

Marmor, J. (Ed.). (1980). *Homosexual behavior.* New York: Basic Books.

Martin, C. L. (1990). Attitudes and expectations about children with non-traditional and traditional gender roles. *Sex Roles, 22*(3–4), 151–165.

Masters, W. H., and Johnson, V. (1966). *Human sexual response.* Boston: Little, Brown.

McDougall, J. (1986). *Theatres of the mind: Illusion and truth on the psychoanalytic stage.* New York: Basic Books.

McKinney, K. (Ed.). (1989). *Human sexuality: The societal and interpersonal context.* Norwood, NJ: Ablex.

McNaught, B. (1988). *On being gay.* New York: St. Martin's.

McWhirter, D. P., Sanders, S. A., and Reinisch, J. M. (Eds.). (1990). *Homosexuality/heterosexuality: The Kinsey institute series.* New York: Oxford University Press.

Mehl, L., Brendsel, C., and Peterson, G. (1977). Children at birth: Effects and implications. *Journal of Sex and Marital Therapy, 3*(4), 274–279.

Melchert, T., and Burnett, K. F. (1990). Attitudes, knowledge, and sexual behavior of high-risk adolescents: Implications for counseling and sexuality education. *Journal of Counseling and Development, 68*(3), 293–298.

Mercier, L. R., and Berger, R. M. (1989). Social service needs of lesbian and gay adolescents: Telling it their way [Special issue]. Adolescent sexuality: New challenges for social work. *Journal of Social Work and Human Sexuality, 8*(1), 75–95.

Monat-Haller, R. K. (1992). *Understanding and expressing sexuality: Responsible choices for individuals with developmental difficulties.* Baltimore: Paul H. Brookes.

Money, J. (1991). The transformation of sexual terminology: Homosexuality in sexological history. *SIECUS Report, 20*(5), 10–13.

Money, J., and Ehrhardt, A. (1972). *Man and woman, boy and girl.* Baltimore: Johns Hopkins Press.

Mott, F., and Haurin, R. (1988). Linkages between sexual activity and alcohol and drug use among American adolescents. *Family Planning Perspectives, 20,* 128–137.

Muehlenhard, C. L., and Falcon, P. L. (1990). Men's heterosocial skill and attitudes toward women as predictors of verbal sexual coercion and forceful rape. *Sex Roles, 23*(5–6), 241–259.

Murphy, S. M., and Kilpatrick, D. G. (1988). Current psychological functioning of child sexual assault survivors: A community study. *Journal of Interpersonal Violence, 3*(1), 55–79.

Myers, M. F. (1989). Men sexually assaulted as adults and sexually abused as boys. 13th Annual Canadian Sex Research Forum Conference. *Archives of Sexual Behavior, 18*(3), 203–215.

National Center For Health Statistics. (1991). *Advance Report of Final Natality Statistics, 1989, 40*(8).

Nelson, J. B. *Embodyment: An approach to sexuality and Christian theology.* Minneapolis: Augsburg Publishing House.

Ornstein, R. (1993). *The roots of the self: Unraveling the mystery of who we are.* New York: HarperCollins.

Orr, D., Langefeld, C., Katz, B., Caine, V., and Dias, P. (1992). Factors associated with condom use among sexually active female adolescents. *Journal of Pediatrics, 120,* 311–317.

Parker, S., and Parker, H. (1991). Female victims of child sexual abuse: Adult adjustment. *Journal of Family Violence, 6*(2), 183–197.

Pellauer, M. D., Chester, B., and Boyajian, J. (Eds.). (1987). *Sexual assault and abuse.* New York: HarperCollins Publishers.

Peplau, L. A., and Cochran, S. D. (1990). A relational perspective on homosexuality. In D. P. McWhirter, S. A. Sanders, and J. M. Reinsch (Eds.), *Homosexuality/heterosexuality: The Kinsey institute series* (pp. 321–349). New York: Oxford University Press.

Peters, D. K., and Cantrell, T. J. (1991). Factors distinguishing samples of lesbian and heterosexual women. *Journal of Homosexuality, 21*(4), 1–15.

Phillips, G., and Over, R. (1992). Adult sexual orientation in relation to memories of childhood gender conforming and gender non-conforming behaviors. *Archives of Sexual Behavior, 21*(6), 543–558.

Pittman, F. S., III. (1993). *Man enough: Fathers, sons, and the search for masculinity.* New York: G. P. Putnam.

Plotnick, R. D., and Butler, S. S. (1991). Attitudes and adolescent non-marital childbearing: Evidence from the national longitudinal survey of youth. *Journal of Adolescent Research, 6*(4), 470–492.

Pocs, O., and Godow, A. C. (1977). Can students view parents as sexual beings? *The Family Co-ordinator, 26*(1), 31–37.

Price, R. H., Cioci, W. P., and Trautlein, B. (1993). Webs of influence: School and community programs that enhance adolescent health and education. In R. Takanishi (Ed.), *Adolescence in the 1990s: Risk and opportunity.* New York: Teachers College Press.

Rathus, S. A., Nevid, J. S., and Fichner-Rathus, L. (1993). *Human sexuality in a world of diversity.* Needham Heights, MA: Allyn and Bacon.

Reiss, I. L. (1966). The sexual renaissance: A summary and analysis. *The Journal of Social Issues, 12*(2), 125–127.

Rubin, I. (1970). *Coping with homosexual fears: The adolescent experience.* In Simmons, J. P. and Krantz, K. E., (Eds.). New York: Macmillan, pp. 98–114.

Sarrel, L. (1989). Sexual unfolding revisited (1989). *SIECUS Report, 18*(5), 4–5.

Scales, P. C. (1987). How we can prevent teen pregnancy (and why it's not the real problem). *Journal of Sex Education and Therapy, 13*(1), 12–15.

Selverstone, R. (1989). Adolescent sexuality: Developing self-esteem and mastering developmental tasks. *SIECUS Report, 18*(1), 1–3.

Serbin, L. A., Powlishta, K. K., and Gulko, J., with commentaries by Martin, C. L., and Lockheed, M. E. (1993). The development of sex typing in middle childhood. *Monographs of the Society for Research in Child Development, 58*(2, Serial No. 232).

Shuster, R. (1987). Sexuality as a continuum: The bisexual identity. In Boston Lesbian Psychologies Collective (Ed.), *Lesbian psychologies: Explorations and challenges* (pp. 56–71). Urbana: University of Illinois Press.

SIECUS (Ed.). (1970). *Sexuality and man.* New York: Scribner's.

SIECUS Report. (1993). Sexual orientation and identity. *SIECUS Fact Sheet on Comprehensive Sexuality Education, 22*(2), 19.

Skolnick, A. S., and Skolnick, J. H. (1992). *Family in transition: Re-thinking marriage.* New York: HarperCollins.

Soskolne, V. S., Aral, L., Magder, D., Reed, D., and Bowen, S. (1991). Condom use with regular and casual partners among women attending family planning clinics. *Family Planning Perspectives, 23,* 222–225.

Stein, T. S. (1993). Overview of new developments in understanding homosexuality. In J. M. Oldham, M. B. Riba, and A. Tasman (Eds.), *Review of Psychiatry* (Vol. 12). Washington: American Psychiatric Press.

Stein, T. S., and Cohen, C. J. (Eds.). (1986). *Contemporary perspectives on psychotherapy with lesbians and gay men.* New York: Plenum.

Steinem, G. (1992). *Revolution from within: A book of self-esteem.* Boston: Little, Brown.

Stewart, A. J., and Lykes, M. B. (1985). *Gender and personality: Current perspectives on theory and research.* Durham, NC: Duke University Press.

Strassberg, D., and Mahoney, J. (1988). Correlates of contraceptive behavior of adolescents/young adults. *Journal of Sex Research, 24,* 531–536.

Strouse, J. S., and Fabes, R. A. (1987). A conceptualization of transition to nonvirginity in adolescent females. *Journal of Adolescent Research, 2*(4, winter).

Summit, R. (1987). Beyond belief: The reluctant discovery of incest. In M. D. Pellauer, B. Chester, and J. Boyajian (Eds.), *Sexual assault and abuse: A handbook for clergy and religious professionals.* New York: HarperCollins.

Takanishi, R. (1993). *Adolescence in the 1990s: Risk and opportunity.* New York: Teachers College Press.

Thornton, A. (1990). The courtship process and adolescent sexuality [Special issue]. Adolescent sexuality, contraception, and childbearing. *Journal of Family Issues, 11*(3), 239–273.

Vasbinder, S. E. (1993). Sexual orientation education and homophobia reduction trainings. *SIECUS Report, 22*(2), 5–8.

Wade, C., and Travis, C. (1994). The longest war: Gender and culture. In W. Lonner, and R. Malpass (Eds.), *Psychology and culture* (pp. 121–126). Needham Heights, MA: Allyn and Bacon.

Wakefield, H., and Underwager, R. (1991). Female child sexual abusers: A critical review of the literature. *American Journal of Forensic Psychology, 9*(4), 43–69.

Weinberg, G. (1973). *Society and the healthy homosexual.* New York: Anchor.

Weinstein, E., and Rosen, E. (1988). *Sexuality counseling.* Pacific Grove, CA: Brooks/Cole.

Whitbeck, L. B., Hoyt, D. R., Miller, M., and Kao, M. (1992). Parental support, depressed affect, and sexual experience among adolescents. *Youth and Society, 24*(2), 166–177.

White, S. D., and DeBlassie, R. R. (1992). Adolescent sexual behavior. *Adolescence, 27*(105), 183–191.

Whitlock, K., and Kamel, R. (1989). *Bridges of respect: Creating support for lesbian and gay youth.* Philadelphia: American Friends Service Committee.

Wilson, P. M. (1994). Forming a partnership between parents and sexuality educators. *SIECUS Report, 22*(1), 1–5.

Wolman, B. B., and Money, J. (Eds.). (1980). *Handbook of human sexuality.* Englewood Cliffs, NJ: Prentice-Hall.

Woods, E. (1991). Contraceptive choices for adolescents. *Pediatric Annals, 20,* 313–221.

Wyatt, G. E., and Newcomb, M. D. (1990). Internal and external mediators of women's sexual abuse in childhood. *Journal of Consulting and Clinical Psychology, 58*(6), 758–767.

Wylie, M. S. (1993). The shadow of a doubt. *Networker, 17*(6).

Index

Abstinence, 172–173
Abuse, 182–212, 241–243
Active mental groping, 184
Adolescence
   physiological changes in, 107–119
   sociosexual experiences in, 119–128
Aesthetic "appreciation," 184
Affection, 233–235
Age difference, sexual abuse and, 187
AIDS, 101, 168, 179–180
Alcohol, rape and, 202
American Psychiatric Association, 91
Androgyny, 42–43

Baby-sitting, 75
Bathing, 4–5
Birth control, 169–170
   parents and, 173–175
   rate of use of, 177
   responsibility for, 177–178
   side effects of, 176–177
Birth rate, 168
Bisexuality, 94–95
"Blue balls," 128
Body hair, 110
Body image, 158–160
Books, sex education, 62, 64, 73–74
Boys
   abuse of, 183
   adolescence growth in, 107
   interest in sex of, 122–123
   masturbation rate among, 16–17
Bras, 110–111
Breasts
   development rate of, 110–112, 162–163
   size of, 112–113
   as status symbol, 161–162

CAR principle, 235

Childhood
   false beliefs about sex in, 60–62
   sexual experience in, 28–41
   sexual orientation variations in, 91–93
Children
   exploitation of, 29
   sexual abuse by, 201–202
   sexual abuse of, 182–212
Classroom assignment, text of, ix
"Coming out," 98–100
Communication, importance of, 231–232, 248–249
Contraception. *See* Birth control
Crushes, same-sex, 95
Culture, encouragement of sex by, 121

Development, early or late, 111–112, 162–163
Disease, sexually transmitted, 168–169
Doctor, playing, 31–32, 37–38
Drugs
   rape and, 202

Education, sex, 59–89
Ejaculation, first, 109–110
Elderly, sex needs of, 8–9
Emotional blackmail, 220–222
Emotions, 50
Erections, spontaneous, 108–109
Exhibitionism, 188
Experimentation, 232
Exploitation, 29, 207–208

Families
   communication in, 249–250
   nudity in, 3
   sexual abuse in, 193–201
   sexual attitudes and, 239
   style of, 1–15
   values and, 243

Fantasy, 119
Farm animals, 62
Fat, feeling, 160
Fathers, sexual abuse by, 197–199
Fear, 179
Fellatio, 153
"Feminine" qualities, 154
Femoral intercourse, 138
Films, sex education, 73–74, 76, 77, 78, 80
Foreplay harassment, 184
Forever, 130
French kissing, 133

"Gaydar," 100–101
Gay men. *See* Homosexuals
Gender roles, 1, 42–58
Genitals
    nursery names for, 59
Girls
    abuse of, 183
    adolescence growth in, 106–107
    interest in sex, 122–123
    masturbation rate among, 16–17
Grandfathers, sexual abuse by, 200
Group interaction, 120–121
Guilt
    about masturbation, 18–19
    consequences of, 240–241
    over playing doctor, 37

Herpes virus type 2, 179
HIV, 183
Homophobia, 97–98
Homosexuals, 244–245
    disillusionment of, 102
    marriage and, 101
    self-image of, 101–102
    social acceptance of, 103–104

Imagery, 119
Incest, 182, 206
In-laws, sexual abuse by, 201
Intelligence, gender and, 52–53
Intercourse
    disappointing, 228–229
    first experience of, 141–143
    initial reaction to learning of, 84
    in long-term, relationships, 225–226
    pressure to have, 137–138
    rehearsing, 140
    timing of, 224–225
Intimacy, 130–153
It's OK If You Don't Love Me, 130

Jealousy, 160–161
Jokes, sex education from, 73

Kinsey report
    on childhood sexual experiences, 28
    on sexual orientation, 93
Kiss, first, 131–132, 138–139

Lesbians. *See* Homosexuals
Locker rooms, 5
Lover's nuts, 128

Macho attitudes, 219–220
Male dominance, 154
Marriage, 225–226, 249
Masculine qualities, 154
Masturbation, 245
    and female orgasm, 17–18
    as first-time adult experience, 23
    guidelines for parents about, 26
    guilt about, 18–19
    lack of, 22–23
    as positive learning experience, 25–26
    "ridiculous stories" about, 19–20
    and stress, 24
    as substitute for sex, 24–25
Menstruation
    discomfort during, 118
    embarrassment about, 116–117
    onset of, 114–115
    "safe" period and, 175
    sex education about, 75–77, 115–116
    slang expressions for, 117–118
Mental illness, homosexuality and, 91
Middle school parties, 123–124
Mothers, sexual abuse by, 196–197
Mystery, 239–240

Necking, 139
Neighbors, sexual abuse by, 188–189, 190–192
Normalcy, 240
Nudity
    in families, 3

Oral sex, 136
Orgasm
    faking, 152
    from masturbation, 17–18
    necking or petting to, 139

Parents
    asking about sex, 64–66, 66–67
    attitudes given along with sex education, 79–81
    birth control and, 173–175
    embarrassment about sex, 63–64
    gender instruction by, 43–51
    gender modeling by, 51–52
    lifestyle differences from, 229–230

Parents (continued)
  and masturbation, 18–20, 26
  and premarital sex, 12–13
  reaction to children's sex play, 35–387
  relationships among, 3
  reporting abuse to, 192–193
  sex education and, 77–78, 82–84
  sexual abuse by, 196–199
  sexual activity between, 5–10
  sexual messages from, 10–12
  values and, 218
Parties, 123–124
Peer pressure, 124–126
  and sexual abuse, 189
  values and, 218–219
Peers
  acceptance by, 165
  and masturbation, 20–21
  sex education from, 70–73
  sexual attitudes and, 239
Petting, 127–128, 139
Physical urgency, 223–224
Planned Parenthood, 173, 175–176
Post office game, 123–124
Pregnancy, 171–172, 214, 215
Premarital sex
  parents and, 12–13
Pre-pubertal pleasure, 38–39
Pretend games, 33–34
Promiscuity, 161
Prostitutes, 207
Puberty, physiological changes at, 107–119

Rape, 202–205, 206–207, 211
Religion, 120
  and homosexuality, 95–97
  and intercourse, 137
  and sex education, 68–69
  and values, 218
Reputations, 126–127

Sanitary napkins, 118–119
Schools
  sex education in, 77–78
  single-sex, 159
Scoring, as stealing, 236
Self-esteem, low, 156–157, 161, 189–190
Self-image
  of homosexuals, 101–102
  sexuality and, 154–167
Self-understanding, 245–247
Sex education, 59–89
  about menstruation, 75–77
  age-based learning guidelines for, 86–88
  first experience and, 123–124
  homosexuals and, 97

  from parents, 64–67
  from peers, 70–73
  religion and, 68–69
  in school, 77–78
Sex Information and Education Council of the United States (SIECUS), 26
Sex play, 29–34, 186
Sex roles, 42–58, 55–56, 90
Sexual abuse, 182–212, 241–243
Sexual activity
  false beliefs about, 60–62
  between parents, 5–10
Sexual harassment, 183–184, 184–186
Sexual identity, 90
Sexual orientation, 91
  in childhood, 91–93
  homophobia, 97–98, 103–104
  mental illness and, 91
  religion and, 95–97
Sexual values, matrix of, 238
Sexual view
  of elderly, 8–9
Shower rooms, 113–114
Siblings
  sex education from, 2, 4, 70–73
  sexual abuse by, 193–195
Silence, prices of, 239–251
Sleeping space, children sharing, 32–33
Social touching, 184
Sociosexual experience
  in adolescence, 119–128
Sports, gender roles and, 49
STDs, 168–169, 179–180
Stress, masturbation and, 24

Talents, 165–166
Tampons, 118–119
Tchambuli tribe, 43
Teachers, sex education and, 79–81, 82–83
Testicles, ache of, 128
Therapy, 210–211
Toilet training, 29
Tomboys, 46–47, 54, 55
Toys, gender roles and, 44, 45, 48

Uncles, sexual abuse by, 200–201

Values, sexuality and, 213–238
Verbal abuse, 182
Very Far Away From Anywhere Else, 130
Virginity, 140–141, 214
Visual aids
  and masturbation, 21–22

"Wet dreams," 109–110
Withdrawal, 170